Race–Ethnicity and Society

Race-Ethnicity and Society

Benjamin B. Ringer
& Elinor R. Lawless

Routledge

New York   London

First published in 1989 by

Routledge
an imprint of
Routledge, Chapman & Hall, Inc.
29 West 35 Street
New York, NY 10001

Published in Great Britain by

Routledge
11 New Fetter Lane
London EC4P 4EE

Library of Congress Cataloging in Publication Data
Ringer, Benjamin B. (Benjamin Bernard), 1920–
    Race-ethnicity and society / by Benjamin B. Ringer with Elinor R.
Lawless.
        p. cm.
    Bibliography: p.
    Includes index.
    ISBN 0–415–90034–4; ISBN 0–415–90035–2 (pbk.):
        1. United States—Race relations. 2. United States—Ethnic
relations. I. Lawless, Elinor R., 1942–   II. Title.
E184.A1R489   1989   89–31910
305.8′00973—dc20   CIP

British Library Cataloguing in Publication Data
Ringer, Benjamin B. (Benjamin Bernard, 1920–
    Race – ethnicity and society.
    1. United States. Race relations, history
    I. Title II. Lawless, Elinor R. 1942–
    305.8′00973

    ISBN 0–415–90034–4
    ISBN 0–415–90035–2 (pb)

To David, Jonathan,
Lia, and Andrew

Contents

Introduction

During the years of President Reagan's administration, racial issues and problems virtually disappeared from the center stage of public discussion and political debate much as they had during the earlier part of the twentieth century.* Most white Americans had come to believe that whatever may have been the nature of these issues and problems historically they were finally resolved by the enactment of the civil rights laws of the 1960s. In fact, even those who resisted passage of these laws in the 1960s adopted this line and with it the rhetoric of the decade as justification for opposing any further remedial action along the racial front. Thus, by the mid-1980s the issue of race had all but vanished from the national agenda. A veneer of tranquility seemed to prevail throughout the society as white America once again asserted its dominance and control over the national agenda and the major institutions of society.

In other words, white Americans had successfully weathered the storm of racial turbulence of the 1960s and the "reverse discrimination" policies of the 1970s which had made them feel and act like the "victims" of government action. In the 1980s they seem more determined than ever to treat these as unpleasant and even ugly accidents or aberrations of history that interrupted the "natural" flow of relations between groups in the American society.

Accordingly, they have dismissed what took place during those years as irrelevant to a better understanding of America's historic relations with its racial minorities. Instead they have sought to return with a vengeance

---

*The possible exception is the last year of his administration when sustained TV and news media coverage of such events as the Howard Beach trial in New York City once again focused some public attention on the issue of racial discrimination and conflict.

to the status quo ante in their thinking. As such, they have become even more convinced than they were in the early 1960s—just before the deluge—that America is today truly fulfilling the promise of the American creed with its "ideals of the essential dignity of the individual human being, of the fundamental equality of all men, and of certain inalienable rights to freedom, justice, and a fair opportunity" (Myrdal 1944:4) to its various ethnic and racial minorities. They are confident that the disparity between the creed's ideals and actual practice about which Myrdal wrote in *An American Dilemma* has finally been eliminated for all and that now it is up to each individual to prove his or her worth.

Most books on race and ethnicity that have been published during this period echo these sentiments. Either they cover those years in a relatively casual manner or treat them as a disruptive, if not destructive, set of historical occurrences. The result has been a trivialization of a watershed set of experiences that in fact challenged the adequacy of the state of knowledge and theory in the field of ethnic and race relations and that raised serious questions about their basic assumptions.

Relatively few scholars, in effect, took advantage of the opportunity offered by this challenge to search for new insights into the study of race relations in America or to reexamine the basic premises in research on these relations. The senior author of this book, Benjamin B. Ringer, undertook such an exploration. During the race riots he soon became convinced that the answers to the fundamental questions raised by them could not be found by merely looking at the present. They were somehow locked into the past. Accordingly, he gave up being a sociologist of the *now* who applied the methodology of survey research to living ethnic actors and became instead a sociologist in history who studied the responses and policies of significant racial actors of America's past. In this manner, he began a voyage of discovery into that past. The odyssey started in the late 1960s and lasted fifteen years. The result was the publication of a monograph that offered a different way of looking at and of conceptualizing what would be better described as the American Paradox than as the American Dilemma. The monograph analyzes in detail how this paradox developed and affected the treatment and life circumstances of specific racial minorities: the blacks, Indians, Chinese, Japanese, and Puerto Ricans. Its title is *"We the People" and Others: Duality and America's Treatment of its Racial Minorities* (Ringer 1983).

During the course of working on the monograph, it became evident that the manner in which many American social scientists have viewed and continue to view the study of race and ethnic relations in America is too narrowly gauged. It neglects a whole array of dimensions and contexts. Accordingly to fill the void new concepts had to be constructed, and older ones reconceptualized. These are woven through the text of the monograph.

This book seeks to bring the various strands that are threaded throughout the monograph into a more general—though not necessarily unified—conceptual framework. As such, it is an attempt to conceptualize what has been learned from the earlier work and to make this knowledge available to scholars and to students in the classroom. This book, thus, is to be considered a supplemental text in the field that hopefully fills significant blank spaces.

As a starting point, this book resurrects from the past a concern, all too frequently lost sight of in today's writings, which is the *they-ness* of race and ethnicity. This refers to the way a *given* ethnic or racial group is perceived and defined by other ethnic and racial groups in society. The *they-ness* includes the beliefs, stereotypes, and the like held by these others about a given ethnic or racial group and also the actions and policies that may be directed against this group.

Today the overriding premise for many scholars is that the working of the American creed has become so pervasive and benign that all we need to study are the internal characteristics of groups which either allow them to make it or cause them to be left behind in the competitive struggle for position and privilege. Formerly Jews were the heroes of this approach; today the Japanese are; always in the rear are the blacks.

And so we find a renewed emphasis on the *we-ness* of ethnicity;[*] how the various kinds of ethnic solidarity and characteristics have helped or hindered groups to overcome the hardships of the past. Accordingly, a deluge of natural histories of specific groups has been written as though these groups were anthropological specimens devoid of a larger societal framework.

Other scholars who are equally enamored with the benign workings of the American creed and who also say the civil rights acts of the 1960s erased racial inequities have followed a different path. For them race has disappeared as an independent variable affecting behavior. Other characteristics of the individual or of his or her position in society have become the determinants of fate.

In focusing on the *they-ness* of race and ethnicity, we do not however go back to the way it was studied in the 1940s and 1950s. Then the study

---

*This book does not overlook the significance of the *we-ness* of ethnicity. In fact, in chapter 1 the authors maintain that what makes an ethnic group a distinctive sociological phenomenon is its *we-they* character. They subsequently develop a typology based on the variations in this twofold relationship. The issue therefore is not the *we-ness* of ethnicity but the absence of sufficient attention to its *they-ness* today.

of *they-ness* was virtually monopolized by the social psychologists who concentrated on the dynamics of prejudice: its cognitive, emotional, and conative components. They also looked for the psychological roots of prejudice. They constructed the F-Scale, devised the concept of authoritarian personality, and concluded that the extremely prejudiced person was basically a sick personality.

Others pursued the trail of discriminatory behavior. They enlarged their analytical framework to include cultural and contextual factors, but they too confined their efforts to the individual or at most to relations between individuals in various kinds of social and institutional contexts. And so a theory of equal status contacts was elaborated. The theory maintained that prejudice would be reduced and friendliness enhanced between individuals from different ethnic and racial groups if they were placed in functional relationships in neighborhoods, at work, or in organizations in which they had to interact with each other as equals.

While each approach has contributed to an understanding of the phenomenon, the events of the 1960s have shown the limitation of defining the study of *they-ness* entirely in these terms. It is no longer adequate to treat ethnic and race relations as though they were primarily products of attitude, stereotype, or interpersonal relations within the community or social order.

Accordingly, this book pays much more attention to the study of *they-ness* within the political-economic order of society than to its study within the interpersonal and social orders. Within each order and within the general stratificational system of society, we are particularly interested in the interplay between race-ethnicity and the structures of power and dominance. Thus the perceptions of *they-ness* that concern us most derive from those in positions of power. For the perceptions and beliefs of the dominant ethnic or racial group are most likely to be translated into actions and policies that vitally affect the life chances and circumstances of a given ethnic or racial group.

In the examination of the political-economic order, we avoid the reductionism of orthodox Marxists and modern-day neoconservatives. We do not transmute race and ethnicity into mere derivatives of the workings of the economic marketplace or of class and its relationship to the means of production. Instead we treat race-ethnicity as a distinctive societal phenomenon that has an inner dynamic of its own.

In addition, we do not reduce the political system to a mere "handmaiden" of the economic system as does the orthodox Marxist or perceive the state as a "neutral referee" for the workings of the market system as in the neo-Adam Smith economics of the neo-conservatives. Accordingly, we do not view the fate of ethnic and racial groups as being determined entirely or even primarily by economic and market forces in society per se. Instead we follow the lead of Gumplowicz, Cox, Fanon, and others and postulate a direct and crucial linkage between race-ethnicity and political forces and factors in society.

This linkage, we maintain, has operated historically in two different causal directions. First is the imprint of an ethnic or racial group on the formation of a state society. This imprint can be much more readily ascertained in the creation of new political societies such as took place during the five centuries of white European expansion throughout the world. In many of these lands the white Europeans created racially segmented colonial societies through their conquest of native populations. In some of these lands they also became colonists and established permanent settlements for themselves. In the process they constructed a political society whose institutions they molded, as was the case of the English settlers and the Spanish conquistadors in the New World.

Second, the dominant ethnic or racial group once in control of a society—newly created or long established—may promulgate policies and enact legal-normative codes and controls that vitally affect the life chances and circumstances of the various ethnic and racial groups already within the territorial boundaries of the society or newly entering either voluntarily or involuntarily.

Obviously where the political society is newly created the two causal sequences may be inextricably linked and both indelibly impressed on the formation of the new society. What is more the legal-normative codes and controls promulgated by the dominant group need not be one kind of thing for all ethnic and racial groups. Both propositions were demonstrated in *"We the People" and Others* (Ringer 1983). In that work it was shown that a duality was imprinted onto the very legal and political foundations of the American society. This duality came from the twofold processes of colonization and colonialization that were generated by the white Europeans' conquest and settlement of the New World.

As colonists, for example, the English created a society whose institutions were molded in their racial, religious, and national image. They took particular pride in the structure of self-governance that they built, first in Virginia and later in the other colonies. In each, the people of the colonist society had certain basic rights and immunities, but only the white colonists could be part of the people.

As colonialists, the English subjected the nonwhites with whom they came into contact to force and fraud; and they subjugated, killed, or drove them off. The Indians, for example, were overwhelmed by force of arms, deprived of their land and resources, and treated as a conquered subject or inhuman enemy. Blacks were involuntarily brought into the colonies as slaves. By the first decade of the eighteenth century in Virginia, blacks as slaves had been completely dehumanized and transmuted into pieces of property. They were enmeshed in a web of legal and extralegal coercive constraints and oppressive controls that placed them completely at the mercy of their white masters.

This duality thrived and grew as the thirteen colonies prepared to oppose the rule of the British government, and it survived the successful outcome of the War for Independence and the creation of the new nation. The colonist heritage, for example, found expression in the Declaration of Independence, the Constitution, and the Bill of Rights as the thirteen colonies were transformed into a federated nation-state, the United States of America. Through this heritage the sovereignty of the people was reaffirmed both in the structures of governance and in the political community.

In contrast, the colonialist heritage found expression in the same kind of structural arrangements that were already in existence. Its racially segmented form and its web of arbitrary legal and political control emerged unscathed with the writing of the Constitution. In fact, it was relegitimized by the Founding Fathers and the First Congress.

In time other racial minorities were caught up in a similar web of arbitrary legal-political control imposed upon them by the dominant white society—a web of control that subjected them to repression and coercion and that enmeshed them in a racial creed of white superiority. Thus, the kind of arbitrary political control that the Founding Fathers had sought to eliminate for the whites in the creation of "We the People" remained for generations as a fact of life for racial minorities. The precise nature of this web of control, however, differed with the individual racial minority. But despite these differences, the basic root for all of these webs was planted in the very foundations of the same society that gave birth to the remarkable people's domain of the Constitution and Bill of Rights.

In short, the Founding Fathers sanctified two political models, not one, in the writing of the Constitution and thereby set the stage for what turned out to be in succeeding generations a herculean struggle between the two for the control of the destiny of racial minorities. Thus, it can be maintained that America's historic treatment of its racial minorities has been both an expression and a product of the dialectical tension between these two models.

The duality thesis, then, opens up a whole new approach to the study of race and ethnic relations. It provides us with an alternative way for examining America's treatment of its racial minorities. As such, it challenges three conventional premises in the field. It maintains (1) that treatment of racial minorities in America was qualitatively, not merely quantitatively, different from that experienced by white immigrants; (2) that racism was not a mere aberration in the American society—largely confined to the South—but was instead built into the very foundations of the American society; and (3) that America's experience with minorities was not unique or found "only in America," but can instead be located within the mainstream of white European expansion, conquest, and settlement as one kind of adaptation of duality. It can accordingly be compared and contrasted with the adaptations of other countries ranging from Australia, New Zealand, and South Africa to those of Latin America.

It would seem, therefore, that the duality thesis has broad applicability as a theoretic and analytic construct even on the international stage. It brings together into a common conceptual framework a variety of historical experiences which share a similar motif. All have been directly or indirectly products of the dual processes of colonization and colonialization generated by the expansion of white Europeans over a span of five centuries.

As we have already indicated, the earliest and most pervasive historical exportation of duality happened during the conquest and settlement of the New World, first by the Spanish, then by the English, and finally by other Europeans. They built their dual societies in South America, Central America, and North America and eventually lost them as these societies became independent nations still bearing the marks of their dualistic heritage.

By the time the white Europeans moved onto the continents of Asia and Africa, they had become, by and large, colonialists who were interested in building an imperial system for their mother country. Accordingly, they constructed only the kind of racially segmented plural society, about which Furnivall [1948] (1956) wrote, with themselves perched at the top as a "sojourner elite." In some places, however, they settled permanently and evolved a colonist society, too. As a result, duality resurfaced in such places as South Africa, Zimbabwe (Rhodesia), Australia, and New Zealand.

In Australia and New Zealand the white Europeans overwhelmed an indigenous population that was pushed to the perimeters of the white society as a racial minority, much as the Indian was in the United States. In South Africa and Zimbabwe the situation was different. Whites built their own society as a small minority among a vast population of subjugated nonwhites. As might be expected, the dual structures constructed in these societies reflected the marked variations in population proportions of white and nonwhite as well as the different historical circumstances.

This book, then, brings together a number of different strands that were explored in the earlier work *"We the People" and Others* (Ringer 1983) and places them into a more general conceptual framework. In the process it seeks to link these strands to the knowledge that had been accumulated in the field, even as it is making a statement for a different approach. This approach would hopefully also provide a general model for the comparative analysis of race and ethnic relations in societies that were products of or influenced by the five centuries of white European expansion.

1 The "We-They" Character of Race and Ethnicity

A major premise of this book is that ethnic and racial groups are not completely autonomous and self-contained entities. They are, instead, part of a larger societal system that influences, shapes, and particularly in the case of racial groups may even define their very character and determine their life circumstances. As such, these groups are continually beseiged by two sets of dynamic forces, which are frequently in opposition to each other: specifically, an internal set that serves to establish and to maintain the group's distinctive we-ness, and an external set that serves to shape and to designate its they-ness. This dualism was recognized by Peter Rose in his book: *They and We: Racial and Ethnic Relations in the United States* (1981). Shibutani and Kwan also embrace this twoness in their definition of the term: "An ethnic group consists of those who conceive of themselves as being alike by virtue of their common ancestry, real or fictitious, and who are so regarded by others" (Shibutani and Kwan 1965:47).

With this dualism in mind, we propose to examine in this chapter first the internal characteristics of an ethnic group, and then shift to a consideration of the role that the larger society plays in delineating the distinctiveness of ethnic and racial groups. Particular attention will be paid to the impact of societal they-ness on the latter.

The Internal Definition of Ethnic Distinctiveness: Its We-ness

A quick glance at the titles of books that have been published in the past several decades would suggest little difficulty in defining what is meant by the term "ethnic group." We have books on Italian-Americans, Jewish-Americans, Afro-Americans, Mexican-Americans, Asian-Americans, and so on; all concentrate on the ethnic character of these specific groups.

1

With so many concrete examples of ethnicity, it would seem that the question, "What is an ethnic group?" would be easy to answer by now. And yet, the opposite is true.

Shorn of its denotative and descriptive concreteness, the term takes an elusive, mystical, and frequently romanticized character. This is clearly evident in an early chapter of *Assimilation in American Life* a book that has done much to provide a meaningful conceptual framework for the study of white ethnic groups in America. In the first few pages of the second chapter, the author M. M. Gordon spans much of man's early history. He invokes the Pleistocene hunter, the Zuni, the Arapesh, Assyrians, Jews, Hindus, medieval English, the early Protestants and the like—all in response to the basic question that he raises in his very first paragraph:

> What does a man answer when he is asked, or asks himself, a question as old as the time when some Pleistocene hunter, strayed far from his reassuring campfire and making his way fearfully through the dark tree-dense forest, came upon a stricken man, bested by his quarry, and realized that he had never seen him before—the first stranger? That question is "Who are you?" (Gordon 1964:19).

In graphic words such as these—sometimes lyrical, sometimes mystical—the author pursues the notion of folk as an essential characteristic of the term "ethnic group."

In a similar vein, another author describes the concept "community" which he subsequently applies to the ethnic group. "In the language of Freud, a community can be said to be derived mainly from subconscious experiences, while an association is derived from direct knowledge" (Francis 1947:395).

Examples can be multiplied: all point to the same conclusion. In trying to get at the essence of an ethnic group, many writers allow their rhetoric to soar. Our purpose at this juncture, however, is not to argue with literary style but to emphasize that the concept itself tends to evoke this response. In fact, as we shall see, the act of defining the concept requires coming to terms with the very features that give rise to this rhetoric.

With this caveat in mind, let us attempt to identify the basic internal characteristics and features of an ethnic group. In so doing, we shall on occasion be as guilty as others of exaggerated romanticism and of talking in somewhat mystical terms. But despite these dangers, our purpose is relatively clear: we wish to view the group from the inside and to identify what appears to be its most distinctive features. We shall at first talk as though the ethnic group could be an entity unto itself, but before too long in this chapter we shall correct this notion.

Communal character of the ethnic group

In stressing the centrality of the notion of folk in their definitions of the ethnic group, most authors are seeking to identify its fundamental nature: it is a kind of human community which is deeply rooted in common sentiments, common experience, and a common history. To get the full flavor of what this means, one has but to examine carefully Ferdinand Tönnies's classic concepts of *gemeinschaft* and *gesellschaft*.

To Tönnies, gemeinschaft relations are essentially relations of the heart; they are based on sentiment, courage, and conscience; their virtues are sincerity, kindness, and faithfulness. In contrast, gesellschaft relations are essentially those of the head; they are based on deliberation, calculation, and ambition in which individuals seek to achieve their own ends and purposes. On the group level, according to Tönnies, gesellschaft is best represented by the city, special-purpose associations, the state, and the metropolis in which convention, contract, legislative law, and public opinion provide the bases for order, law, and morality. In contrast, on the group level, the gemeinschaft is governed by understanding, concord, custom, and belief or creed.

He distinguishes three kinds of gemeinschaft: that of blood, of place, and of mind. The gemeinschaft of blood he identifies with kinship and the biological ties that bind human beings into a common genetic pool. The gemeinschaft of place results from the sharing of territory that produces "collective ownership of land." The gemeinschaft of mind is reflected in common values, ideals, and bonds that come to be expressed through sacred beliefs and to be "represented by sacred places and worshipped deities" (Tönnies 1940:48).

So suggestive is Tönnies's treatment of the term *gemeinschaft*, that it provides a conceptual setting in which we can locate the ethnic group. As E. K. Francis says, "If we adopt for the moment Ferdinand Tönnies' typological dichotomy *Gemeinschaft* and *Gesellschaft*, we would have to classify an ethnic group as a rather pure type of *Gemeinschaft*" (Francis 1947:395).

As with Tönnies's trichotomy of blood, place, and mind, so it is possible to trace the basic sources that give rise to the ethnic group, though its precise origins may be lost in the mists of history. First, however, just as Tönnies's concept of gemeinschaft is rooted in the family and kinship system, so are the latter the basic building blocks of the ethnic group. They are the anchor and link to a larger communal system of the present and of the past. And yet the ethnic group is more than a kinship and clan system; historically, it grew out of people who shared territory, sacred belief systems, and biological characteristics.

Gordon considers these shared characteristics as the basic ingredients of

Robert Redfield's "classic model of the 'folk society'" (Gordon 1964:23). In this manner Gordon identifies the folk society as the prototypic community for the ethnic group.

In each of these prototypic communities, then, the three elements of territory, sacred belief system, and biological characteristics reinforced each other to accentuate the distinctiveness of that community in relation to others. This reinforcement was in large measure an expression of the fact that these tribal or folk societies functioned throughout much of man's early history as relatively independent, isolated "political entities" characterized by a relatively homogeneous population, economic self-sufficiency, and what Durkheim called "mechanical solidarity."

In more modern history, the interplay among these three factors becomes more complex. This is particularly true as they relate to ethnic groups in the modern nation-state. Territoriality becomes translated into nationality, sacred belief system into religion, and biological characteristics into race. Each of these factors can and does become the principal organizing basis around which distinctive ethnicity is established. Thus the saliency of the shared characteristic may vary between and among ethnic groups as their defining feature.

And yet it is also possible to describe each group in terms of the other characteristics as well. Gordon does just that when he argues that race, religion, and national origins are the "competing models of ethnicity" in the twentieth-century nation-state. He also adds membership in the nation-state itself as another component of ethnicity.

> The American who answers Who He Is, answers, then, from an ethnic point of view, as follows: I am an American, I am of the White or Negro or Mongoloid race, I am a Protestant, Catholic, or Jew, and I have a German or Italian, or Irish, or English, or whatever, national background. In practice, it is probable that these discrete categories are attached to the self not separately or serially but in combination (Gordon 1964:26).

However, when Gordon shifts to a discussion of "our conventional language of ethnic identification within the nation," he omits being an American as part of this identification.

> This American is a white Protestant Anglo-Saxon; that one is an Irish Catholic (white race understood), this one a Negro Protestant (African background understood), that one is a Russian Jew (white race understood). This is the way we identify each other and ourselves when we think, ethnically, about Who We Are within the national boundaries (Gordon 1964:26).

For Gordon, then, race, religion, and national origins constitute the "conventional language of ethnic identification within the nation." We agree with this usage. But we would go a step further and say that these are the only defining features of ethnicity that he has to offer. For ethnicity, as he himself suggests, focuses on group differences within the political and territorial boundaries of the nation-state. Small wonder that he does not mention present membership in a nation-state as part of the person's ethnic identification. We are accordingly puzzled over his rationale for including it in his earlier, more general statement on ethnicity. We shall have much more to say on this issue later.

The role of the past

Another distinctive feature of the ethnic group is that it has a history. This not only gives the group a common ancestry and descent but also becomes a significant basis for organizing the present. The temporal dimension obviously accentuates the role of the family as a major link between the present and the past. As such, membership in the ethnic group is primarily a function of birth—a matter of ascription rather than of voluntary choice.

And yet despite the importance of the temporal dimension, the factual origins of the group are frequently shrouded in mystery. It is extremely difficult to trace the causative unfolding of common ancestry for the contemporary character of the ethnic group. Much more significant is the function that the presumed ancestry plays in maintaining the present for the group. It underlies the central collective representations, core myths, and belief systems that serve to provide cohesion for the present. Francis argues that "the real racial composition" and actual history of a group are less important than are its assumed common descent and beliefs about the history. "The device of myths to establish a common ancestry for an ethnic group is a very ancient one. At all times man seems to have tampered with the mystery of biological heredity" (Francis 1947: 396).

These myths and belief systems in connecting the present with the past not only insure the continuity of the group but also make the past a living and vital part of the present. In the process, the tendency is to emphasize the perceived presumed heroic nature of this past; the accuracy of these memories is less important than the memories themselves.

> For a person who identifies with an ethnic category, its history provides a backdrop before which to review his own conduct. The history of any group consists of those collective memories shared by its members of the glorious deeds of their forebears, of their unfair persecution, and of the decisive events that resulted in its present situation. This historical past often includes fictitious accounts, but the way in which the history of a group is remembered is far more important than what it has actually been. Those who identify can

conceive of themselves as a part of something larger than themselves, something of far greater importance (Shibutani and Kwan 1965:43).

In many respects, then, the historical past is selectively read and interpreted from the perspective and from the needs of the present. Nowhere is this more apparent than among ethnic groups who are seeking to redefine their current status and image. For example, blacks in the 1960s were not content with challenging their current position in American society but were equally intent upon winning a new interpretation of the blacks response to slavery. They angrily denied the contention that blacks were submissive and passive under slavery; instead they insisted that many blacks were hostile and rebellious and only the superior force of a repressive white society succeeded in crushing overt expressions of this antagonism. In a similar fashion many American Jews angrily denounced the contentions of Hannah Arendt and others that many European Jews passively accepted their fate under Hitler. And so the examples can be multiplied. Ethnic groups feel the need to stress a heroic image of their past, as though such an image is essential for mobilizing their energies for the struggles of the present.

Thus the historical past of an ethnic group is not something that is relegated to its archives to be viewed as a curious but interesting relic. Instead it functions to organize the sentiments, needs, aspirations of the present. Consequently to understand fully the meaning of the past for an ethnic group, it must be seen as filtered through the prism of the present. As such the past and present are inextricably interwoven in the life of the ethnic group, and the interaction between the two does much to define the group's vision of its future.

The ethnic group and cultural distinctiveness

As a people with a history, the ethnic group is further characterized by a distinctive culture. The distinctiveness of the shared values, beliefs, institutions, style of life, and general design for living varies in scope and inclusiveness among ethnic groups. For example, the Amish in Pennsylvania exhibit a cultural distinctiveness that ranges from the family and kinship system to religious, economic, social, educational institutions—in short, virtually the whole gamut of institutional practices and values. On the other hand, it would be more difficult to identify the cultural distinctiveness of the third- and fourth-generation Irish, other than their sense of Irishness and the wearing of the green on St Patrick's Day.

Yet despite these great variations in cultural distinctiveness among ethnic groups, it is equally evident that each ethnic group—no matter how removed from others it may be or on what bases it is organized—has at the very center of its values and beliefs a cluster of "truths" which basically justify the group's existence. This sacred core of beliefs may be of a religious nature as with the role of Judaism for Jews or Catholicism for Catholics. But it may also be derived from secular sources. An example is the role of the homeland for national-origin groups—Ireland for the Irish, Israel for the Jews. Another example is the phrase "Black is Beautiful" for the blacks. Certain symbols, values, and beliefs in taking on a sacred character, may come to represent the very essence of the concept of folk and give a sense of mission and destiny. These sacred values and symbols are located at the very center of what sustains feelings of pride and ethnocentrism. At times the idea is expressly stated as in the "chosen people" concept of the Jews.

Structural components

All too frequently sociologists seek to define the structural characteristics of an ethnic group in oversimplified terms. The concept itself is frequently treated as though it were a distinctive structural category when in fact it is a distinctive sociological phenomenon to which a variety of structural terms may be applied; as such it may reveal a structural complexity which is not immediately apparent. It is equally obvious that the structural complexity varies with the ethnic group: its size, location, history, and the like.

Perhaps the least complicated structure would be found where all members of an ethnic group occupied a common territorial area and comprised for all intents and purposes a relatively inclusive and total community. Within such a setting an ethnic group would approximate Redfield's folk society. Such a community might involve firsthand knowledge of total membership and an elaborate network of kinship and primary group ties which would be anchored in a sacred system of beliefs and values. These arrangements tend to be tribal by nature and can be found among tribes in newly independent nations of Africa, the Indian tribes on the frontiers of Brazil, and various American tribes such as Navaho and Sioux, and the Murngin of Australia.

It is important to note however, that to find examples of such relatively small groups we have to seek out what may well be limiting cases for the concept of ethnic group. In short we have to select examples from what amounts to man's early history.

In most cases, the total membership of a given ethnic group does not occupy a common territory but is distributed—though not randomly—over a wide geographic area either within one country or among many countries. In either case distance and other kinds of people separate those of the same ethnic group. Within each of the larger geographic areas some members of a given ethnic group will tend to cluster in certain sections and develop a sense of community. Such communities then comprise the nuclei for the broader ethnic entity.

The nuclear ethnic community

Some of these nuclear communities may approximate the total inclusive type of community of the folk society variety. These are likely to be located in rural settings and to be relatively isolated from the rest of society. An example is an old order Amish community in Pennsylvania, Ohio, or Indiana.

As Hostetler says, the Amish community resembles Redfield's folk society in its possession of the "qualities of distinctiveness, smallness, homogeneity, and self-sufficiency" (Hostetler 1968:21). He maintains that the unifying framework for the Amish society is religion. "Religion permeates daily life, agriculture, health considerations, and the application of energy to economic ends. Religious beliefs determine the conceptions of the universe, the self, and man's place in it. Religion is 'an ever present dimension of experience'" (Hostetler 1968:10). As such it is the generating source for the mores of the community and the fundamental axis of communal solidarity.

Life in such nuclear communities takes on a special character, according to Hostetler.

> By living in closed communities where custom and a strong sense of togetherness prevail, an integrated way of life, a folklike culture has been formed. Continuity of conformity and custom is assured and the needs of the individual from birth to death are met within an integrated and shared system of meanings. Oral tradition, custom, and conventionality perform an important part in maintaining the group as a functioning whole. The participant believes religion and custom are inseparable. Conviction and culture are combined to produce a stable human existence (Hostetler 1968:11).

Inclusive and isolated as such ethnic communities may be, they nevertheless are not completely closed to external influences. Even the Amish community must cope with the outside world. For example, it has had to come to terms with its economic relations with the larger society.

> In finding markets for crops and products, the little Amish community is linked with the economy of the larger industrial nation. It is not a communal society with an exclusive economic system, and ownership is not unlike the prevailing economic system in American life (Hostetler 1968: 20).

However the Amish community has sought to control the disruptive influences of such contacts by developing patterns and practices which help sustain its internal order.

In a similar manner the community, though subject to governmental regulations and dealings, has sought to limit and to control governmental intervention in its internal affairs.

Self-sufficiency is the Amish answer to government aid programs, such as farm subsidy and social security benefits. Amish leaders repeatedly go to Washington to seek freedom from federal aid (Hostetler 1968:20).

They fear the disruptive influences of dependence upon government for meeting any of their needs. Accordingly they seek to take care of their own "in times of stress, fire, sickness, old age or death" (Hostetler 1968:21).

Perhaps one of the Amish community's most serious struggles has been with the public school system. It has felt itself particularly threatened by the requirement that its children attend high schools which would bring them into contact with non-Amish children and with the standards and values of the outside world. In its *Wisconsin v. Yoder* decision of 1972, the U.S. Supreme Court agreed that Amish parents were not obliged to send their children to formal high schools until the age of sixteen in accordance with the compulsory education laws of Wisconsin. Accordingly, the Court granted the Amish the right to assume full responsibility for the education of their children after the latter completed the 8th grade in public schools—a requirement the Amish did not contest. In this manner the Amish were allowed to continue, without interference from public officials, their "system of learning-by-doing" which, according to Chief Justice Burger, appears to be "an 'ideal system' of education in terms of preparing Amish children for life as adults in the Amish community" (406 US 1972:223).

Thus far the Amish community has been able, through increased efforts, to protect itself from these various forces of change and to maintain a distinctive way of life. How many more generations it shall be able to do so remains open to question, but it still can be reckoned as one of the more successful efforts at ethnic survival.

As we move from these examples of relatively isolated, total ethnic communities in rural settings, it is also possible to identify relatively total ethnic communities within urban settings. In such settings the boundaries of the communities tend to be contiguous with those of others in some sort of ecological arrangement. Robert E. Park and his colleagues at the University of Chicago identified these as natural areas in his urban studies of Chicago in the 1920s. Inside these areas first-generation immigrants, whether Italian, Irish, Jewish, or other, sought to build what Wirth calls ghettos, within whose boundaries a relatively full life experience could be lived. Louis Wirth in his classic work *The Ghetto* (1966) described life within these enclaves.

Protective though these walls were, they were nevertheless even less closed to external forces than were those of the more isolated rural communities. Tensions were constant along the ethnic boundaries; one group vying with the other for space and resources. In more recent times, Suttles in his work on the Adams area presents a more systematic analysis of these tensions and the jockeying for space and dominance along the boundaries (1968). Institutions from the larger society, be they schools, police, or welfare agencies have penetrated the boundaries and become part of the environment. Furthermore, even in the early urban ghettos, many inhabitants spent their workday outside the ghetto, frequently in the company of their fellow ethnics, but nevertheless exposed to features and facets of the larger society. The net result was that these ghettos were under constant pressure and influence from forces generated from the outside.

The instabilities and problems created by outside forces can best be seen in those instances where ghetto residents sought valiantly to preserve a total way of life. One such example would be the Hasidic communities in Williamsburgh and Crown Heights in Brooklyn, which seek to retain their integrity as religious communities. In time some segments have found the urban pressures too overwhelming. In order to retain their inviolability they moved to more congenial surroundings in northern New Jersey, New York state, and elsewhere. More frequently ghetto residents did not have such a stake so that the first-generation ghettos became dispersed and functioned essentially as creations of bounded time and space.

Dispersion of the ghetto of the first-generation immigrant did not generally mean the dissolution of the ethnic enclave; instead there arose what Kramer and Leventman have called the "gilded ghetto" of the second and third generation (1961).

However these ethnic communities were and are more open to the influences of the larger society. Many members cross the boundaries of the community to satisfy important interests and needs. Occupations and jobs become increasingly pursued in the larger society. Educational, cultural, and recreational interests also involve such participation as well as involvement in nonethnic community and other types of voluntary associations. Even within the ethnic community, values and life-styles modeled after those of the larger society take on an increasingly important role.

These ethnic communities no longer contain an inclusive and total life experience; they are more aptly described as open-ended or partial ethnic communities. We find increasing numbers of members of an ethnic group—including those who retain their ethnic identity—move out from the community itself and become randomly distributed throughout the larger society.

These variations among ethnic communities can be described in terms of a continuum. At one end are the inclusive and total communities of the Amish type and at the other the open-ended and partial communities of the second- and third-generation suburban ethnics. Beyond that would be a random distribution which would signify the dissolution of the ethnic community.

Despite these variations, it is evident that these nuclear ethnic communities share a common function; they serve as the basic energizing and revitalizing source for the ethnic group as a whole. As Gordon suggests, they perform this function largely through the network of primary relations, through the pivotal role of the family and kinship system, and through other institutions that are located within its boundaries. In a microcosm, then, these nuclear communities provide for the individual member and for the group the immediate existential stage on which the drama of the "folk" is played out. In some respects, it resembles the atom which reflects on a small scale the workings of the universe.

This is particularly true of nuclear ethnic communities—whether inclusive or partial—located in suburbia, small towns, and working-class neighborhoods in the city. Middle-class ethnics in the city may, however, operate on a somewhat more general level of involvement through networks of organizations that have only incidentally a neighborhood or community base.

Most ethnic groups include a number of such localized nuclear communities of varying size and inclusiveness which may be scattered over wide areas—even worldwide. Most of these nuclear communities have virtually nothing to do with each other, but all recognize their being part of a larger entity; of being part of the same folk as reflected in common institutions, culture, and the like.

In this respect the ethnic group in its totality resembles a kind of nation in which loyalties to the whole might be of a more abstract, symbolic nature if they were not mediated through intense sentiment experienced on the more local level in and through networks of informal and formal relations. Small wonder then that William Petersen prefers the concept "ethnic sub-nation" to that of "ethnic group" (1971).

Associational character of the ethnic group

Thus far we have dealt with the communal character of the ethnic group. However, within the ethnic group—both on a local and general level—there tends to develop a variety of formal and informal associational arrangements which reinforce ethnicity either through the ethnic goals they pursue and/or through the homogeneity of their ethnic membership. As Gordon says,

> within the ethnic group there develops a network of organizations and informal social relationships which permits and encourages the members of the ethnic group to remain within the confines of the group for all of their primary relationships and some of their secondary relationships throughout all the stages of the life-cycle (Gordon 1964:34).

Within the nuclear community, the scope and character of such associational and institutional arrangements will depend on the degree of inclusiveness and totalness of the community and its class level.

For example, in the inclusive or total nuclear community virtually all activities—religious, economic, regulatory, social, and recreational—reinforce the ethnic character of the community. These are largely carried out through networks of informal and primary relationships which function as the basic system of order and structure in the community. This is clearly illustrated in the case of the Amish community.

The nuclear community in the case of the Amish is the "church district," which according to Hostetler is the "primary, self-governing unit, wherever Amish live. The rules of life are determined by this local bandlike organization, which is kept small by the ceremonial functions of assembling in a single household and by the limitation imposed by horse-and-carriage travel" (Hostetler 1968:12). There is a clear-cut structure of leadership with the bishop, the highest and most responsible position, and then the minister and deacon. Other than this there is almost no other formal organization. These officials are the ceremonial and religious leaders, but they cannot act arbitrarily. "The officials may informally come to an agreement on disciplinary matters, but they cannot make decisions that are binding without the consent of the assembled members" (Hostetler 1968:13).

The rules and order, "which are formulated by each district, cover the range of individual experience" (Hostetler 1968:14).

> Smallness in the Amish community is maintained by a functional unit no larger than a group of people who can know each other by name, by shared ceremonial activity and by convention. Like the Redfield model, the Amish community "is small, so small that either it itself is the unit of personal

observation or else, being somewhat larger and yet homogeneous, it provides in some part of it a unit of personal observation fully representative of the whole" (Hostetler 1968:14–15).

Within the social system, the family through its multiple functions plays a central role in the control of the individual and in the ceremonial life of the community. Virtually all activities in the community are performed through networks of informal relations. Even "leisure and ways of social enjoyment are met by the informal institutions within the community" largely carried out through the family and kinship system (Hostetler 1968:19).

Within the relatively inclusive ethnic community of the first-generation immigrant we also find marked reliance on informal networks of relationships as the major mode of life. This is true even in more recent studies of working-class and low-income ghettos such as those by Gans, *Urban Villagers* (1962), and Suttles, *The Social Order of the Slum* (1968). But alongside these networks, we also find in the urban setting the growth of organizations such as mutual aid societies, theater groups, burial societies, and the like. Each perform some needed function for the community, but all retain their primarily expressive functions of relating person to the community. Expressing even more significantly this dual function of fellowship and larger goals is the ethnic church and temple that stand at the center buttressed by the family as the core institutions in the community.

Once we reach the "gilded ghetto" of the second and third generation located in middle-class suburbs associational life takes on a more formal and special purpose character. Even as the community itself includes less of the total life experience of the ethnic members, a proliferation of voluntary associations tends to develop. Many of these are local chapters of general ethnic organizations such as B'nai Brith and Knights of Columbus which have explicitly ethnic goals and sponsorship; others take on the quality of an ethnic group through having a preponderance of membership from that group though the goals may be nonethnic in nature as in the case of PTAs, neighborhood improvement associations, and the like. The ethnic community becomes honeycombed by formally organized, special purpose associations that frequently have to compete with their nonethnic counterparts for the time, loyalty, and money of the ethnic members.

In certain respects a parallel structure of associations may develop within the ethnic community similar to that in the larger community. But unlike the colonial plural society of Furnivall (1956) and Smith (1965) in which these parallel structures are noncompetitive, ethnic members may move across boundaries so that these parallel structures frequently compete with each other for membership. But the response to the alternatives tends to be selective. In Lakeville, for example, Jewish women prefer sectarian auspices in their health and welfare affiliations, but nonsectarian auspices for their youth-serving affiliations. Their community and civic organizations are nonsectarian but their cultural and social organizations are sectarian. Thus the crossing of boundaries becomes widespread (Ringer 1967: ch.6 passim).

Despite the proliferation of these special purpose associations, the basic cohesion of the nuclear ethnic community still depends upon the networks of informal ties that connect segments of the community and upon the church and synagogue in its multiple roles as a place of worship and as a social center for members of the congregation.

Many of these ethnic organizations transcend the local nuclear communities and operate on the broader societal stage. If they seek a mass ethnic membership, then they tend to have chapters in the various nuclear communities. If mass membership is just incidental to their professed purpose and function, then their national headquarters becomes the main center of activity; examples are the American Jewish Committee, NAACP, and The Urban League. Such groups either function to coordinate and to deal with matters internal to the ethnic group or more frequently they operate on the boundaries of the ethnic groups and focus on relations with the outside world. As such they take on the instrumental function of pursuing the interests, needs, and defense of the ethnic group.

The proliferation of special purpose associations reflects the growing division of labor and function that develops within ethnic groups as they become more societalized and depend more on these associations to express their interests both inside and outside the ethnic boundaries. These associations are frequently organized on the Weberian rational authority principle. As such they resemble other bureaucratic structures in society that recruit and are run by professionals and officials whose basic claim to position is their technical competence and their contribution to organizational goals. In the process, these associations run the risk of taking on a gesellschaftlike quality and of so routinizing and rationalizing their interests that they lose contact with the sentiment and communal character of the ethnic group itself. On occasion, movements may arise within the ethnic group to protest this "over-rationalization and societalization" of ethnic group interests and to restore emotional fervor to the ethnic group. Some observers claim this may be one of the reasons for the emergence of the Jewish Defense League. However, we still know little about the actual or potential conflict or tension between the process of societalization by which the ethnic group mobilizes its energies to realize more effectively its interests and the underlying sentiment and communal character of the ethnic group.

These associations, both local and general, comprise the major elements of what Gordon calls the ethnic subsociety. Their importance for the ethnic group cannot be overstated. In addition to a more efficient and effective pursuit of group interests, they also serve the important function of making visible the broader unity of the ethnic group despite its segmentation into nuclear communities.

Furthermore these associations can be ranked according to their relative prestige and power within the ethnic group and also how they are responded to by the larger society. Where the ethnic group undergoes such a process of societalization, then power and influence tend to be concentrated in an "establishment" of instrumentally organized, special purpose associations.

Most ethnic groups in modern society undergo a process of societalization which produces a proliferation of special purpose associations. One of the more challenging questions for study is the effect this societalized structure has on the underlying communal character of the ethnic group. This relationship is filled with stresses and strains that have barely begun to be understood.

The ethnic group as a public and political interest group

Increasingly the ethnic group in modern society also functions as a public whose attention and interest is aroused on controversial and political issues before the general body politic. This is most evident when the ethnic group in its collective role as citizen and interest group seeks to bring pressure either collectively or through social agents on public policy and through the ballot on the officeholder. The significance of this conception is that it allows us to identify the process whereby the ethnic group becomes politicized and translates its interests and opinions into relevant channels of influence on the larger society.

According to Glazer and Moynihan, ethnicity has in fact become one of the most potent mechanisms in modern society for mobilizing sentiment in the pursuit of collective group interests and of concrete political ends. They insist that it has even come to challenge "the primacy for such mobilization of *class* on the one hand and *nation* on the other"—both of which have been presumed to be more in tune with organizing interest and sentiment in modern society (Glazer and Moynihan 1975:18).

In many countries, particularly those of the Third World, Glazer and Moynihan argue that ethnicity has been responsible for overt conflict and bloodshed; in others it has expressed itself in a more "peaceful" struggle for power and for the allocation of resources. But whichever the form it has taken, ethnicity, they conclude, has moved front and center on the political stage of modern society, and most racial and ethnic groups have organized themselves to pursue their interests on this stage.

The ethnic group as a subsociety in the larger society

As we have already indicated, ethnic groups vary according to the extent to which they function as relatively self-contained, autonomous communities in which all the vital life activities of its membership are performed; however, by definition, none is a completely autonomous social, economic, and political entity. This notion that the ethnic group is a subpart of a larger societal entity is clearly conveyed in a number of definitions of the term itself. Ware, in her article on ethnic communities in the *Encyclopaedia of the Social Sciences* in 1937, says, "Ethnic communities are groups bound together by common ties of race, nationality or culture, living together within an alien civilization but remaining culturally distinct" (p. 607). Morris, in the updated 1968 article on ethnic groups for the *International Encyclopedia of the Social Sciences*, reaffirms this notion:

> An ethnic group is a distinct category of the population in a larger society whose culture is usually different from its own. The members of such a group are, or feel themselves, or are thought to be, bound together by common ties of race or nationality or culture. The nature of an ethnic group's relationship with the society as a whole, and with other groups in it, constitutes one of the main problems in describing and analyzing such societies (Morris 1968:167).

Gumplowicz goes so far as to argue that the ethnic group as a distinctive sociological phenomenon was the product of conquest and the creation of the state society. Wagley and Harris basically agree with the Gumplowicz thesis. They too contend that ethnic groups emerged relatively late in human history, that prior to that time human beings lived in relatively small autonomous tribal-like societies in which they shared common values, sentiments, territory, and history. These societies were organized around the principle of Tönnies's gemeinschaft, Durkheim's mechanical solidarity, and Redfield's folk society. As such they were relatively homogeneous without any provision "for incorporating into a single social unit groups of individuals who are not related by descent or by marriage, who follow different customs, who stress distinctive values, and who, in sum, are an alien people" (Wagley and Harris 1958:241–242).

The formation of state societies, approximately five thousand years ago, created the basis for a more heterogeneous society.

> Only with the development of the state did human societies become equipped with a form of social organization which could bind masses of culturally and physically heterogeneous "strangers" into a single social entity. Whereas primitive peoples derive their cohesion largely from a common culture and

from kinship and other kinds of personal ties, state societies are held together largely by the existence of a central political authority which claims a monopoly of coercive power over all persons within a given territory. Theoretically, with a sufficiently strong development of the apparatus of government, a state society can extend law and order over limitless subgroups of strangers who neither speak the same language, worship the same gods, nor strive for the same values (Wagley and Harris 1958:242).

In this manner, many of the small autonomous societies were transformed into ethnic minorities within the larger societal system.

Yet the growth of the state form of organization did not entirely replace the principles by which unity is achieved among primitive peoples. On the contrary, if a thoroughgoing replacement had indeed taken place, [ethnic] minorities, as we know them today, would not exist. In reality, many of the subgroups have continued to regard themselves as distinctive units within the total society, not because they inhabit the same territory and are subject to the same apparatus of government, but because they share cultural traits different from others and reckon themselves, in a sense, as kinsmen by descent (Wagley and Harris 1958:242).

In time, the state society may seek to develop a notion of itself as a people and thereby come to be defined as a nation. This has led some observers to include under the ethnic rubric the nation, which can be defined as a community whose boundaries are presumably coterminous with those of the state society. A number of these observers however seem to be inconsistent in this usage. Gordon and Francis, for example, cannot quite make up their minds whether to include or to exclude the nation from the category of ethnic group.

Their confusion is understandable. For, though ethnic groups and the nation may share certain communal characteristics that make them seem similar, their relationship to the state society is qualitatively different. An ethnic group is merely part of the state society whereas the nation stands as a representation of the state society as a whole. And the relationship between part to whole—either in the form of the state or of the nation itself—is problematic and varies in time and place with a specific ethnic group and with the specific political society involved.

Therefore, to subsume the nation under the ethnic rubric is to obscure an analytic distinction that merits independent study and that is crucial in the world today. We agree with Wagley and Harris and others that it is better to distinguish the two concepts and to treat them as separate structural terms. Thus we join those who would confine the term ethnic group to subgroups, subsocieties, or even subnations within the more general state society or nation-state. We shall have more to say about ethnicity and the nation-state in later chapters.

The External Societal Designation of Ethnic and Racial Distinctiveness: Their They-ness

Thus far we have concentrated on those forces and factors internal to the ethnic group that contribute to its cohesiveness, structure, and distinctiveness. The ethnic group is also part of a larger political economic system with which it must come to terms. At the least, the ethnic group must show an adaptive capacity to this larger system if it is to survive. But what is even more significant, the larger society actively sets the terms of adaptation and furthermore actively influences and shapes the very character of the group itself, particularly if it is also a racially distinctive group. In some instances the larger society recognizes the distinctiveness of an ethnic or racial group but defines and interprets this distinctiveness in its own way; in other instances it "creates" a distinctiveness, and in still other instances it may refuse to recognize and/or to legitimate the distinctiveness of a group which so views itself. Whichever alternative it takes, the larger society affects the very structure and character of the target group.

> In fact, we know that the subjection of a group of people to a common political organization may directly, or more often, indirectly, by imposition of common laws, religion, language, feeling of loyalty, etc., not only forge together different ethnic elements into a new ethnic group but also divide an ethnic group or deliberately alter its structure, culture, and character (Francis 1947:397).

In other words, an ethnic group develops into what Sumner calls an in-group with a defined sense of we-ness. The ethnic group is quite aware that beyond the boundaries of the we-ness is a *they*. This *they* may be specific groups of others, but from our present stance the most important They for the ethnic group is the larger society itself. This capital They plays a vital role in the very being and functioning of the ethnic group, a fact of which the ethnic group is fully cognizant. There is an inextricable connection between the two. As we have already indicated, Peter Rose recognizes this fact in the very title of his book: *They and We.*

Allport puts the matter somewhat differently.

> Every line, fence or boundary marks off an inside from an outside. Therefore, in strict logic, an in-group always implies the existence of some corresponding out-group. But this logical statement by itself is of little significance. What we need to know is whether one's loyalty to the in-group automatically implies disloyalty, or hostility, or other forms of negativism, toward out-groups (Allport 1954:40).

In our judgment the answer would be no, but we also feel that the most relevant part of the statement is in the first sentence; namely that the boundary around an ethnic group separates a *we* on one side from a *they* on the other; and from the perspective of an ethnic group the most important They is the larger society itself.

However, just as the ethnic group defines those outside its boundaries as a They; so can it be said that those outside the boundaries of the ethnic group—the larger society, in effect—tend to designate the ethnic group itself as a They. And this designated *They-ness* of the ethnic group can be seen as part of larger society's effort to establish and/or to maintain some sort of boundary between itself and the designated ethnic group.

According to Allport, the larger society, in defining the ethnic group tends to use categories that are (1) monopolistic: include all kinds of elements in definitions whether essential, nonessential, and even false beliefs; (2) value-laden: saturated with emotional overtones and judgments of goodness and badness; and (3) rigid: exhibit a reluctance to modification even with new information; new information tends to be selectively incorporated to retain preexisting categorization (Allport 1954).

The we-ness and they-ness of an ethnic group

When an ethnic group defines itself as a distinctive group it must face the fact that the larger society also perceives it as a distinctive entity. To the one, though, this distinctiveness refers to "we"; to the other, a "they."* A dynamic tension exists between this "we-ness/they-ness" character of the ethnic group which plays an overriding role in determining the life circumstances of the ethnic group.

However, despite this apparent agreement on the designation of distinctiveness, major differences exist between the ethnic group and larger society over the specifics of this definition. For example, on the cognitive level, larger society's definition of the ethnic group is primarily a function of its own beliefs about the group, which may not basically correspond with the group's own beliefs about itself nor even with the "real nature of the group." In effect both may differ greatly in their answers to such questions as: What are the essential defining characteristics of the ethnic group? What are its values and goals? What are the basic characteristics of its membership? The larger society tends to oversimplify the answers, to use what Allport calls "monopolistic categories" in defining the group. By the same token the ethnic group's beliefs about itself may or may not correspond to the "realities" of the

---

*We shall henceforth reserve the term *They* as the label outsiders bestow on an ethnic group, and we shall use the term *Them* as the label an ethnic group gives to outsiders.

situation, but they frequently stand in opposition to those of the larger society.

Equally, if not more significant, are the differences that characterize the evaluation of this distinctiveness by both. The ethnic group positively values its distinctiveness; often the larger society evaluates it negatively. As we shall see in the next chapter, some ethnic groups may be positively valued by society. Thus the we-ness that is a plus to the ethnic group is transmuted to a minus by the larger society in its view of the ethnic group as a they. Even the standards of judgment vary between the two with each selecting a standard which is more in keeping with its own scale of priorities and values. Thus a dynamic tension is virtually built into the we-ness/they-ness character of the ethnic group from which the group never fully escapes.

The larger society's conception of the they-ness of the ethnic group has serious consequences for the ethnic group. For the larger society tends to accept the "validity" of its own definition and seeks to impose it in its relations with the ethnic group. Its conception of the they-ness of the group, for example, will govern its treatment of the ethnic group which in turn affects the life circumstances and opportunities of the ethnic group in the larger society. In addition, its conception may serve to erect or reinforce insular barriers around the ethnic group. Such barriers can have positive consequences for the internal cohesion of the group by forcing its members on each other and reinforcing loyalty. However, history offers many examples of where sustained and overwhelming pressures by the larger society have fragmentized and pulverized ethnic solidarity. Under certain circumstances the larger society may seek to impose its definition of membership, even at the expense of the ethnic group's own definition. For example, Hitler labeling persons who had disappeared into the German community as Jews even though they and other Jews no longer considered themselves as Jews.

Even where this they-ness reinforces the internal solidarity of the ethnic group, the negative evaluations of the ethnic group by larger society may still seep in and affect an ethnic group member's conception of himself. Inasmuch as such evaluations may highlight the designated "inferiority" of the group, it may produce uncertainties and mixed feelings among these ethnic group members as to who they really are and how good they are. Kurt Lewin's statements on self-hate are pertinent here (1948).

The less clear-cut an ethnic group's sense of folk, of we-ness with its accompanying ethnocentricity, the more vulnerable are its members to such unfavorable societal designations. Most vulnerable are those groupings that are under sustained and continuing pressure from the larger society.

They-ness and racial distinctiveness

Historically, society's designation of an ethnic group as a *they* has frequently been a response to an already established sense of we-ness of the ethnic group. This is frequently the case with those ethnic groups whose solidarity is based on grounds of religion or nationality. However, colonial history contains many examples of a society's designation of they-ness being instrumental in "creating" the conditions for the subsequent development of we-ness in a group. Thus, society may define as a distinctive category (a they) an aggregate of people who lack common culture, an internal structure, and a sense of folk, but who share certain distributive characteristics, and by forcing them into a common environment of arbitrary and discriminatory treatment, creates a sense of shared fate and identity among them. This has been more or less the history of relations between peoples with different racial characteristics in which one racial group subordinates another.

> A more conspicuous case is the American Negro. Although most of the slaves were seized on the west coast of Africa, they were from a number of different ethnic groups. In the beginning those who worked together on the same plantation spoke so many different languages that they had to learn English in order to communicate with each other. Regardless of ethnic identity they were assigned the same status, and after four centuries as a minority group American Negroes now conceive of themselves as being of a kind. Thus, minority groups arise from differential treatment based upon classification. People who find themselves set apart eventually come to recognize their common interests (Shibutani and Kwan 1965:202).

This categorization of a they, unmindful of the internal differences of the group, became a prevailing feature of the white Europeans' colonial activities.

> In Colonial Africa, for example, all natives were treated alike, but they certainly did not conceive of themselves as being of a kind. They had deeply-rooted tribal affiliations, and conflicts among their ancestors reached back far beyond the arrival of the first white man (Shibutani and Kwan 1965:41–42).

And so racial boundaries were established which in many ways superseded internal variations on either side.

The same story unfolds in the American treatment of Indians. The Kluckholns describe graphically the process as it unfolded among the Navaho.

> It has not been established that there ever was a "Navaho Tribe" in the sense of an organized, centralized, "political" entity.

> Just as there is no complete cultural or "racial" unity, so also The People are only beginning to have what may accurately be designated as a "tribal" or "national" consciousness. Previous to 1868, the largest unit of effective social cöoperation seems to have been a band of Indians who occupied a defined territory and acknowledged the leadership of a single headman. These local bands acted without much reference to other such units . . . . When The People were all treated as a unit by the United States Government and were assigned a common Reservation, this doubtless had the effect of promoting tribal cohesiveness (Kluckholn and Kluckholn 1962: 122–123).

Thus colonial conquest and enslavement frequently established and reinforced racial boundaries between groups so that, according to Shibutani and Kwan, *"new classifications of human being develop to coincide with the evolving pattern of differential treatment"* (Shibutani and Kwan 1965:202). This differential treatment under colonialism profoundly affected the life circumstances and chances of the subordinated racial group and bestowed upon it a pariah status of a kind that qualitatively distinguished its fate from that accorded groups divided on grounds of nationality and religion. For example, the definition of they-ness that the white Europeans imposed on many of these subjugated racial groups literally stripped them of basic human qualities. As Winthrop Jordan (1974) reports, white Europeans in the seventeenth and eighteenth century compared black Africans to animals, called them libidinous savages, and with the burgeoning of the slave trade transmuted them into the ultimate form of dehumanization: they became chattel property to be bought and sold.

In the early stages of colonial conquest this they-ness may be unaccompanied by a sense of we-ness within the designated category, but in time this asymmetrical definition of distinctiveness may give way to a growing sense of internal solidarity. The Kluckholns describe such a transformation among the Navaho.

> Whatever tribal feeling The People have today rests upon the following factors: a common language; a common designation for themselves as The People as distinct from all others; a cultural heritage which is, *in general*, the same; a territory with a certain topographical unity, where the occupants are mostly Navahos and where many mountains and other natural features are enshrined in a common mythology; the fact that almost all The People constitute a single governmental administrative unit with a single elected council for the whole tribe. The system of clans and linked clans also makes for unity, to the extent that they have cross-regional representation and make legion the number of individuals whom any given Navaho addresses as "my relative." To some degree, all of these factors point to a general tendency: The People are becoming increasingly conscious of common background, common problems, a common need to unite to protect their interests against the encroachment of whites (Kluckholn and Kluckholn 1962:123).

In a similar manner it is possible to trace the growth of a sense of folk and we-ness among the black Americans. Unfortunately crucial features of this development are largely unknown and are still the subject of serious controversy. Yet certain of these features can be identified. From a fragmented, aggregate of diverse peoples living in a state of relative anomie under slavery, there slowly emerged among them a sense of folk.

The nullification of they-ness and the delegitimization of the ethnic group

To many ethnic groups their treatment as a they by the larger society makes their life and position in society a difficult one; they become targets of prejudice, discrimination, exploitation, and ill-treatment. And yet in some perverse manner, their they-ness also protects them. At the least this designation recognizes that they *exist* and are deemed identifiable groups—perhaps of pariah status—but at least within the framework of society.

The case for the protective function of they-ness for racial groups, particularly for the black under slavery, is less clear-cut. A number of scholars maintain that because white slaveowners invested so heavily in the black as their source of labor, they were unlikely to destroy arbitrarily or irrationally their investment. Thus, they claim, the black had a modicum of protection. He was given the right to *survive* in society as long as he did not actively challenge his status as property and as a nonperson.

Throughout history, however, occasions have arisen where a larger society has even sought to deny the right of an ethnic group to survive. It has gone so far as to reject the ethnic group's right to exist within its boundaries. It has done so by refusing to recognize the ethnic group as a they or by withdrawing previous recognition of it as a they. In some instances larger society has sought to act on this denial or delegitimization of the ethnic group by exterminating it, as in the case of the Jews in Nazi Germany or the Huguenots of France. In other instances it has expelled the group from its boundaries as was the frequent fate of Jews in medieval Western Europe. And in still other instances it has sought to assimilate forcibly the ethnic group, as was the case of the Jews of Spain.

Success in these efforts by larger society has meant of course the dissolution of the ethnic group; but history also reveals occasions where an ethnic group with a distinctive sense of we-ness has attempted to survive under these conditions of societal nonthey-ness. By becoming a nonthey, the ethnic group is even more at the mercy of the larger society than as a they; it can never escape an awareness of the larger society in its efforts to survive and to avoid detection. In the process, its very character and nature became transformed as it takes on the characteristics of what Georg Simmel defined as a "secret society" (1950).

One of the most dramatic examples of this internal transformation is to be found among the Marrano Jews of medieval Spain. Prior to the late fifteenth century Jews were recognized as a pariah religious community whose members, though, were able to attain high positions in government, medicine, and public affairs. Beginning with 1480, systematic efforts were made to either expel or convert them to Christianity. By 1492, virtually all who continued to profess Judaism were expelled; only those who had converted and had become New Christians remained. Many of these, despite their public roles as Christians, continued to practice their Judaism in private. They were labeled Marranos and became the major objects of surveillance and concern during the Inquisition. Discovery by the Inquisitors resulted in death for the Marranos. They were punished, however, not as practicing Jews but as heretics. In fact, professing Jews did not come under the scope of the activities of the Inquisition. In effect, the larger society even pursued a policy of nonthey-ness in their punishment. Marranos were not defined as really Jews at heart but as deviants in the Christian community who were heretical in their practices.

So oppressive did surveillance become and so severe the threat of punishment that the Marranos were forced even more into a clandestine existence. For purposes of safety and protection they became fragmented into small groups, consorted among their own kind, married among themselves. They had to give up any outward visible signs of Judaism, prayer books could not be kept in the household. They had to divest themselves of the various written, symbolic, and other forms of Judaism that traditionally had been a major source of continuity from generation to generation. In its place they had to depend on oral transmission of practices, which by the second and third generation had become so transformed that all that remained in essence was a belief in monotheism and a sense of group cohesion.

In time, they became transformed into a new ethnic group. As Kamen says, "the later *conversos* possessed little or no religion, and they became a nameless community, replenished only now and then by immigrant Portuguese judaizers, but otherwise sorry remnants of a great and martyred race" (Kamen 1965:22).

Nullification of they-ness and absorption of the ethnic group

At the other extreme of nullified they-ness, we have a more benevolent situation in which the larger society may mute or even forego its designation of they-ness. Over time members of an ethnic group may even move away from a sense of we-ness. The net result is that boundaries between the two become permeable and individual members of the ethnic group gain acceptance and are absorbed into the larger society. Should a sufficient number of ethnic group members follow this path, then in time the ethnic group may disappear as a distinctive entity and its membership become absorbed into the larger national identity.

In some respects, this describes the path of voluntary assimilation which may be the normative model of the larger society and may become the accepted model of the ethnic group. In the United States, despite its egalitarian-assimilationist values, this has happened only selectively to certain nationality groups. Except for the symbolic residue of ethnic distinctiveness, third and fourth and beyond generations of Northern Europeans, including Germans, Irish, and the like, have become more closely bound with a national identity of being an American than with their ethnic group of national origin.

Such situations, however, can no longer be treated or subsumed under the rubric of ethnic situations. They have become something else.

A typological summary

We have thus identified four kinds of we-ness/they-ness situations that characterize relations between an ethnic or racial group and the larger society. These four situations are summarized in the following table, "Types of ethnic situations as defined by internal and external definitions of distinctiveness."

Ethnic Group Definition of We-ness	Societal Designation of They-ness	
	Yes	No
High	First and second generation national-origin groups.	Secret societies: Marranos of Spain
		Jews in Nazi Germany
	Religious groups. (1)	(3)
Low	Racial groups in early days of colonial conquest by white Europeans (2)	"National Identity": Fourth-generation Irish, etc. (4)

In cell (1), we find agreement over the distinctiveness of the ethnic group; to the ethnic group, a clear sense of we-ness; to the larger society, a clear-cut designation of they-ness. In the American experience examples in cell (1) would be the immigrant national origins groups and religious ethnic groups. In cell (2) we find that society clearly designates this category of people as a they, though the group itself may have no real sense, at least initially, of being a we. The most significant examples for this cell would be nonwhite racial groups in the early days of colonial conquest by white Europeans. In time many of these groups, as in the case of the black and the American Indian in the New World, developed a strong sense of we-ness and took on the other internal characteristics of an ethnic group. As a result, their defining features today are virtually indistinguishable from those that characterize the national-origin and religious groups of cell (1).

In cell (3) we find a more deviant type of situation in which, despite societal efforts to make a nonthey out of an ethnic group, the group nevertheless persists in trying to maintain its cohesion and we-ness. As we have seen, in the process it takes on the character of a secret society.

Cell (4) takes us outside of an ethnic situation; for neither society nor the ethnic group retains a sense of distinctiveness about the group. The ethnic group has ceased to exist as a distinctive entity and has become absorbed into a larger national identity. The significance of this cell is that it describes one kind of outcome for ethnic identity as boundaries between the group and society become permeable and the amalgamation that Park (1950) once foresaw as the probable ultimate fate of ethnic groups in America is realized.

Racial and ethnic groups: combined or separate categories

Before concluding this chapter, we'd like to address ourselves to a question that is more than a mere exercise in semantics. Should racial groups be subsumed under the general rubric of ethnic group as are religious and national-origin groups?

A number of sociologists would answer in the affirmative. They are particularly impressed with the we-ness associated with many racial groups today. These groups, in effect, also share the communal, cultural, and structural characteristics identified with ethnicity. And so we find sociologists like Gordon who have adopted this approach. Glazer also agrees with this inclusive usage.

> Thus one possible position on ethnicity and race, and the one I hold, is that they form part of a single family of social identities—a family which, in addition to races and ethnic groups, includes religions (as in Holland),

language groups (as in Belgium), and all of which can be included in the most general term, ethnic groups, groups defined by descent, real or mythical, and sharing a common history and experience (Glazer 1971:447).

Other scholars disagree and keep the two terms separate. Warner, for example, contrasts the cultural characteristics of ethnic groups with the physical characteristics of racial groups. Van den Berghe argues that both are socially defined groups: the ethnic group "on the basis of *cultural* criteria," (van den Berghe 1967a:10) and racial groups "on the basis of *physical* criteria" (van den Berghe 1967a:9).

Feagin insists that on the surface the disagreement between the two sets of scholars seems to manifest itself only over the internal characterization of we-ness with which they depict racial and ethnic groups. But, he continues, on a deeper and less obvious level the disagreement is over basic assumptions about the they-ness imputed to each group.

> Those who prefer the broader definition often argue that the experiences of people defined as nonwhite are essentially similar to the experiences of white groups. Some have argued that in the United States the situation and experiences of nonwhite Americans are essentially similar in kind to those of white immigrant groups. Often a further assumption is that the experiences of both white and nonwhite groups are adequately explained using the same theoretical framework—usually an assimilationist framework. Researchers who prefer the narrower definition, who see ethnic groups as a category separate from racial groups, usually have different underlying assumptions. These include the view that the experiences of non-European racial groups have been distinctively different from those of European groups (Feagin 1984:9).

We would make the point even more strongly than does Feagin. The they-ness imputed to racial minorities by the dominant American society has been qualitatively different from the they-ness imputed to white ethnic minorities. True, the latter have experienced historically considerable deprivation and discrimination in America but not the kind of exclusionary and dehumanizing treatment that deprived racial minorities of even the most basic rights and amenities for much of U.S. history. So imprinted has this differential treatment been onto the very foundations of the American society from the colonial period onward that we have constructed a theory of duality to account for this differential treatment. In succeeding chapters we shall explain and elaborate upon this thesis of duality. Accordingly we shall keep the two terms separate, although on occasion when we shall be looking at matters common to both racial and ethnic groups we may for the sake of simplicity use the term "ethnicity" only.

2 Race-Ethnicity and Types of Dominance

In the last chapter we dealt in general terms with the relationship between race-ethnicity and society. Within the framework of larger society, racial and ethnic groups are neither randomly distributed nor equally valued and accepted. Instead they are located in the hierarchical structures of society according to the extent to which they have access to or possess basic kinds of dominance and/or according to the way they are manifestly "valued" in society.

In this chapter we shall first examine the majority-minority status of racial and ethnic groups. We shall then proceed to a more systematic analysis of the relationship between race-ethnicity and the basic types and structural contexts of dominance in society.

Race-Ethnicity and Majority-Minority Status

A conventional way for distinguishing the relative position of racial and ethnic groups in society is to use the labels majority and minority. As elaborated by Wagley and Harris (1958), some groups assume such a preeminent position in society through numbers and/or through power that they tend to be identified as a majority or dominant group. Most other groups occupy disadvantaged and subordinated positions and come to be designated as minorities.

The difficulty in using this terminology is that the two terms combine the dimensions of numbers and of power when in fact the relationship between the two dimensions may vary with different countries. In the United States, for example, the two dimensions have historically been in agreement. The majority group has been characterized by both dominance and large numbers; the minority by subordination and small numbers. In formerly colonialized countries as in Africa and Southeast

Asia the relationship between the dimensions has been the inverse. Those numerically in the majority (the indigenous population) have been subordinated; those numerically in the minority (Europeans) have been dominant. Wagley and Harris still prefer the majority-minority designations for these situations, but their primary emphasis is obviously on differential power. Schermerhorn (1970), however, prefers the term *elite* for the group that is a statistical minority but is in position of dominance in a society and the term *mass subjects* for the group that is a numerical majority but is in a subordinated position. Diagram 1 illustrates the ways in which these dimensions are related.

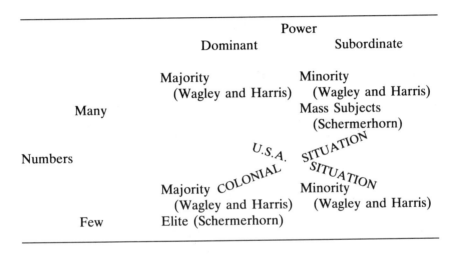

Whichever terminology one adopts, however, the crucial factor is relative dominance or subordination, not mere numbers. That will be our primary emphasis, too.

The majority as national model

The significance of racial or ethnic majorities rests not only on their possession of the basic instruments of control in a society, but also on their impact on the values and identity of the nation as a whole. Wagley and Harris offer a succinct statement of what this means.

After describing the growth of the modern state society which consists of a number of racial-ethnic groups, each of which regards itself as a distinctive unit within the total society, they go on to say,

> certain of these sub-groups, especially the more numerous and more powerful ones ... have tended to act as if the state society to which they

29

belong ideally ought to consist of their own physical and cultural type; and as if the state were merely the territorial expression of their own people or "nation" (Wagley and Harris 1958:242).

Thus it can be argued that the dominant group seeks to impress its own brand of truth, virtue, and beauty on the larger society, to monopolize elite positions, and to require adoption of its styles and values by those who wish to gain acceptance in that society. Yet, despite the success of its efforts, this distinctive racial-ethnic stamp may be transformed over time into a more universalistic ethnically neutral value system. This will be discussed in Chapter 4.

Minorities and subordinated status

Most racial-ethnic groups in a society, however, do not occupy such a favored position. Many find the channels to privilege and power blocked, and they occupy subordinated positions economically, politically, and socially. These racial-ethnic groups are labeled minorities. Though the term minority has been applied to virtually all racial-ethnic groups that suffer some disadvantage in society, the extent and kind of disadvantage varies. Racial minorities, for example, have suffered historically from a more arbitrary and legally sanctioned exclusion and discrimination in America than have the white immigrants. Among the least disadvantaged are third- and fourth-generation Irish.

Despite these differences, it is evident that in varying degrees minorities do not share equitably in the distribution of power, privilege, and property. This arises in large measure from deliberate policies of exclusion and discrimination; even if these policies wane or become selective, these groups are confronted by a differential opportunity structure that penalizes them in their pursuit of privilege, power, and property.

Dimensions of Dominance and Structural Contexts

We have indicated that racial-ethnic groups can be divided into those in a dominant position in society (majority) and those in a subordinate position (minority). These distinctions, however, are too gross; they treat the term dominance in too global a manner. Various sociologists have argued that there are different types of dominance in a society; the most often mentioned are power, property, and prestige. They also maintain that these types of dominance bear special relationships to different structural contexts in society; the most frequently mentioned distinction is between the political-economic order and the social order. Accordingly, the study of the relationship between race-ethnicity and dominance becomes a more complex matter than is suggested by the labels majority and minority. This relationship varies significantly with the specific type of dominance and structural context.

The political-economic order: sources of dominance

To a number of scholars the crucial consideration in the study of the structure of inequality or dominance in a society is what happens in the political-economic order. However, the forces that are viewed as instrumental in the creation and maintenance of the structure of inequality depends upon which realm of the order is stressed: the economic or the political.

Marx and Weber: Class and the Economic Realm

For Marx, the major arena that determines the allocation of position and power in society is the economic. He considers the political arena as a part of the superstructure of society and what happens there is derivative of what happens in the economic. According to Marx, the economic sphere is rended by a basic conflict of interest that sets the stage for a historic struggle between classes. As he wrote in his *Communist Manifesto*, "The history of all hitherto existing society is a history of class struggles" (Marx and Engels [1848] 1935: 21). To Marx this struggle develops over man's relationship to the means of production. On the one side are the owners and controllers of these means; on the other are those who are dependent on these means of production for their livelihood and life chances but who do not own or control them.

To Marx these two groups comprise the basic contending classes in society: the former labeled the oppressors; the latter, the oppressed. According to Marx, the specific character of these antagonistic classes varies with the historical epoch. At one time the struggle was between freeman and slave; at another, between patrician and plebian; at still another, between lord and serf. The struggle that occupied most of Marx's attention in his works was that which arose under capitalism between bourgeoisie and proletariat. In each period, however, the issue between the classes was basically the control over the means of production which to Marx was the key to the exercise not only of economic but also of political power in society.

Although Marx never fully developed his concept of class, Weber undertook that task almost three-quarters of a century later. In doing so he sought to distinguish those processes and principles that serve to stratify the economic order from those that serve to stratify the social order. His concept of class focuses exclusively on what happens in the economic sphere of society. "With some over-simplification, one might thus say that 'classes' are stratified according to their relations to the production and acquisition of goods" (Weber [1922] 1946:193).

To Weber then the economic order is stratified into a hierarchically arranged set of classes. Each class includes "(1) a number of people [who] have in common a specific causal component of their life chances, in so far as (2) this component is represented exclusively by economic interests in the possession of goods and opportunities for income" (Weber [1922] 1946:181). Weber then added another crucial element to his definition: all the above must come about "(3)... under the conditions of the commodity or labor markets" (Weber [1922] 1946:181). In other words, people who perform a comparable function or occupational role in the economic order tend to occupy a similarly advantaged or disadvantaged bargaining position in the competitive marketplace and accordingly share similar opportunities and ways of earning income as well as for rewards for services. As such they constitute a class in Weber's sense.

According to Weber, the class situations that arise from the market frequently lead to a fierce competitive struggle between the propertied and the propertyless, between management and labor. But unlike Marx, Weber did not view revolution or overt conflict as an inevitable consequence of this struggle; only as other historical and cultural conditions were present did this arise. Further, the market as the pervasive mechanism for allocating and distributing economic goods and services was likely to occur only in some societies, according to Weber. Specifically these were likely to be capitalist societies that had transformed the major factors of production of land, labor, and capital into commodities for hire and sale in the marketplace.

Within the framework of Marxian and Weberian class analysis, race and ethnicity seem to play little if any independent role in determining position in the structure of inequality—any effect being ultimately reducible to an economic class effect. Even with Weber's market mechanism, race and ethnicity have at most an indirect effect. They may reflect the relative "readiness' of a given group to take advantage of the labor market—the market itself being considered impersonal, neutral, and unaffected by racial and ethnic considerations.

Gumplowicz: Ethnicity and the Political Realm

Scholars who stress the political arena tend to view matters differently. They focus on other forces and factors as being instrumental in the creation of the structure of inequality. One who has made political conquest and ethnicity the heart of his theory is Ludwig Gumplowicz; his major works were written toward the end of the nineteenth century.

According to Gumplowicz, mankind for much of its early history lived within small compact societies characterized by "association and simple consanguinity with the resultant community of language, religious ideas, customs and mode of life ... " (Gumplowicz [1899] 1963:222). Gumplowicz labeled these preliterate societies "primitive hordes." During this period these hordes lived isolated from each other. Occasionally they engaged in "simple plundering raids," including the practice of women stealing (Gumplowicz [1899] 1963:196), otherwise they had little contact.

But there came a time in human history, Gumplowicz asserted, when more warlike societies undertook "expeditions for the permanent subjection of the foreign horde and the acquisition of territory" (Gumplowicz [1899] 1963:196). In the process a complex societal system was created which was based on "the subjection of one social group by another and the establishment of sovereignty" (Gumplowicz [1899] (1963):199). This complex societal system, Gumplowicz called "the State"* (Gumplowicz [1899] 1963:199).

"The activities of the State as a whole," he continued, "originate in the sovereign class which acts with the assistance or with the compulsory acquiescence of the subject class." The attention of the State "is directed against other states and social groups. Its object is always defence against attacks, increase of power and territory, that is, conquest in one form or another. And its motive in the ultimate analysis, lies ... in the impulse to secure conditions favorable for existence ... " (Gumplowicz [1899] 1963:199).

Within the State the superior class imposes the burden of manual and other forms of labor—often compulsory—upon the subject classes in order to achieve its political and economic goals and to live a better life than it otherwise could. "As a rule, this leads to oppression and can always be considered as exploitation" (Gumplowicz [1899] 1963:199). In this way, Gumplowicz concluded, " ... the foundation of ethnically composite States [is laid] in human necessities and sentiments. Human labor being necessary, sympathy with kindred and tribe and deadly hatred of strangers led to foreign wars. So conquest and the satisfaction of needs through the labor of the conquered, essentially the same though differing in form, is the great theme of human history from prehistoric times to the latest plan for a Congo State" (Gumplowicz [1899] 1963:203).

---

*Throughout this book we shall adopt a more limited usage for the term "State." We shall confine it to the structure and system of governance and legal-political authority of society and not expand it to include the total structure and system of society as does Gumplowicz.

As a result, Gumplowicz was convinced that the internal stratification of the State or classes as he called them "arise originally out of different ethnic elements or by the permanent organization of such as are at different stages of development at the time of their union" (Gumplowicz [1899] 1963:218). "Such classes antedate the State and are the more easily maintained in it because their differences are both anthropological and moral" (Gumplowicz [1899] 1963:216). Gumplowicz also believed that once the State came into being "a process of differentiation" created other classes as well (Gumplowicz [1899] 1963:216). These classes might also take on the "group-making" characteristics of the "primitive horde" and develop a strong sense of moral solidarity and common class interests as have the ethnically defined classes from the very beginning (Gumplowicz [1899] 1963:223).

Within the State, relations between the various classes are tense and conflictual. "Each group exerts whatever power it normally possesses and tries to have its relative position recognized in the State in form of rights. But every right is made the basis of renewed efforts. Human desires are constantly growing and no social group ever rested content with what it had obtained. On the contrary, present attainments are used to increase power and satisfy new desires" (Gumplowicz [1899] 1963:226). Thus, "the struggle between social groups, the component parts of the State, is as inexorable as that between hordes or States. The only motive is self-interest. In *Der Rassenkampf* we describe the conflict as 'race-war' for such is is inexorable animosity that each group that is able, tends to become exclusive like a caste, to form a consanguineous circle. In short, it becomes a race" (Gumplowicz [1899] 1963:227).

The struggle is primarily played out on the legal-political stage. "The superior classes, as we have seen, cannot rest content with the fact of superiority. Political relations need to be confirmed. Might must be turned into right ... " (Gumplowicz [1899] 1963:230). The other classes also organize in order to influence the political and legal process.

> The proximate end of organization is to establish a legal norm for the mutual relations of the groups, to confirm by right the commanding position which has been acquired or is striven for. Hence it is clear that the organization which has acquired the right of legislation in the State occupies the most powerful position, and that it is the aim of every other organization to participate in the same right (Gumplowicz [1899] 1963:228).

In the final analysis then, Gumplowicz accepts a conflict model of society as does Marx, but he departs from Marx in his emphasis on race-ethnicity, conquest, and the political process as major forces in the struggle for power in society. A further distinction is that each uses as his analytical model a different type of society—though both thought that they were developing a general theory applicable to all societies. Gumplowicz, for example, focuses on two types of societies: those in the early stages of State formation and those that appear much later during the feudal or monarchical periods, particularly in Western Europe. Marx in turn was preoccupied with industrial capitalistic societies, particularly as they were developing in Europe in the nineteenth century.

However, with the colonial and imperialistic expansion of capitalist societies during the late nineteenth and early twentieth centuries, even observers who called themselves Marxists had difficulty applying the orthodox mode of Marxian analysis to the objects of this expansion. One such observer was Frantz Fanon who developed his own distinctive brand of what can be called "ethno-Marxism."

Frantz Fanon and "Ethno-Marxism"

More a radicalized ideologist and man of action than a scholarly observer, Frantz Fanon nevertheless developed penetrating insights into the workings of the colonial society. His major contribution was his effort in *The Wretched of the Earth* (1968) to adapt a Marxian mode of analysis to the colonial situation, the result of which made him an "intellectual hero" to the Third World and to the black nationalist movement in the United States.

Fanon accepted in broad outlines Marx's conflict theory of society and his thesis that historically this conflict has been expressed in a struggle between the powerful and the powerless, the haves and have-nots. He took exception, however, to Marx's contention that the generative source for this conflict was in the economic arena while the political arena was but part of the derivative superstructure built from the particular economic foundations of the society. He insisted that the reverse was true in the colonial society. For, he argued, the struggle in that society derived from its conquest by an alien race and continued to be fought in the political arena as the white colonialist imposed upon the nonwhite native control over the instruments of coercion and government and used this control to exploit the economic resources and wealth of the colony. In short, political domination led to economic domination.

Thus he argued that Marx's contention that the basic cleavage in society was between the economic class that owned and controlled the means of production and the economic class that did not, had to be modified in any analysis of the colonial society. There, the basic cleavage was between a white colonialist race who had seized the colony's economic wealth and the nonwhite colonialized race who was dispossessed. "In the colonies the economic substructure is also a superstructure. The cause is the consequence; you are rich because you are white, you are white because you are rich" (Fanon 1968:40). In short, the interlocking of race and class, according to Fanon, was the result of the drive by the racially dominant group to monopolize all sources of power in the colonial society.

To Fanon the rule of the white colonialist was even more repressive than was the rule of the bourgeoisie under the capitalism Marx wrote about. The colonialist lacked any of the national, cultural, and territorial interests and values that the bourgeoisie ostensibly shared with the subordinated classes in capitalist society and by which they were able to claim legitimacy for their rule and to appeal for the loyalty and support of the subordinated classes. (Fanon acknowledged that Marx believed that this appeal to "false consciousness" was bound to fall on deaf ears eventually.) As a result, the colonialist elite had to rely heavily and continually on the use of force and violence to keep the colonialized in line. In turn, the colonialized, according to Fanon, were even more estranged, antagonistic, and resistant to colonialist rule than was the proletariat to the rule of the bourgeoisie. Thus, relations between the two in the colonial society, Fanon contended, were more tense, more raw, more conflictual, and based more on naked power than were relations between dominant and subordinate classes under capitalism.

Cox and Others: Political Class and Power

Unlike Fanon, Cox sought to adapt the basic tenets of Marxist analysis to his study of race relations in the modern capitalist society. He stated, in effect, that

> racial exploitation is merely one aspect of the problem of the proletarianiza-
> tion of labor, regardless of the color of the laborer. ... The capitalist
> exploiter, being opportunistic and practical will utilize any convenience to
> keep his labor and other resources freely exploitable. He will devise and
> employ race prejudice when that becomes convenient. As a matter of fact,
> the white proletariat of early capitalism had to endure burdens of
> exploitation quite similar to those which many colored peoples must bear
> today (Cox 1948:333).

And yet Cox identified, as did Fanon, the political arena—not the economic marketplace—as the major stage for the class struggle. Specifically his basic construct was "political class" which he defined as "a power group which tends to be organized for conflict ... " (Cox 1948:154). He went on to say that "as a power group, the political class is preoccupied with devises for controlling the state" (Cox 1948:155).

He considered this struggle for political power basic to understanding race relations in the capitalist society: " ... racial antagonism is essentially political-class conflict" (Cox 1948:333). The dominant political class, he argued, uses the apparatus of the State to enact policies and to institute practices whose intent is to divide the working class along racial lines. Accordingly, it actively promotes "race prejudice." In fact, Cox insisted, "race prejudice may be thought of as having its genesis in the propagandistic and legal contrivances of the white ruling class for securing mass support of its interest. It is an attitude of distance and estrangement mingled with repugnance, which seeks to conceptualize as brutes the human objects of exploitation" (Cox 1948:475).

Thus, Cox introduced an "attitude-value" component into his study of race relations. This component, he insisted, did not rise spontaneously in the marketplace or among the proletariat who in fact share common class interests, nor is it a product of tradition, mores, or even community sentiment per se. It is instead imposed from without by the dominant political class. Race prejudice then is the result of a deliberate state policy of debasing and devaluing one group of people in the eyes of others. In this manner Cox made the political arena and control of the State and its legal-normative apparatus central to his study of race relations.

Other scholars have also elaborated and reconceptualized the study of power in modern society. They generally recognize the importance of position in the economic structure of society; however, most also point to the importance of position in other societal structures as well. Dahrendorf (1959), for example, has identified the major class division in society as between those who wield power and authority by virtue of their offices in basic institutions and structures of society and those who are the objects of this power and whose life circumstances and opportunities are influenced by its exercise. Mills (1959), in turn, has defined the economic, political, and military as the major pyramids of power in American society, the most important being the economic. Those who occupy strategic command posts in pivotal organizations that are located at the top of these pyramids run the society, according to Mills. These are " . . . men whose positions enable them to transcend the ordinary environments of ordinary men and women; they are in positions to make decisions having major consequences" (Mills 1959:3–4). Mills also believed that these three types of elite have coalesced in modern America into a single power elite that is bound together by an intricate set of overlapping cliques and common values and social backgrounds. Their common racial and ethnic ties play a central role in the solidarity that they have developed. Mills's power elite in the American society is almost exclusively white Anglo-Saxon Protestant.

Weber: prestige, status, and the social order

In confining his concept class to the economic order, Weber was in effect preparing the groundwork for treating the processes and principles of stratification in the social order as an analytically distinct area of study. According to Weber, the social order of a society tends to be stratified into a hierarchical arrangement of status groups according to some scheme of social evaluation that defines social honor and prestige for that society. (The roughly equivalent term in American sociology is social class.) This scheme of evaluation is incorporated into the cultural-value system particularly as it is interpreted and fostered by those in the socially dominant position. The extent to which other strata accept the terms and criteria of the evaluational system may vary under given societal conditions—a matter that will concern us in the next section.

Where an elite has succeeded in entrenching itself in the social order over time, it seeks to "usurp status honors" to use Weber's terms, and to protect this usurpation by establishing and maintaining almost impenetrable social boundaries between itself and other strata in society. As such, it develops a distinctive life-style which is rooted in tradition and glorification of the past. It practices exclusivity by restricting social intercourse to its own kind, and by confining marriage to within the status group. It insists that only by being born into the elite group can a person legitimately be part of it. In effect, this group seeks to extend its claim to elite status from the past to the future through the principle of birthright and hereditary transmission of these rights. As such it brings the past into the present by its emphasis on family lineage; and the present into the future through its reliance on endogamy.

Ultimately though the success of a social elite in maintaining its position depends upon its ability to monopolize the basic sources of wealth and power in the political-economic order. This is largely so because its life-style, as Veblen (1899) has indicated, is based on the presumption of wealth and because its special claims to privilege requires special treatment from those in political authority. To the extent that a social elite does control these other sources then the workings of the marketplace are restricted in favor of the principle of birth and hereditary rights.

However, there are many instances historically of a social elite that has lost control over the political-economic order and has disappeared—only to be replaced by new claimants to social honor and prestige. This situation may have relevance for landed aristocratic societies of the past, including the antebellum South, and perhaps even the caste society in India of the near present, but it bears only some resemblance to what has been happening in the American society. The closest approximation is in the study by Warner and Lunt of the New England community of Yankee City (1941). And yet the description does alert us to certain features of the structure of stratification in the social order. It indicates that the more favored social classes seek to develop a distinctive style of life and to restrict their social intercourse to those whom they call their own. Only among those defined as social equals are they likely to develop their friendships, their cliques, their social clubs, and even to contract their marriages. It also indicates that ascriptive criteria play a role—though of varying significance—in the evaluative scheme of honor and worthiness: that is, criteria that are a function of birth and over which the individual has no control. Examples are kinship, family lineage, religion, race, and even national origins.

However where the principle of the marketplace and not that of hereditary right governs the workings of the economic order, other claims to status may be generated which are more in the control of the individual, such as income and wealth. Possession of these resources may itself be esteemed in a society, but even more significantly their possession allows the person to command goods and services that undergird the life-style of a class, and as such give one an important claim of access to that class. Veblen (1899) made much of the device of conspicuous consumption as a major mechanism for staking claims to social position in society. Even Weber recognizes the importance of wealth in the status system. As he says, "'status groups' are stratified according to the principles of their *consumption* of goods as represented by special 'styles of life'" (Weber [1922] 1946:193). Weber contends that the status order would be threatened at its very roots if acquisition of wealth in the marketplace were enough to bestow the same status honor and position as does birth and inherited life-style. Accordingly, "all groups having interests in the status order react with special sharpness precisely against the pretensions of purely economic acquisition" (Weber [1922] 1946:192).

Thus there is a built-in tension between the ascriptive criteria of birth and family lineage and the criteria of wealth in the social order which is recurrently expressed in history. For example, the nouveaux riches have always been a troublesome group for a social elite that based its claims to status on an inherited life-style. The character of the problem obviously varies with the extent to which a hereditary social elite is able to monopolize the basic sources of power and wealth in the society. In those societies where such an elite has lost its control over these sources or in societies whose social orders are not dominated by a hereditary elite, wealth assumes greater importance as a claim to high social standing.

When we turn to race-ethnicity, its role in the social order varies with the relative importance of the ascriptive criteria. In a social order dominated by such criteria, race-ethnicity fits neatly into the scheme of things, in part because it is itself an ascriptive characteristic and in part because it is one of the evaluative criteria that reinforces the established distribution of honor and prestige. However, in social orders in which newly acquired wealth from the marketplace provides a potent claim toward social standing, the situation is more complex. On occasion even a member from a disesteemed minority may win wealth in the marketplace, but in trying to convert it to an equivalent position in the social order, he will find his race-ethnicity stands in his way, for even in that situation ethnicity continues as one of the criteria of social evaluation. As a result, the social standing of such a minority member will tend to be lower than his wealth would seem to indicate. This will be shown in the next section.

Ethnicity and the Social Order

In recent decades a number of observers have been interested in examining the role that ethnicity plays in the stratification of the social order. One popular approach has been to view ethnic groups as arrayed in a hierarchical structure and to treat this structure as relatively distinct from social class stratification. Gordon, for example, argues that

> American society is criss-crossed by two sets of stratification structures, one based on social status, economic power, and political power differences, regardless of ethnic background, the other a set of status and power relationships based precisely on division of the population by racial, nationality background, and religious categories into "Old Americans," Negroes, Jews, Catholics, Japanese-Americans, Italians, French-Canadians, etc. The two systems must be kept conceptually separate, for otherwise the nature of their interrelationships cannot be discovered (Gordon 1963:252).

Lieberson also follows Gordon's approach: "ethnic differentiation may be the basis of a stratification system" (Lieberson 1970:172). However, Lieberson has expressed uncertainty about the extent to which such treatment is analytically desirable. "Does an ethnic stratification system differ significantly from those based on economic, age, or sex characteristics? Or is ethnic stratification but another form of general stratification?" (Lieberson 1970:172). But he then goes on to treat ethnic stratification as literally an independent type of stratification in society.

The connection between these two "analytically distinct" stratificational structures is of crucial significance to Gordon and others. It is as though they were asking, "What happens when an ethnic stratificational structure is 'superimposed' analytically upon the underlying system of stratification in the social order?" The answer is quite clear when we turn to the colonial and caste societies. Racial-ethnic stratification tends to correspond and to reinforce the system of occupational, economic, social, and political stratification of the society as a whole. This will be demonstrated in the next chapter. It also does something else; it intersects these strata vertically as well. The result is a horizontal and vertical segmentation of the society along racial-ethnic lines which produce, according to Furnivall [1948] (1956) and Smith, (1965) a plural society.

However, observers who have sought to apply this approach to the American society have come up with somewhat different results. Perhaps the closest approximation to the "vertical-horizontal" segmentation of the plural society is to be found in the study of black-white relations in a community in the Deep South that was conducted by Davis, Gardner, and Gardner.

In that study the authors found a distinct "castelike" cleavage that separated the subordinated black group from the superordinate white group. However, the authors also found that the whites had not succeeded in monopolizing "all the pleasant and profitable jobs" (Davis, Gardner, and Gardner 1941:4). Thus some blacks had been able to obtain these jobs and have a better income than some whites. The net result is that the racial cleavage did not follow a horizontal path as it would have if all blacks remained in the subordinated position, instead it described a diagonal path. The results are shown in the diagram below.

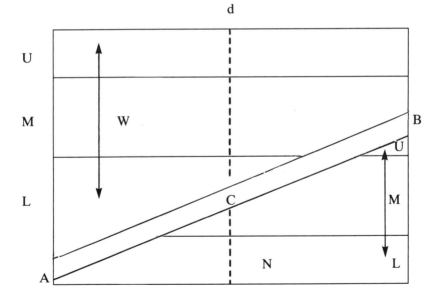

The arrangement of these parallel lines

> expresses the essential skewness created by the conflict of caste and class in
> the South. The gradual elaboration of the economic, educational, and
> general social activities of the Negro caste since slavery (and to some extent
> even before) has created new groups which have been vertically arranged by
> the society until certain fairly well-marked class groups have developed
> within the Negro caste. As the vertical distance of the Negro group has been
> extended during the years, the top Negro layer has been pushed higher and
> higher. This has swung the caste line on its axis (c), so that the top Negro
> group is higher in class traits than the lower white groups and is so recognized
> (Davis, Gardner, and Gardner 1941:10–11).

In other studies of communities, the axes of religious and national
origins as well as race were seen to intersect vertically the horizontal
social class layers of the community. Perhaps the most clear-cut example
of this kind of finding was in Hollinghead's study of New Haven. He
reported that

> Around the socio-biological axis of race, two social worlds have evolved—a
> Negro world and a white world. The white world is divided by ethnic origin
> and religion into Catholic, Protestant, and Jewish contingents. Within these
> divisions there are numerous ethnic schisms. The Irish hold aloof from the
> Italians, and the Italians move in different circles from the Poles. The Jews
> maintain a religious and social life separate from the Gentiles. The horizontal
> strata that transect each of these vertical structures are based upon the social
> values that are attached to occupation, education, place of residence in the
> community, and associations. Thus ethnic origin, occupation, education, and
> residence are combined into a complicated status system ... that is highly
> compartmentalized (Hollingshead 1952:685).

Gordon was so impressed with the idea that vertical substructuring was
becoming a significant feature of American society that he called for a
new construct to label this phenomenon. He coined the word "ethclass"
to describe this vertical intersection of the horizontal stratifications of the
social class by ethnicity. As he elaborated, "thus a person's *ethclass* might
be upper-middle class white Protestant, or lower-middle class white Irish
Catholic, or upper-lower class Negro Protestant, and so on" (Gordon
1964:51).

On the surface, Gordon's and Hollingshead's formulations have a
persuasive simplicity. And yet on closer inspection they have a major
flaw: they fail to take into account the role of ethnicity as a dimension of
social class itself.

Both would obviously agree that ethnicity has a significant indirect
influence on social class. For example, the kind of occupation, education,
income, or residence a person may have—all significant dimensions of

social class—are affected in part by the racial or ethnic group in which the person happens to be born. To illustrate, the black's life chances and opportunities to acquire better jobs, education, and income are obviously much lower than are those of the white Anglo-Saxon Protestant. On that account alone he would be unlikely to acquire the monetary and other claims that could be translated into the life-style of a higher social class, say the middle class. Thus his race handicaps him in his struggle for the claims to higher status. Within this context it can be argued that it is the absence of these claims, and not his race, that is the immediate "cause" of his exclusion from this higher class.

But what if he, the Jew, or the Italian manages to overcome these barriers and succeeds in obtaining the claims toward a life-style in accord with this higher status, does his race-ethnicity disappear as a factor in his social class position? All that we really learn from Gordon and Hollingshead is that the blacks, Jews, and Italians at these various "class" levels are likely to segregate themselves within their own racial and ethnic communities. Perhaps this is all that we would need to know if we were dealing with the "plural society" of Furnivall [1948] (1956). But it is an incomplete answer when we turn to the American scene. For people do try to cross these boundaries and what happens to them when they do? For example, what happens to the presumably middle-class Jew when he tries to join the country club of the middle-class Protestant? What happens to the middle-class black when he tries to invite the middle-class white to his home? The answer is frequently rejection. In effect, ethnicity operates to limit the kinds of social relationships these people have with each other. Most assuredly, the white Anglo-Saxon Protestants do not see these Jews and blacks as their "social equals"; they do not see these others as eligible to belong to their clubs, cliques, and the like despite similarities in occupation and income. Are these considerations of little significance in any attempt to describe the social class structure in the American society? Obviously they are significant. We contend that race-ethnicity functions as an important dimension along with others in the very structuring of social classes within the American scene; it helps define the social class in which the person is accepted within the larger community.

A clear example of what we are talking about can be seen in the work of W. Lloyd Warner. More than any other observer, Warner has provided empirical evidence to support the contention that ethnicity in a competitive class society functions as one of the operating dimensions in the assessment of social class position. Warner did not set himself the task of demonstrating this, but if we examine carefully some of his findings that are reported in *Social Class in America: The Evaluation of Status* [1949] (1960), we can find significant confirmation of our contention.

In his studies of social class in American communities, Warner depended very heavily upon the reputational technique. In the various communities he investigated, he recruited in each a group of judges to help him to establish the social class configuration in that community and also to locate specific individuals within the various classes in this configuration.

Warner called this procedure Evaluative Participation (E.P.). To Warner this procedure was an effective way of getting at the system of social stratification in the community.

> Each of the rating techniques combined in the E.P. method for stratifying a community and for placing families and individuals at their proper level in the status system of a community can play a decisive part in the process of determining the social stratification of a community or determining the status of an individual or family (Warner [1949] 1960:36).

He was convinced of the superiority of this approach because he believed that it was based

> on the propositions that those who interact in the social system of a community evaluate the participation of those around them, that the place where an individual participates is evaluated, and that the members of the community are explicitly or implicitly aware of the ranking and translate their evaluations of such social participation into social-class ratings that can be communicated to the investigator (Warner [1949] 1960:35).

Such a procedure, Warner realized, was extremely time-consuming and expensive; consequently, he sought to develop a simpler measure of a person's social class which would be highly correlated with the Evaluative Participation technique, but which could be constructed from more readily obtainable kinds of information. He devised the Index of Status Characteristics (I.S.C.) which he stated was "primarily an index of socio-economic factors" (Warner [1949] 1960:39). Warner however left little doubt that he considered the E.P. technique a truer measure of social class. "This entire analysis has assumed, of necessity, that the E.P. indicated the 'correct' social-class placement of each individual or family studied. This was necessary, since the E.P. was at least presumably, the *best* indication available of the actual social class of each family." (Warner [1949] 1960:211). As a result, Warner used the E.P. scores as intrinsic parameters of the social class system; he frequently wanted to know how well the I.S.C. scores predicted these parameters.

The Index of Status Characteristics initially included weighted information on six characteristics: occupation, amount of income, source of income, education, house type, dwelling area. However, Warner found that he could reduce the six characteristics to four and get almost as high a degree of predictability. Therefore he finally decided upon occupation, source of income, house type, and dwelling area. When he correlated the Index of Status Characteristics with Evaluative Participation in his study of Jonesville, he obtained a multiple correlation of .974 for the six characteristics and .972 for the four characteristics. These correlations, however, were obtained within the group Warner called "Old Americans."

He encountered, however, difficulties when he sought to correlate the Index with Evaluative Participation for various ethnic minorities within his study. For example, he found very little discrepancy between the average I.S.C. and the average E.P., but a markedly significant amount of error at the top and lower ranges of the scale. Specifically he had only 16 per cent incorrect class placements for Old Americans but for Scandinavians, Poles, and Southern Mountain Whites, the errors ranged from 25 to 55 per cent. Further, placement and position within class were correct for 42 per cent of the Old Americans, 23 per cent of the Scandinavians, 0 per cent of the Poles, and 33 per cent of the Southern Mountain Whites. What is even more interesting, for our purposes, is the fact that in the higher ranges the I.S.C. was putting the person from the ethnic minority in a higher class than was scored on the Evaluative Participation measure.

Subsequently Warner revised his I.S.C. scores to bring them into greater correspondence with the predicted E.P. social class placement, and it is here we begin to note a very interesting difference. In his weighted total of the four status characteristics, a score value of 1 to 22 put a person into Class A if he were an Old American: the lower end range of that Class A was scored 18 to 22. When Warner revised his weighted totals for Scandinavians, for example, we find that the total that would have placed an Old American in the lower range of the Class A-, place the Scandinavian in the middle of Class B+, not even in the upper part of the class, B++. Similarly, a score of 24 to 30 which placed an Old American at the upper ranges of the class B+, put the Scandinavian in the very lower ranges of that class B-.

In sum, the Scandinavian needed to score 9 or 10 points higher on the I.S.C. than did the Old American to be considered in the same social class. Interestingly, no Scandinavians fell into the highest social class, A, none was even found in the highest range of Class B. Translated into descriptive terms this means that the Scandinavian had to be in a correspondingly higher occupation, had to have a more established source of income, and/or had to live in a better house or dwelling area than did an Old American in order to be considered on the same social class level.

A similar pattern was found among the Poles, none of whom was considered to be in a social class higher than D++. To be in that class the Pole needed an I.S.C. score of 39 to 53—a score that would have put him in the lower range of Class C if he were an Old American.

What Warner was in effect showing is the cost in quantitative terms to a Scandinavian of being a Scandinavian to a Pole of being a Pole, to a Southern Appalachian White of being a Southern Appalachian White in a social stratificational system which is weighted in favor of the Old American who is predominantly a white Anglo-Saxon Protestant.

Although Warner did not treat ethnicity as intrinsically connected with the status order of the community, it is evident from the above that his judges did indeed introduce—at least implicitly—ethnicity as one of the dimensions by which they evaluated the social class position of the persons in the community.

If we were now to redraw the social stratificational order of the community, we would accordingly find that instead of merely horizontal strata, in those strata where ethnic groups enter into the system as in Class B for Scandinavians, the strata would describe a steplike character. Let us illustrate this for the Old Americans and Scandinavians through Class C.

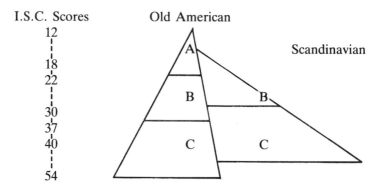

The relative importance of ethnicity as a dimension of stratification can be expected to vary with the relative significance of other ascriptive characteristics in the stratificational order. For example, in Warner and Lunt's classic study of Yankee City, a community in New England (1941) family lineage and kinship were more important determinants of elite social status than were money and wealth. Interwoven in this cluster of ascriptive criteria was ethnicity. Thus, the upper-upper class consisted exclusively of Old Yankees of Protestant persuasion; they also virtually dominated the lower-upper class: only a few Irish families, the oldest ethnic minority in the community, had been able to penetrate this social class.

In Jonesville, a community in the Midwest (1949), Warner noted the absence of an "aristocratic elite"; accordingly he failed to distinguish an upper-upper class as he did in Yankee City, instead he merely talked about an upper class. In this setting, wealth and other nonascriptive criteria took on an increased importance as claims to social standing. It increased the possibility of some kind of status transaction taking place; that is, a person might be able to use his higher economic standing to compensate for his lower ethnic standing in order to gain access to a given social class that was primarily dominated by persons of higher ethnic but lower economic standing than he. This happened as we have already seen in the case of some Scandinavians. Such a transaction can be illustrated in following diagram. "Social class position of Scandinavians and old Americans according to level of ethnic and economic standing." For the sake of simplicity we merely divide each of the two dimensions into two categories: high and moderate as would apply to a comparison of Old Americans and Scandinavians in Jonesville.

		Ethnic Standing	
		High (Old American)	Moderate (Scandinavian)
Economic Standing	High	Social Class A	Social Class B
	Moderate	Social Class B	Social Class C

Thus, Old Americans who had a high economic standing did not allow any Scandinavians, no matter how high their economic standing, into their social world; just as Old Americans of moderate economic standing excluded their economic peers among the Scandinavians. The only identifiable social transactions took place between members of both groups whose position was high on one dimension and low on the other.

In effect, Warner's work, particularly that done in Jonesville, demonstrates something else besides the role of ethnicity as a dimension of the social stratificational order; it also suggested the relevance of a transactional model for dealing with relations between ethnicity and other dimensions of stratification. Such a model would seem to have particular relevance in studies of intermarriage which frequently involve an economically mobile man from an ethnic minority marrying a woman of lower economic standing from the dominant group.

Gordon also expressed an acute awareness of the possibility of status transactions in which ethnicity functioned as part of a bargaining arrangement with other status characteristics. He lamented the absence of research into such exchanges. The likelihood of such status transactions in the American scene calls into question another major contention of Hollingshead and to a lesser extent Gordon: namely, that the boundaries between ethnic groups are relatively impenetrable. In fact, it appears at times as though they were describing a kind of racial segmentation that closely resembles that found in the plural society of Smith (1965) and Furnivall [1948] (1956). And yet the differences between the two situations are profound.

As Smith maintains in Chapter 3, a fundamental feature of the colonial plural society is that each segment of that society is characterized by its own distinctive cultural system. Few of the subordinated segments attempt to model their values and life-style after the dominant segment, whose efforts to disseminate deliberately its "way of life" meet with limited success. As a result there is little interpenetration of values and culture between segments. Even Hollingshead and Gordon would agree, that this does not apply to the American Scene. The history of most American minorities is relatively rapid acculturation to the values and standards of the social class structure of the dominant society. Gordon himself realizes how permeable are the cultural boundaries between the white ethnic minority and the dominant society. In elaborating on his concept "ethclass," which we have already seen involves the intersection of ethnicity and social class, Gordon commented that cultural differences between social classes are more important than are those between ethnic groups.* "This means that people of the same social class tend to act alike and to have the same values even if they have different ethnic backgrounds. People of different social classes tend to act differently and to have different values even if they have the same ethnic background" (Gordon 1964:52).

The situation seems quite different when we turn to the question of the social boundaries between ethnic groups. Most observers of the American scene agree that kinship, friendship, and other primary group relationships tend to be restricted to the ethnic group. "With regard to social participation in primary groups and primary relationships, people tend to confine these to their own social class segment within their own ethnic group—that is, to the ethclass" (Gordon 1964:52).

True as this is today, observers have also noted that members of racial-

---

*By absorbing these cultural styles and values, ethnic minorities have also become in effect "integrated" into the normative framework with its criteria and standards of evaluation that encompass the stratificational order of society as a whole. As a result, a consensual scheme of evaluation can be seen as characterizing the American society. According to Rex (1970) and Smith (1965), this does not happen in the colonial plural society. Each segment retains its own evaluative scheme; no consensual framework develops that would reflect commonly shared values and standards.

ethnic groups, particularly those who are economically and socially mobile, tend to engage in a variety of interactions with persons and groups outside their racial-ethnic boundaries. They tend to participate in community-related activities and organizations and become socially acquainted with others. In effect, the enlargement of these spheres of acquaintanceship and contact that transcend ethnic group membership seems to be a striking feature of contemporary America. Even at this "quasi-social" level then, ethnic boundaries are being penetrated.

3 Race-Ethnicity and Systems of Stratification

In distinguishing types of dominance and structural orders in a society, it has become evident that marked variations occur in the interplay between the different criteria and principles for allocating positions and rewards within and between these orders. We shall now move to an even larger framework, namely, the society itself in which this interplay assumes a characteristic pattern. By doing this we shall be in a better position to answer our basic question, "What is the role of race-ethnicity in the stratificational system of a society?" The stratificational systems that we shall now look at are those found in the caste, colonial plural, and modern competitive societies.

Caste System

One of the most explicit linkages, between race-ethnicity and the structure of stratification in a society is found in a caste system. Before we pursue this connection, let us first examine some of the characteristics of the system itself. The society that we shall have specifically in mind is India.

A caste system is a rigidly stratified set of culturally distinct ascribed status groups which are organically linked to the system through a religio-value schema that "sanctifies" their position and function. Each of these groups is characterized by a corporate consciousness and a way of life that distinguishes it from the others. "The members usually share a group name; always they interact with one another in characteristic ways; always there are symbols of group membership ranging from skin colour to cultural features such as language, occupation, dress, place of residence, and the like. Only members of the group are one's peers. Where group affiliation is relevant, individual attributes are irrelevant" (Berreman 1967:48).

50

Membership in these status groups is determined through parentage. At birth then "an individual is assigned his lifelong and unalterable status ... a status which he shares with others of similar birth who are therefore assigned to the same group" (Berreman 1967:48). (The principle of endogamous marriage insures that this fixed status will continue into the next generation.)

In this manner the individual is anchored to "a fixed social milieu." It provides him "with a permanent body of associations which controls almost all his behaviour and contacts. His caste canalizes his choice in marriage, acts as his trade union, his friendly or benefit society, his slate club and his orphanage; it takes the place for him of health insurance, and if need be provides for his funeral. It frequently determines his occupation, often positively, for in many castes the occupational tradition is very strong indeed, commonly negatively, since there are many pursuits, at any rate in the case of all but the lowest castes, which he cannot follow, or can follow only at the cost of excommunication from the society to which he belongs ... " (Hutton 1963:111). The caste also regulates what the individual is to do and how he is to do it in the most minute detail from birth to death. Accordingly, a person is engulfed in a set of ceremonials, rituals, and mores that define truth, virtue, and beauty for him.

Once such a total cultural and communal environment has been created, a status group, according to Weber, has attained its "purest form" of expression and has been transmuted into a "closed 'caste'" whose way of life is embedded in and expressed through religious symbolism, ceremony, and ritual. This also applies to relations between castes. "Status distinctions are then guaranteed not merely by conventions and laws but also by *rituals*. This occurs in such a way that every physical contact with a member of any caste that is considered to be 'lower' by the members of a 'higher' caste is considered as making for a ritualistic impurity and to be a stigma which must be expiated by a religious act. Individual castes develop quite distinct cults and gods" (Weber [1922] 1946:188–189).

To Weber, a hierarchy of status groups can only attain the highly stratified character of a caste system if the caste cleavages correspond to underlying ethnic differences. Caste and ethnic community become synonymous. "The 'caste' is, indeed, the normal form in which ethnic communities usually live side by side in a 'societalized' manner. These ethnic communities believe in blood relationship and exclude exogamous marriage and social intercourse" (Weber [1922] 1946:189).

In many instances, the ethnic character of the group antedates its entry into the caste system. Hutton maintains that "the caste system has afforded a place in society into which any community, be it racial, social, occupational or religious, can be fitted as a co-operating part of the social whole while retaining its own distinctive character and its separate individual life" (Hutton 1963:115).

Hutton then goes on to identify tribal communities that have become incorporated into the system. Most have retained their ancient tribal names much as the Gujar has. Others have taken other names. The Huns, for example, "have been absorbed into Hindu society under the guise of Rajput clans." This process has continued until relatively recent times: tribes becoming castes such as "Koli in western India, Chuhra in the Punjab, Dom in the United Provinces and elsewhere ... and so forth" (Hutton 1963:115–116).

Sectarian religious groups have also been absorbed into the system. Hutton describes how this has come about, even for religious groups that were "formed in defiance of and in protest against the caste system." He offers as "a typical instance of the religious sect turned caste ... the Lingayats, a caste which started as the followers of Bāsava, a teacher of the twelfth century who preached the repudiation of caste. They wear as the symbol of their faith a small silver box containing a stone phallus (*linga*), 'the loss of which is equivalent to spiritual death'" (Hutton 1963:117–118).

Other castes have arisen from nonethnic sources. They have come primarily from "occupational groups which have migrated from one part of India to another and formed a new caste group in the new area which has become completely separated from its original caste. This appears to have happened more than once in the case of Brahmans as well as of labouring castes like weavers or oil-pressers. New castes have also been formed by the segregation of subcastes or of occupational groups within castes, and these have been accepted as independent castes just as tribes and peoples have been" (Hutton 1963:116).

These occupational castes resemble in part the medieval guilds in their elaborately kept occupational secrets and ritualized behavior and intense solidarity. But in time they come to encompass the total life of their members as does any other caste. In short, they take on the character of a religio-ethnic community with its own distinctive style of life and what Weber calls a sense of honor and dignity. In effect, the caste, whether it started that way or not, becomes an ethnic community which perpetuates itself over time. Thus, ethnic divisions are woven into the very fabric of the caste system. The system either coopts already existing ethnic groups such as tribes and religious sects into its structure, or generates ethnic communities from those castes whose initial communality may have been occupational in nature.

To Weber, the caste structure links what otherwise might be ethnically segregated groups, with unconnected coexistences to the occupational and social structure of society through a system of super- and subordination.

> The caste structure brings about a social subordination and an acknowledgement of "more honor" in favor of the privileged caste and status groups. This is due to the fact that in the caste structure ethnic distinctions as such have become "functional" distinctions within the political societalization (warriors, priests, artisans that are politically important for war and for building, and so on) (Weber [1922] 1946:189).

In this manner castes are arranged in a hierarchical order that reflects a "system of differential evaluation, differential power and rewards," and a differential assessment of intrinsic worth. It reflects, in other words, "a system of institutionalized inequality" in which one's opportunities and expectations are fixed and immutable. For lower castes this means generally a life of poverty and continual struggle for survival and subsistence as a debased group in a society that virtually allows no escape during one's lifetime.

However, instead of the kind of alienation, dissatisfaction, and even protest that could conceivably be generated from such conditions, a number of observers report what appears to them as general acceptance by even the lowest castes of their position and functions in society. Some see the system, as does Hutton, as a functioning organism within which the various castes and subcastes operate as individual cells or organs.

What serves to integrate this incredibly complex ethnically divided structure (it is estimated that there are 3,000 castes in India) is according to many of these observers the presence of a basic religio-value schema to which all segments of the society subscribe. It sanctifies fulfillment of present caste obligations, and in the fulfillment of these duties it promises a better future in the next life through reincarnation. Thus, "the belief in *karma* ... renders the superficially inequitable distribution of functions acceptable as being part of the divine order of the universe and a transient episode in the prolonged existence of the individual soul, which by acquiring merit in one existence may rise in the scale in the next, or which may be suffering from a degradation in caste merely by reason of its transgressions in a previous life. ... The very nature of the system discountenances and discourages attempts to surmount existing barriers of rank or occupation or to break down those barriers by intermarriage or by freedom of social intercourse generally ... " (Hutton 1963:121–122).

A number of students of the Indian caste system, however, consider the image of a harmonious, consensual "organism" as an oversimplification. They point to significant stresses and strains which even in its days of stability characterized the system. DeVos, for example, would do away with the "single linear hierarchical view of caste in India." Instead he sees the Indian society as split vertically, as well as horizontally. On one side of an imaginary vertical division, which I call the caste line, is a social stratification which is related to class, defined in terms of political and economic domination, and on the other side is a hierarchical system related to the stratification of the "sacred," which has to do with the value structure of the society—that is to say, its ideology and what is usually expressed in the religious system (DeVos 1967:20).

DeVos argues that position in one hierarchy may not necessarily be congruent with position in the other.

one may find political dominance by a group lacking high religious validation; and, conversely, high religious rank unconnected with political power. In Indian caste society the Kshatriya (warriors) were traditionally the dominant element in the secular realm, whereas the Brahmans presided over the sacred elements of the culture. Brahmans may, at the same time, be ritually elevated but economically powerless. They may become far from the centre of political power, but through their religious "potency" maintain a high position in the social hierarchy (DeVos 1967:20–21).

DeVos, however, does not press his argument of incongruence for those at the bottom. Those castes are at the bottom of both hierarchies. Sinha goes a step further when he questions the extent of incongruence among those at the top of both hierarchies. He argues that preeminence in the sacred order, for example, requires reinforcement of position in the secular order. Otherwise, status in the sacred order is bound to suffer in time. "Even the Brahmans in an area cannot maintain their ritual dominance very long unless they maintain equivalent levels on the power and economic dimensions. In other words, caste is not as peculiar a type of stratification as would appear if we focused only on its ritual aspects. There is some kind of interaction between the sacred and the secular spheres and a fair amount of congruence between them observable today, and I suspect that it has been like that in past periods also" (Sinha 1967:22).

Perhaps the most significant reservations are expressed by scholars concerning the extent to which the Indian caste system functions on a consensual basis—a common belief in the legitimacy of the hierarchical caste arrangements. Some scholars, including Berreman, place greater emphasis on the coercive power in the hands of the dominant castes in maintaining order within the system—"power ... [that is] expressed physically, economically, politically and socially" (Berreman 1967:54).

Despite this, Berreman recognizes the existence of a consensual framework, but he calls it "limited consensus." He maintains that there is a general agreement on the "facts" of the caste arrangements. They agree, for example, on who belongs to which caste and on the "publicly accorded status" of each caste. In addition, "they agree on the hierarchical meaning ascribed in the society to particular attributes and behaviour." There is, however, much less agreement on the legitimacy of the caste system. Specifically, they disagree "on the legitimacy of the hierarchy or, more commonly, on the place their group has been accorded in it; on the legitimacy of the criteria of ranking; on the legitimacy of the requirements and rewards of rank, and so on" (Berreman 1967:55).

Sinha adds another dimension. He states that despite the pressures for conformity, coordination, and cooperation, "the recorded studies of caste communities offer much evidence of jostling for power, prestige and economic advantage among the castes." The tensions that are generated, Sinha continues, are kept in check "partly through movements toward group mobility and partly through the coercive force of the power structure, which was controlled by the rulers belonging to the upper castes" (Sinha 1967:97).

Beyond the competitive struggle for advantage that Sinha mentions and the coercive exercise of power by the dominant caste groups to which Berreman alludes, there is also the chronic source of inner tension that must pervade the various lower castes. On the one hand is the need to protect themselves from the negative evaluations and pressures of higher castes and the pushing upward of still lower castes. On the other is the ethnocentric concern to maintain and to foster their own sense of dignity and honor. Weber maintains that "even pariah people who are most despised are usually apt to continue cultivating in some manner that which is equally peculiar to ethnic and to status communities: the belief in their own specific 'honor'" (Weber [1922] 1946:189).

By maintaining their own sense of dignity, the lower castes reinforce their sense of we—ness and thereby protect themselves from the opprobrium of the higher castes. Yet, these internal standards of evaluation do not depart significantly from the basic assumptions and premises of the broader consensual schema. They primarily introduce a sense of special destiny or mission in the broader scheme of things whose fulfillment will be rewarded in the next world. As Weber concludes, "the sense of dignity of the negatively privileged strata naturally refers to a future lying beyond the present, whether it is of this life or of another. In other words, it must be nurtured by the belief in a providential 'mission' and by a belief in a specific honor before God" (Weber [1922] 1946:190).

The situation is significantly different when we turn to the colonial plural society.

Colonial Plural Society

Another society in which a close linkage exists between ethnicity and stratification is the colonial society. Coming into existence as it does through conquest by a technologically and militarily superior ethnic minority as was the case in the conquest of Africa, the Western Hemisphere, and Southeast Asia by white Europeans, such a society is characterized at least in its early stages by marked occupational class and status divisions that correspond to basic racial distinctions. So significant are these racial-occupational divisions that an observer such as J. S. Furnivall made them the central features of his view of the colony as a "plural society." Furthermore, in the hierarchical arrangement of the racial-occupational strata the colonial society resembles the caste society, but there is a significant difference between the two. Unlike the caste system, it lacks a belief-value system that binds the various parts of the society into an integrated whole and that makes the subordinated groups more receptive to the authority of the dominant group. As a result, coercion and force are the central features of the dominant group's control of the colonial society.

J. S. Furnivall and the plural society

Perhaps one of the most important efforts to provide a conceptual framework for dealing with the racial bases by which colonial societies tend to be organized is that of J. S. Furnivall. His book *Colonial Policy and Practice: A Comparative Study of Burma and Netherlands India* [1948] (1956) offered an extended treatment of his concept "plural society." So significant do we consider his contribution that we shall discuss his work at some length; then we shall consider M. G. Smith's elaboration of the concept, John Rex's further specification of the role of race in the colonial society, and finally, the paternalistic mold that may develop in such a society as discussed by Pierre van den Berghe.

Furnivall stressed the profound impact of Western political control and capitalism upon traditional societies, those organized around personal authority, custom, and a self-subsistent economy. According to Furnivall, the introduction of Western law and administration, particularly when they were accompanied by direct rule as was British control of Burma, tended to undermine and virtually destroy the organic native society that was built around the village, its headmen, and customary rules and procedures. The indirect rule of the Dutch in the Netherlands East Indies allowed the normative system of the native to continue to function but only under the domination of the Western legal system. Even there, the organic basis of the native society underwent disruption and fragmentation.

The unleashing of capitalistic economic forces, Furnivall continued, also contributed to the dissolution of the social will and social structure by undermining the traditional economy and by fostering a "market mentality" of self-interested quest for individual gain. This was particularly true under the direct rule of the British in Burma. Under the indirect rule of the Dutch in the East Indies, economic forces were somewhat held in check by customary procedures and traditions which allowed an occasional expression of collective concern and will.

In breaking down the traditional sources of solidarity, these colonialist societies created a "consensual" vacuum, for they failed to generate any common social will of their own. As a result, these societies became fragmented into racial segments. Each segment lived, by and large, unto itself behind its territorial, cultural, and social boundaries and met the others only as political and economic necessity warranted. In short, they were transformed, according to Furnivall, into plural societies.

> In Burma, as in Java, probably the first thing that strikes the visitor is the medley of peoples—European, Chinese, Indian and native. It is in the strictest sense a medley, for they mix but do not combine. Each group holds by its own religion, its own culture and language, its own ideas and ways. As individuals they meet, but only in the market-place, in buying and selling. There is a *plural society* [emphasis added], with different sections of the community living side by side, but separately, within the same political unit (Furnivall [1948] 1956:304).

What further fragmented these plural societies, according to Furnivall, was the fact that "even in the economic sphere there is a division of labour along racial lines. Natives, Chinese, Indians and Europeans all have different functions, and within each major group subsections have different functions."

This pattern, he insisted, was to be found throughout the Tropical Far East: whether the dependency was under "Spanish, Portuguese, Dutch, British, French or American rule," or whether the native populations were "Filipinos, Javanese, Malays, Burmans and Annamese;" or "whether the objective of the colonial power has been tribute, trade or material resources; under direct rule and under indirect. The obvious and outstanding result of contact between East and West has been the evolution of a plural society" (Furnivall [1948] 1956:305).

Furnivall feared that collective social will and action were also disappearing within these racial segments, not merely between them. He saw a breakdown in relations within these segments and an inexorable process of atomization taking place which transformed these segments from communities into crowds.

What produced this atomization and segmentation? According to

Furnivall, the unleashing of capitalistic economic forces with their emphasis on self-interest and profit raised "mammon" to the level of a common deity and placed people, even of the same racial group, into a competitive relation with each other. As a result, these people came to resist banding together for the collective whole and were turned instead into an atomized mass intent upon the pursuit of their self-interest in the marketplace. The marketplace then, rather than a consensual value scheme, bound these people together, but the marketplace also mirrored in sharp outline the basic tensions and conflict generically related to a plural society.

Furnivall offered a graphic description of this process in his research on Burma. He showed that the Burmese had become a propertyless people. They had lost their land and were now nothing more than "sharecroppers." They resented their present status and directed their anger against those whom they believed responsible for their plight. They were particularly hostile toward the Indian "middlemen" who were moneylenders and merchants. A lesser target for their antipathy was the white colonialist. He was too far up the pyramid of political and economic power for them to have the same kind of abrasive contact they had with the middlemen.

Persuasive and dramatic as Furnivall's description was of the plural societies of Burma and also of Indonesia, his claim that racial segments of the two societies had become so fragmented and their internal relations so atomized that they were incapable of collective action seemed to be contradicted by other conclusions he also drew. For example, in another section of the book, he referred to the survival of social and religious customs and traditions within the various racial segments as though they were still functioning as a collective umbrella for the segment. He also mentioned growth of nationalistic forces within some of these segments. It would appear that despite the economic self-interest and its atomizing effect on the internal group relations, some ties of a noneconomic nature continued to bind the persons into a cohesive whole in at least some of the racial segments.

Another point that merits mention is Furnivall's contention that the plural society need not remain a totally coercive, exploitative system as was the case in Burma under the British; it may also develop paternalistic features as was the case in the Netherlands East Indies. There, the Dutch pursued a policy whereby the dependent population was protected from excessive economic exploitation. The Dutch implemented this policy through the use of indirect rule and through the setting up of special categories of professionals and administrators whose function was to see that the needs of the subject populations did not go entirely unheeded.

M. G. Smith and the cultural segmentation of the plural society

As can be seen in the title of his book *The Plural Society in the British West Indies* (1965), M. G. Smith adopted Furnivall's concept, but he also did more. He elaborated the concept and applied it to a wider range of societal situations than did Furnivall.

To Smith the crucial feature of the plural society was its division into separate social and cultural sections, each of which was characterized by a distinctively different system of basic institutions: "This basic institutional system embraces kinship, education, religion, property and economy, recreation, and certain sodalities" (Smith 1965:82). These differences, according to Smith, organized the society into a hierarchically arrayed mosaic of total communities, each capable of providing for its members the entire range of life experience.

His most detailed illustration of a plural society was Jamaica. It consisted, he stated, of three layered sections; a small white section was at the top; at the bottom was a black section which included about four-fifths of the population; and in between, a brown section. Smith then went on to describe in elaborate detail the various basic institutional differences among the various sections.

Smith agreed with Furnivall that a plural society lacked a common institutional framework and a common value-belief system that embraced all sections and classes within the society. Smith also recognized, as did Furnivall, that a plural society required the existence of some mechanism by which order and control could be maintained. Accordingly, he argued, the society depended on an overall governmental structure, whose control was in the hands of the dominant cultural section as was the control over the economic means of production.

Smith insisted, however, that each of the subordinated sections did not merely rely upon control by the dominant section but each in turn evolved its own system of internal control and status that reflected its own traditions and values, which frequently were not in accord with those evolved by the other sections.

> The distribution of status within each cultural section rests on common values and criteria quite specific to that group, and this medley of sectional value systems rules out the value consensus that is prerequisite for any status continuum. Thus the plurality is a discontinuous status order, lacking any foundation in a system of common interests and values, while its component sections are genuine status continua, distinguished by their differing systems of value, action, and social relations (Smith 1965:83).

In short, Smith recognized that within each of the cultural sections a sense of dignity and of worth developed which frequently ran counter to that which the dominant section sought to impose upon the society as a whole.

Smith eventually addressed himself to two questions: How did these plural societies originate? What perpetuated them? Smith's answers were somewhat ambiguous. First he rejected Furnivall's thesis that plural societies "were limited to the modern colonial tropics and were products of Western economic expansion." He insisted that "the Norman conquest of Britain, and the Roman conquest before it, certainly established plural societies, and there are many other instances that cannot be attributed to Western economic activity" (Smith 1965:88–89). Smith then went on to enumerate plural societies of the past. Conquest and consolidation may be involved "but this is not always the case" (Smith 1965:89). Voluntary or involuntary migration may also play a role in the creation of a plural society.

In stressing cultural segmentation, Smith sought to avoid the overly deterministic view that inextricably linked the emergence of plural societies with racial differences. In other words, he wished to deflate the notion that wherever you have a racially differentiated society you are likely to have a plural society. For example, he insisted that not all multiracial societies became plural societies, instead they might remain heterogeneous societies, or they might form "a common homogeneous society, as for instance among the Hausa-Fulani of northern Nigeria" (Smith 1965:89).

However, in tryng to mute a deterministic view, he overstated the case. For even he recognized the fact that "modern plural societies are multiracial, and that these racial groups tend also to be culturally distinct." But, he insisted, in some instances these imputed racial differences were the result of social definition and not of biological origin and as such expressed symbolically the basic cultural divisions of that society. Accordingly, he continued, a plural society may be characterized by "culturally distinct groups that belong to the same racial stock expressing their differences in racial terms. This seems to be the case in Guatemala, Haiti and among the Creole folk and elite of the British West Indies. History provides us with many other examples, such as the Normans and Anglo-Saxons, the English and the Scots or, most recently and most elaborately, the Nazi ideology" (Smith 1965:89).

Finally, Smith emphasized, even more than Furnivall did, the coercive control that the dominant section exercised over the other sections of the plural society. This control, he admitted, might go unchallenged through much of the society's history, but it would nevertheless produce an uneasy calm between the subordinated and dominant sections. In time political consciousness might develop within some of the subordinated sections and express itself in nationalistic longings and ultimately in a challenge to the status quo through violence, rebellion, and revolution. In view of this potential, Smith saw an inherent instability in the structure of a plural society.

John Rex and the dual colonial societies

The third theorist, John Rex, concurred with Furnivall on the racially plural character of the colonial society and on the role of conquest in its creation. However, he placed even greater emphasis than did Furnivall on the unequal distribution of power and privilege that produced a hierarchical arrangement among the various racial segments in the colonial plural society.

Rex also agreed with Furnivall and Smith in their contention that the colonial society lacked an overall value-belief system which could integrate the various segments and strata in society into a unified whole as in the caste system.

> The important thing when we turn our attention to colonial society is the absence of overall value-consensus, the fact that one stratum or segment dominates the others, and that one of the dimensions on which the various segments or strata have to be differentiated concerns the degree to which they are legally free and capable of controlling their own economic destiny. In this sense we should say that power is an extremely important factor in colonial societies. If such distinctions are really viable, however, we should say that our concept of power is a zero-sum concept, since quite clearly the more one group has the less is available to the other (Rex 1970:69).

As a result, Rex continued, the colonial society had to rely heavily on a political and governmental structure in order to bring the parts of the society together; and its ruling racial elite had to depend upon control of the instruments of coercion to insure compliance. Further, Rex attributed, even more than Furnivall and Smith did, a similar unifying function for economic institutions; he also viewed coercion as the major mechanism of control in the economic order.

In effect, Rex stressed, even more emphatically than did the other two, the power differentials within the colonial society and the potential for coercive, exploitative, and conflictual relations contained therein. However, Rex also recognized that relations between dominant and subordinate segments in the colonial society might under some conditions become relatively harmonious. In fact, one of the major distinctions he drew was between colonial societies "structured in terms of class conflict" and those structured "in terms of a particular kind of estate order" (Rex 1970:78).

The former situation is likely to arise, according to Rex, "where there is a large settler population including farmers and employed workers living in a colonial context," as in the case of South Africa and Algeria. In such instances, he continued, "the farmer and settler element amongst the settlers is likely to form a class in something like the Marxian or Weberian sense and defend its interests not merely in the market but in the political sphere. Native labour is thus forced into a position of having less control over the means of production and is potentially a separate class." In this manner, racial and class divisions mutually reinforce each other, and the ensuing struggle between the two groups assumes the form of "a conflict between physically distinguishable groups acting in terms of their material interests" (Rex 1970:74).

Such an "ethno-Marxist" struggle is unlikely to develop in colonial societies where the settler population is either small or virtually nonexistent or where alien ethnic and racial groups perform the function of "middlemen" or "secondary capitalists." In such situations peaceful accommodation may come to characterize relations between the various segments. Rex called the resulting societal structure a colonial estate system or an ethnically plural estate system. According to Rex, stability in such a society is maintained as long as it remains under the protection of the colonializing power, particularly if the power pursues a policy of benevolent paternalism in its relations with the colony. Furnivall clearly agreed with this in his obvious preference for the paternalistic rule of the Dutch in the East Indies to the more coercive rule of the British in Burma.

Pierre L. van den Berghe and paternalistic race relations

The theorists we have already discussed all left some room in their plural theories for the development of a normative overlay and code that would mitigate some of the harsh coerciveness of the colonial society. Van den Berghe made this code central to the type of race relations he labeled paternalistic. The code defined rights and obligations of dominant and subordinated strata to each other and was structured on a "master-servant" or "parent-child" relationship. It accepted without question the right of the dominant group to rule, and it maximized the distance between ruler and ruled "by an elaborate and punctilious etiquette involving nonreciprocal terms of address, sumptuary regulations, and repeated manifestations of subservience and dominance" (van den Berghe 1967a:27).

In turn, the master class was presumed to have certain obligations toward the subordinated strata. Its dealings with this strata were to be motivated by more than exploitative self-interest; they were also to be conditioned by concern over the welfare and the need to protect the subordinated group. According to the dominant group, the subordinated strata needed this because they were incapable of taking care of themselves; they were regarded "as childish, immature, irresponsible, exuberant, improvident, fun-loving, good-humored, and happy-go-lucky; in short, as inferior but lovable as long as they stay in 'their place'"(van den Berghe 1967a:27).

In effect, benevolent paternalism was the normative model for the society. However, the extent to which paternalism was indeed practiced by ruling groups varied. In some societies paternalism was built into the very fabric of the society as in the case of the caste system in India; in other societies it was primarily expressed through public and administrative policy as in the case of the Dutch East Indies; in still others it extended into legal, religious, and other major societal institutions as in the case of colonies in the New World conquered by Spain and Portugal. And in still other societies the paternalistic code operated on the more informal level of relations between master and slave as in the case of the South before the Civil War. However, no matter how narrowly or widely defined were the institutional or other areas of society in which the paternalistic code in fact operated, it served as the idealized model for the society as a whole of what relations between super- and sub-ordinated groups should be like. So significant did van den Berghe consider this paternalistic model that he identified it as one of the two basic systems of race relations in society; the other was the competitive type of race relations.

The extent to which the subordinated strata accepted this view of the world and of themselves also varied within and between societies. The caste system represented the most extreme case of general consensus built usually around a commonly shared religious set of beliefs; even the lower castes presumably accepted their inferior status as fitting and proper. Within colonial societies, conformity to the paternalistic code was also found among the subordinated groups. They knew how to defer to the master, to act servilely, to conform to his demands, and to play the part of a "carefree child." However, the extent to which they inwardly accepted the validity of the paternalistic system and the "truth" of their own innate inferiority is a question still being argued. In those societies which Rex would label as colonial estate societies, the process of "sambofication" may have spread fairly extensively throughout the lower groups; however, in virtually all colonial societies it could be expected that behavioral conformity to the code was much more frequent than were inner feelings and convictions about the validity of the code; the cost of expressing negative or hostile convictions through nonconforming behavior was just too high given the generally repressive character of the society.

In effect, the presence of a normative "overlay" on the colonial society may have mitigated some of its harsher features; the paternalistic code may have facilitated accommodation and varying degrees of harmony between strata; and in the case of the caste system even provided for an integrated and stable structure. Yet in most instances the code functioned as a veneer for what was essentially a repressive, coercive system in which fear and resentment were inherent features—though overt conflict may have been less frequent.

The Competitive Class System and Modern Society

Thus far we have examined societal systems in which race-ethnicity has a direct and manifest connection with the structures of power and privilege. Now we should like to turn to a societal system in which the relationship between race-ethnicity and these structures is more complex and not as easy to identify.

Modern society and the growth of large-scale bureaucratic structures

In his definition of "competitive type of race relations" van den Berghe asserts that it "is characteristic of industrialized and urbanized societies with a complex division of labor and a manufacturing basis of production " (van den Berghe 1967a:29). In other words, he identifies a distinctive type of racial-ethnic relations with the modern urbanized society in contrast to the paternalistic relations that he identifies with the industrially backward colonial society. Before we examine this distinctive type and in general the role of ethnicity in the modern urban society, let us first look at some of the structural features of this society that are relevant to our concern.

A number of students of society have commented on the character and nature of the basic structural transformation that has occurred to society in recent history. Tönnies sees this as a change from a society organized around the principle of gemeinschaft to a society organized around the principle of gesellschaft: in other words, from a society in which kinship, blood, territory, and tradition were central to a society in which market relations, self-interest, rationality, and contract are central. To Durkheim [1893] (1947) the change has been from a social cohesiveness based on shared values and experiences gained from living in a common territory— or what he called mechanical solidarity—to a cohesiveness based on shared values and experiences gained from a common occupational function—or what he called organic solidarity. Weber focused on the changing character of authority from traditional to legal rational bureaucratic.

Parsons, Etzioni, and Keller go a step further and emphasize the changing scale of organization: the growth, in other words, of large-scale, special purpose associations organized on the principle of rational efficiency. Etzioni comments at length on the importance of such organizations in modern society:

> Our society is an organizational society. We are born in organizations, educated by organizations, and most of us spend much of our lives working for organizations. We spend much of our leisure time paying, playing, and praying in organizations. Most of us will die in an organization, and when the time comes for burial, the largest organization of all—the state—must grant official permission (Etzioni 1964:1).

To Keller the growth of the importance of formal organizations and of institutional differentiation has heightened the importance of Weber's depiction of the basic features of the bureaucratic structure. "Specialization, limited spheres of competence, hierarchies of offices, specified responsibilities, rights, rules and rewards, are all elements of the rise of bureaucratization in the world" (Keller 1963:73).

These structures have become the primary basis for organizing occupational, economic, and political activities and interests in modern society. To Robin Williams this has meant the introduction of radically different principles for structuring the economic and political system from those found in the ethnic, kinship, and territorial community systems. The former system is organized around the "principles of achieved, competitive placement ... of impersonal universalistic norms, and of highly specific, narrowly defined relations among persons" (Williams 1964:356). The latter system continues to revolve around ascribed status (fixed by birth), diffuse rights and duties, and particularistic loyalties.

To Parsons this shift has resulted in

> the general weakening of many of the historic bases of ascriptive status such as religion, ethnicity territorial location ... In general, these changes have favored the rise to prominence of collectivities and roles (organized about functional specificity and universalistic standards of selection and performance) to a paramount position in the occupational system and in most modern authority structures (Parsons 1970:19).

In effect, modern society has witnessed the growth of large-scale occupational, economic, and political bureaucratic associatons divorced from the principles and boundaries that define ethnicity and kinship. These associations are characterized by a hierarchically arranged set of roles. Each of these roles tends to be defined in terms of function, duties, and rights and to require a certain level of technical skill, competence, and knowledge for their performance.

Claims to these positions are presumably gained through the efforts of the individual: his capacity and opportunity to acquire the necessary "credentials," technical skills and competence, and the like. In short, the position is not his by right of birth per se. Thus another distinctive feature of the modern society is its emphasis on achievement rather than ascription as the means of staking claims to position in the various structures.

Another distinctive feature of this system is that the process of selection for these positions and the distribution of rewards is presumably done through the workings of an impersonal evaluative mechanism which merely weighs those considerations directly relevant to potential or actual performance. The prototypic mechanism for modern society is the competitive marketplace where the monetary value of a good or service—whether these are labor, land, or capital—is set by the impersonal workings of the law of supply and demand. Within the bureaucratic structure, the model is also an impersonal and universalistic scheme for the evaluation of performance and for the recruitment and assessment of personnel. These may take the form of examinations, objective performance records, and the like. If these mechanisms were to operate perfectly, then rewards would be distributed objectively according to scarcity value in the marketplace, and according to merit in the bureaucratic structure.

The presence of these features in the occupational and economic structure of society—roles defined in terms of technical competence, claims to these roles through efforts of the individual, and an impersonal evaluative mechanism for placement of personnel and distribution of rewards—does not in itself tell us who will be allowed to acquire the necessary "credentials" to enter and to participate in the various parts and levels of the occupational and economic structure. For just as democracies have existed as in the case of Greece with the rights of citizenship guaranteed to only a small portion of the population, so have there been occupational and bureaucratic structures where the rights of "citizenship" have been confined to relatively few. For example, we have already noted that bureaucratic structures existed in the colonies, but entry into and movement through it was confined to the colonial and certain favored segments of the native population. Nazi Germany developed an immense bureaucratic structure that excluded non-Aryans.

Thus a society can restrict eligibility to relatively few, or it can extend eligibility so that it includes virtually all segments and groups. To the extent that the latter happens the more likely are we to approximate a relatively "pure" competitive class society. Parsons believes in the inherent tendency of a modern competitive class society to universalize eligibility. Only he uses the term "equality" instead of the term "eligibility." He argues that this takes place through the gradual extension of the doctrine of equal opportunity and treatment into a variety of sectors in modern society such as the legal, the political, the occupational, and even to a certain extent, the social. So pervasive does Parsons view the pressure for and the extension of equality that he comments:

> It amounts to saying that the modern societal community shall be "basically" a "company of equals" and hence, so far as empirically possible, legitimate inequalities shall be "won" from a base of equal opportunity and that the rewards which go to differential statuses and achievements shall be justified in terms of functional contribution to the development and welfare of the society. (Parsons 1970:33).

What Parsons is saying is that universalizing equal opportunity does not mean equality of rewards. In fact, Parsons's major thesis is precisely the opposite: namely, the more pervasive equality of opportunity becomes in modern society the more likely will it serve to legitimize inequality. Presumably, those who have gained positions of power and privilege within these structures will be viewed as having done so on their own in equal competition with all others as evaluated by impersonal and objective mechanisms in the marketplace or in the bureaucratic structures.

We have been able to identify five distinctive structural and normative features of the modern competitive society.

1. relative separation of the occupational-economic sphere from the kinship-ethnic sphere: each of which is organized around different principles
2. tendency to define roles in the occupational sphere in terms of technical competence
3. claims to these roles based on individual effort and achievement;
4. emphasis on impersonal evaluative mechanisms to distribute rewards and personnel
5. tendency to universalize eligibility to compete for the various roles.

Such an occupational world, were all the above features operative, would conceivably allow the individual to function outside the boundaries and influence of his ethnic group membership. Ostensibly the individual should be able to do as well as his innate capacities and opportunities permit. If this were indeed the case, and if ethnicity were of no relevance in this world of individual achievement, then we would expect in time to find members of the various ethnic and racial groups randomly distributed throughout the occupational structure. Each group would, in effect, have its share of better and worse jobs and of higher and lower income positions. The net result would be proportional representation at each occupational level for each group according to its numbers in the total work force. This would, in the final analysis, be the natural and logical outcome of a meritocratic society in which race and ethnicity had indeed become irrelevant for eligibility, allocation of position, and distribution of rewards. Members of the various groups would indeed share equally in the inequalities of society.

The American and Racial Creeds

Even before the structural transformation of America into the kind of modern industrial society that we have just described, a legal-normative code that served as a framework for this transformation had already begun to evolve during America's colonist days and was firmly imprinted in the formation of America as a federated nation-state. This American creed, the label used by Myrdal, incorporated the "ideals of the essential dignity of the individual human being, of the fundamental equality of all men, and of certain inalienable rights to freedom, justice, and a fair opportunity . . ." (Myrdal 1944:4).

The tenets of this creed, Myrdal continued, have been

> written into the Declaration of Independence, the Preamble of the Constitution, the Bill of Rights and into the constitutions of the several states. The ideals of the American Creed have thus become the highest law of the land. The Supreme Court pays its reverence to these general principles when it declares what is constitutional and what is not. They have been elaborated upon by all national leaders, thinkers and statesmen. America has had, throughout its history, a continuous discussion of the principles and implications of democracy, a discussion which, in every epoch, measured by any standard, remained high, not only quantitatively but also qualitatively. The flow of learned treatises and popular tracts on the subject has not ebbed, nor is it likely to to so (Myrdal 1944: 4–5).

Thus the American creed represents to Myrdal a set of high ideals that is identified with the American people as a nation and is legitimated as the supreme law of the land by the Constitution as interpreted by the Supreme Court. Fulfillment of this creed would indeed have made America into a meritocratic society in which individual achievement and not racial or ethnic group membership would have been rewarded. Instead, according to Myrdal, America has been confronted historically by what he called an "American Dilemma"—the disparity between its ideals of individual achievement and equality and the practices of racial discrimination and inequality. These practices, with their attendant expressions of racial prejudice and racist beliefs, were also part of the American experience. However Myrdal believed that they were connected to narrow economic, social, or sexual interests and jealousies.

In short, he assumed that these beliefs reflected the prejudices, antipathies, and selfishness of various white groups and individuals. They were "valuations on specific planes of individual and group living, where personal and local interests; economic, social, and sexual jealousies; considerations of community prestige and conformity; group prejudice against particular persons or types of people; and all sorts of miscellaneous wants, impulses, and habits dominate his [the white's] outlook" (Myrdal 1944:xlvii).

Myrdal even states that these racial beliefs may be of even greater importance than the American creed in the day-to-day behavior of people and groups. However, he contends that they have not been elevated to prescriptions of a legal-normative code by the whites who hold them, but have instead become transmuted into presumptive factual statements of reality. Thus one order of belief and valuation, the American creed, is used to define a higher order of what ought to be; and the other, used to justify a lower order of what presumably is—a distorted and false view of reality.

This point of view is shared by many white scholars of ethnicity—even today. They operate from the basic premise that prejudice and discrimination have been irrational and aberrant responses in a society whose core value system is the American creed. For example, the classic studies of the authoritarian personality conducted in the early 1940s by Adorno and others at the University of California concluded that prejudice served important psychic and emotional functions for "sick" personalities; hence their need to scapegoat ethnic and racial minorities. Other observers applied the label of abnormality and even of sickness to their studies of hate groups from the Ku Klux Klan to the Asiatic Exclusion League.

Perhaps the largest component of the American society stamped by various scholars with the label of abnormal and aberrant was the Deep South with its Jim Crow societal structure built on the racial creed of black difference and inferiority. So convinced were many scholars from Dollard and Park to Myrdal that the racial situation in the South was alien to an American dedicated to the normal workings of Myrdal's American creed, that they grafted the concept *caste* onto their vocabulary of race as a label for this regionally residual network of black-white relations. Other scholars are convinced, as is Sowell, (1981) that under the benign workings of the American creed, ethnic and racial groups are themselves entirely responsible for what happens to them in the labor market.

What Myrdal and these scholars have failed to realize is that these racial beliefs were more than by-products of white man's baser nature. They were imprinted into the very founding of colonial America and became part of a distinctive legal-normative code that sanctified domination and discrimination of black and later of other racial minorities by the white. The code was legitimated in the writing of the Constitution and later reaffirmed after a brief period of suspension during the first period of Reconstruction by the Supreme Court as law of the land. (America's duality is discussed in later chapters.*) Thus, by the end of the nineteenth century discrimination and segregation were deemed the law of the land in the private and institutional arenas of society, both South and North. Though the immediate targets of this lawful discrimination were racial minorities, the effects of this lawfulness spilled over and contaminated the life circumstances of the white immigrant, too. Few were the white immigrants who did not find their access to jobs, colleges, and professional schools blocked or severely limited.

From the 1940s onward, however, doors began gradually to open to certification and to occupational opportunities that had been previously barred. As we have already mentoned, Parsons insists that the norm of equal access has extended into various sectors of society in a manner that has vastly enlarged the company of those eligible for entry. Perhaps the most visible and dramatic expression of this has been at the level of the federal government.

Initiated by the Supreme Court's Brown decision of 1954, the process of transforming the racial creed from a legitimate to an illegitimate code of behavior was completed by Congress a little more than a decade later. In rapid succession Congress passed the Civil Rights Act of 1964, the Voting Rights Act of 1965, and the Fair Housing Act of 1968. However, unlike the Supreme Court, Congress did not confine the transmutation to actions of the state and/or its agencies only, but extended it also to actions of public consequence by individuals and organizations in the major institutional environments of the political, economic and social realms of the people's domain. In so doing, Congress explicitly and clearly affirmed the right of blacks to share with whites equality of access, opportunity, and treatment within these environments.

In effect, Congress had mandated that all the major institutional environments of the people's domain were to be governed under a common legal-normative framework based on racial equality and the American creed. Thus, the normative task begun in the first period of Reconstruction seemed to have come to fruition at last during the height of the second period of Reconstruction.

The executive branch of the federal government even began to

---

* For a much more elaborate and documented discussion of the duality thesis see Ringer (1983).

implement policies such as affirmative action that sought to redress some of the continuing effects of the past racial inequities. These policies proved too much for most white Americans. Under the slogan of "reverse discrimination", opposition to these measures mounted dramatically so that by 1981 a historian was able to proclaim that America's second period of Reconstruction had given way to a second period of Redemption. "In both the nineteenth and twentieth century, a period of turbulent change was succeeded by a desire for 'stability,' followed in turn by an open assault on achievements enshrined in Federal Law and the Constitution that had appeared irreversible" (Foner 1981:23).

For many white Americans, then, the civil rights acts of the 1960s seemed to have created a tabula rasa on which all past racial inequities had been wiped clean; no further action was deemed necessary along the racial front. America was now, they insisted, the racially neutral meritocratic society that the Founding Fathers had presumably meant it to be from the beginning.

Tempting as this belief may be, the dominant whites have yet to face a sobering fact. Many of the racial inequities imprinted from America's past are still deeply engraved in its institutional arrangements and continue to contaminate any truly meritocratic allocation of position, reward, and privilege. Under the circumstances, the "meritocratic" system as presently constituted in America does not function in the kind of objective and rational manner that most white Americans would like to believe it does and should. In an article for *Society* early in 1976, Ringer stated:

> It can be argued that defenders of the merit system all too often treat it as though it were a fully automated, self correcting foolproof machine or perhaps computer which sorts individuals into occupational slots and differentially rewards them according to a mathematical formula, rationally and objectively derived, quantitatively described, and universalistically and impersonally applied (Ringer 1976: 25).

Ringer then went on to identify a number of nonrational and subjective components contained in the system. He concluded that these components are not racially or ethnically neutral; instead they favor the already advantaged racial and ethnic groups and tilt the system even more in their direction. Thus ethnicity and race continue to play an important role—directly or indirectly—even in those occupational structures in which position is presumably based on individual achievement and merit.

> They [the supporters of meritocracy] fail to realize that merit is a dynamic system in which people make decisions about its vital features. What is to be defined as technical competence? What should be the criteria of evaluation?

How is an individual to be scored on each of the criteria? How should these scores be weighted? The hope, of course, is that these decisions will be rational and objective and will lead to the goal of excellence and merit. But the fact is that these decisions contain so many subjective and non-rational elements which reinforce the position of those people who are already favored. As a result, the merit system operates like a political system and not like the self-regulatory economic market system of Adam Smith (Ringer 1976:25).

4   Racial-Ethnic Dominance and the Nation-State

In the last two chapters we examined the relationship between race-ethnicity and the structures of power and stratification in society. In the process we continually alluded to the importance of the political system and its legal-normative framework in determining the fate of racial and ethnic groups.

In this chapter we shall examine how a dominant racial-ethnic group may in turn affect the character of a society and its political system. Such a group is not likely to be content with merely having a favored position in society; it will also seek to impose its will on the whole of society and to mold society in its image. As such it may try to monopolize the instruments and offices of the *state* and thereby make its rules the law of the land. Such a group may also seek to place its imprint on the general culture, symbols, and life-styles of the society and thereby have a determining influence on the whole society as *nation* and *national community*.

This relationship between a dominant ethnic or racial group and the whole society, either as a state or as a nation, has an inherent complexity and variability. For example, white Europeans succeeded for hundreds of years in dominating through conquest the state structures of colonial societies, but they have rarely been able to develop a sense of common purpose in these societies either because they did not try or because they tried and failed. This is also true at the other end of the scale. Ethnic and racial groups that enter at the bottom of society invariably come under the rule and control of the political state of that society, but whether they identify with or are allowed to become part of that society varies with the group and with the society.

Thus nation and state become important representations of the whole society to which ethnic and racial groups relate separately or jointly. Yet

73

many scholars have failed to recognize the importance of this dual representation for the study of ethnic and race relations. In the first part of this chapter we shall deal with this matter. But so important do we consider this distinction between nation and state as representations of the whole society that we shall devote the next section of this chapter to an examination of the two concepts. We shall conclude this chapter with an analysis of the impact of the dominant racial and ethnic group on both nation and state.

The Distinction Between the Dominant Racial-Ethnic Group and Society: The Need for Reconceptualization

All too frequently scholars of ethnic and racial minorities have neglected to deal clearly and systematically with the distinction between the dominant racial or ethnic group of a society and the society itself. Sometimes they use the terms interchangeably. As an example, a reader confronted by the phrase dominant society or dominant group as applied to the United States is frequently unclear whether the reference is to the WASP or to the American society generally.

Other times, scholars treat as a bilateral relationship what is better treated as a triadic relationship. This type of confusion appears in one of the more sophisticated attempts to develop an inclusive conceptual scheme for the field of comparative ethnic and race relations. The problem though does not emerge at the level of basic definitions. Specifically Schermerhorn in his book *Comparative Ethnic Relations* clearly accepts the premise that ethnic groups are part of a larger society.

> Each society in the modern world contains subsections or subsystems more or less distinct from the rest of the population. The most fitting generic term to designate this fraction of the whole is "ethnic group." An ethnic group is defined here as a collectivity within a larger society having a real or putative common ancestry, memories of a shared historical past, and a cultural focus on one or more symbolic elements defined as the epitome of their peoplehood (Schermerhorn 1970:12).

Several pages later he clearly states that when he uses the term society, he really means the nation-state.

> Finally, a word about the term "society." For the purposes at hand, I am deliberately excluding the broader, generic meaning for a more limited one. ... Thus in the modern world, it seems most appropriate to define a society as a nation-state, i.e., a social unit territorially distinguished from other such units, having a set of governmental institutions of a central character preeminent over local political controls, and empowered to act for the entire unit in external relations (Schermerhorn 1970:14).

Thus to Schermerhorn ethnic groups are parts or subsystems of nation-states.

Within the nation-state, according to Schermerhorn, one of these ethnic groups can be identified as the dominant group. It is "that collectivity within a society which has preeminent authority to function both as guardians and sustainers of the controlling value system, and as prime allocators of rewards in the society" (Schermerhorn 1970:13). The size of the dominant group in a society may be large or small; it may be confined to a "restricted elite" or include a majority of the population. Virtually all other ethnic groups in a nation-state occupy subordinate positions, Schermerhorn refers to them as minority groups or as mass subjects depending upon how large a proportion of the nation-state they compromise.

Having completed his "preliminary definitions," Schermerhorn then goes on to raise what he considers to be the central question for comparative research in ethnic relations. "What are the conditions that foster or prevent the integration of ethnic groups into their environing societies?" (Schermerhorn 1970:14). By the end of the paragraph he shifts his term of reference from "environing societies" (or nation-states) to "dominant group." Thus he states, "As presented here, integration is not an end-state but a *process* whereby units or elements of a society are brought into an active and coordinated compliance with the ongoing activities and objectives of the dominant group in that society" (Schermerhorn 1970: 14). He spends considerable time dealing with relationships between subordinate and dominant ethnic groups in a society. But he finds that for some of the questions he wishes to deal with he has to come back to his original definition: "... integration will be regarded as a process whereby units or elements of a society are brought into a more active and coordinated compliance with the ongoing activities and objectives of the total society at any given period of time" (Schermerhorn 1970:58).

This shifting back and forth of his terms of reference reflects Schermerhorn's tendency to conceptualize his problem in terms of sets of bilateral relationships. He is obviously most interested in the bilateral relationship between subordinate and dominant ethnic groups; on occasion he expresses an interest in the bilateral relationship between an ethnic group and the society (here he comes closer to the approach we suggest below). In doing this he fails to recognize that in many societies the most important relationships between dominant and subordinate groups are rarely bilateral. They do not involve direct confrontations between the two as one ethnic or racial group against another; instead these relationships are mediated through the positons each has in various structures of society and their identification with and involvement with these structures. Thus a member of the dominant group does not usually confront members of minority groups as a representative of the dominant ethnic or racial group but as an agent of the larger society. In addition, he tends to define his rights and to define the obligations of the minority group in terms of the broader societal system and not on the narrower grounds of ethnicity. For example, the president of the United States who is generally a WASP does not address himself to the second- and third-generation Jew or Italian as a WASP but as an American. What appears to be a bilateral relationship between dominant and subordinate groups is in fact a triadic relationship which involves the relationship of each to the society itself.

There are two basic kinds of triadic relationships that shall be of special interest to us: (1) that between the society as a *nation* or *national community* and the dominant and subordinated racial and ethnic groups and (2) that between the society as a *political state* and the two kinds of racial or ethnic groups. The significance of these relationships should become evident later in this chapter. However, we shall first wish to examine more closely the concepts of nation and of state.

Society as a Political State

In identifying his usage of the term society with that of the nation-state, Schermerhorn is saying that relationships between dominant and subordinate groups cannot be fully understood unless they are placed within the political and cultural framework of society. However, in defining the concept nation-state he places special emphasis on the governmental and political features of this framework. In effect, what he primarily does is give a definition of the *state* part of the *nation-state* concept. This becomes evident if we look at several definitions that have been used by various sociologists in defining the concept *state*. Hoult, for example, in the *Dictionary of Modern Sociology* defines a state as a "politically organized society especially one that functions through a government which claims ultimate authority in the area subject to its jurisdiction" (Hoult 1969:315). Max Weber defines it in similar terms: "A compulsory political association with continuous organization ... will be called a 'state' if and insofar as its administrative staff successfully upholds a claim to the *monopoly* of the *legitimate* use of physical force in the enforcement of its order" (Weber [1922] 1947:154).

By defining the term as he does Schermerhorn falls into an error which MacIver would have scholars avoid. He cautions against treating the state as though it were also the nation.

The state is frequently confused with the community. In reality the state is *one* form of social organization, not the whole community in all its aspects . . . .The confusion of community and state is increased by the usage of the same term to indicate either. Thus "United States" refers either to our national state association with its governmental apparatus or to the national community which it governs (MacIver and Page 1949:13).

MacIver insists that which distinguishes the state from the nation and from all other associations is *"its exclusive investment with the final power of coercion"* (MacIver and Page 1949:456). In short, it has a monopoly on the legitimate use of force. As a result, MacIver continues,

> the state alone can establish an effective and basic order in a complex society. The state can maintain such an order because of the peculiar attributes which we saw that it and it alone possesses. On the one hand its law is binding on *all* who live within an entire geographical area; on the other hand it possesses the ultimate right of enforcement. The establishment and maintenance of a universal order are thus an essential function of the state, its function par excellence (MacIver and Page 1949:458–459).

The development of the state, particularly as described in MacIver's terms, is a relatively recent historical phenomenon. Gumplowicz argues that the state emerged relatively early in history when one primitive horde conquered and placed another under permanent subjugation. Wagley and Harris conjecture that the state first emerged about five thousand years ago with the birth of "mankind's first cities"; these witnessed the coming together of different kinds of people in one territorial area. "Only with the development of the state did human societies become equipped with a form of social organization which could bind masses of culturally and physically heterogeneous 'strangers' into a single social entity" (Wagley and Harris 1958:242). For much of this period of history, this occurred without the heterogeneous mix of people and groups developing a sense of collective unity and identity within the boundaries of the state. As a result, Wagley and Harris adopt the term *state society* to describe the situation. They reserve the concept of nation-state for a later historical variant of the state society.

For our purposes the crucial period in the development of the state society began in Europe about 600 years ago with the breakdown of the feudal system. From about the twelfth through the seventeenth century, the history of Europe, particularly that of France and England, showed remarkable growth of the state as the basic apparatus for centralized political authority within ever expanding territorial boundaries. Examination of the dynastic struggles within the two countries reveals an inexorable movement toward increasing the power of the king at the expense of the nobility, toward a more centralized administration and legal structure and political economy, and toward improved means of communications and transportation. These along with other centralizing tendencies served increasingly to bring together people from different regions, classes, and ethnic groups into a single unified political framework and made them subject to the same laws and decrees.

The purpose of this enlargement was to enhance the power and the glory of the dynastic state by extending the rule of the king over an increasing number of people as his subjects. In extending its control and territory, however, the dynastic state society was in fact laying the groundwork for its eventual transformation into the nation-state.

The State as Nation

According to a number of scholars, the dynastic state did not take on the character of a nation until the people within the political boundaries of the state saw themselves as a distinctive collectivity and community and located the source of political authority and legitimacy within that conception—and not within the divine right of kings or a special relation between ruler and subject. This did not occur in Western Europe until the eighteenth century. According to Kohn (1961) its clearest manifestations were in England first and in France later. The emergence of the national community meant therefore that the people saw themselves as part of a community that transcended their more parochial group and communal memberships.

> In our present-day civilization the nation remains the largest effective community. By this we mean that the nation is the largest group which is permeated by a consciousness of comprehensive solidarity. There are interests extending far beyond national frontiers, including, perhaps, those most vital to man's own welfare; and there are international associations of many kinds, the United Nations and many less comprehensive. But as yet there is no international *community* in any effective degree, a point that becomes clear when we remind ourselves of the fundamental bases of all communities (MacIver and Page 1949:296).

The sentiments that tied together members of the national community were steeped in a sense of common destiny and purpose. Although the concept of the nation was abstract and removed from the immediate senses of the populace, its capacity to elicit strong emotions and sentiment, particularly in time of crisis was virtually unlimited. MacIver and Page comment upon two basic forms this sentiment has taken: patriotism and nationalism.

National sentiment however was itself the product of a cultural process that expressed itself in a variety of forms and contents. It was built on a common language, on the creation of an art, literature, philosophy, history, and law that stressed common ties and origins. The result was the building of a national culture.

Znaniecki comments upon the process by which a national culture comes into being and flourishes. He views it as primarily a product of the intellectual elite in a society.

> In every instance hitherto investigated, the formation of a national culture society starts with a relatively small social nucleus whose influence slowly spreads until it eventually reaches millions of people. This nucleus is not constituted by any authoritative organized group, be it the government of a state, or the clerical hierarchy of a church, or an association of members of an economically dominant class. It originates with independent *individual leaders* in various realms of cultural activity, who gradually create a national culture in which a plurality of traditional regional cultures becomes partly synthesized. We call them leaders because and insofar as they attract circles of voluntary followers. They frequently gain also the support of socially powerful sponsors or patrons—princes, magnates, church dignitaries, men of wealth, statesmen, military commanders, heads of political parties.
>
> As the national culture grows, these leaders, their followers, and sponsors who participate in its growth form an increasingly coherent intellectual community activated by the ideal of a culturally united and socially solidary national society, which should include all the people whose folk cultures are presumed to be essentially alike and who are supposed to share the same historical background. The realization of this ideal is expected to overcome the cultural isolation of local and regional communities, political divisions, religious differences, class conflicts (Znaniecki 1952:24–25).

Znaniecki then goes on to discuss the contribution of various segments of the intellectual elite and intelligentsia: such as men of letters, historians and ethnographers, national ideologists, artists, musicians, and scientists.

Over time institutions and other societal structures have also tended to solidify the sense of national community. Of particular importance has been the growth of educational systems which link the people to the culture and occupational order of the national society and which imbue them with values and beliefs that transcend local and provincial loyalties and connect them with the larger community. Similarly, social, economic, and political institutions have tended to strengthen the ties with the national community just as have improvements in the means of communications and transportation. The net result of the convergence of all these factors has been the development of the nation as a viable community within the boundaries of the political state of many societies.

Despite the fact that nation and state have become inextricably interwoven in many societies, this linkage is neither inevitable nor necessary. There are still many societies in which the two are distinct. Furnivall's colonial plural society represents, as we have seen, a society with a well-developed state structure without even a rudimentary sense of national community. By the same token recent history contains many examples of people who identified themselves as national communities but who lacked a state apparatus of their own and were, instead, the subjects of other rulers whom they decried. The history of Central and Eastern Europe is replete with such examples. The period of post-World War I and of the League of Nations can be seen as the apex of the struggle of national minorities for political autonomy and independence.

The Nation-State and the People's Domain

The linchpin that connects nation and state is, as we have already seen, the people who stand as a collective expression of the linkage between the two. Nowhere is this symbolism more clearly enshrined than in the preamble to the United State Constitution whose first words are "We the People . . ." The Constitution then proceeds to establish the construct of a federal government and to spell out in detail its sphere of jurisdiction. Governmental activities and functions that were not specified were left to the states. In effect, what was created were two governmental structures, each charged with its own area of responsibilities. Both derived their authority and legitimacy from the consent of the people.

To highlight this, the Constitution, and the Bill of Rights that was subsequently appended to it, spelled out the rights and immunities of the people. They were to have access to the legal and judiciary system and were to be protected from the arbitrary exercise of governmental authority. They were granted the right of trial by jury of their own peers; they did not have to testify against themselves; they were guaranteed due process of law, and the protection of their property. Further, they were granted the right of access to and participation in the political system. They were guaranteed the right "to petition the Government for a redress of grievances" (*The Constitution* 1872:21) and to vote directly for members of the House of Representatives and indirectly for members of the Senate and the president. Most were eligible to stand for public office.

And finally the people had rights that would allow them to interact freely with whomever they wished in their communities. They could worship as they pleased and with whomever they pleased. They could assemble peaceably and say what was on their mind without fear of legal and political authority and also publish the newspapers they wanted. In addition they could remain "secure in their persons, houses, papers and effects, against unreasonable searches and seizures" (*The Constitution* 1872:21). In effect, the rights of the people transcended the legal and political system and included the national community as well.

In this manner then the sovereignty of the people was reaffirmed in both the political state and in the national community. In both they shared equally in the various rights and were in effect citizens of both. In sum, according to the Constitution and the Founding Fathers, the people are the citizens of the United States. And with the addition of the Bill of Rights a domain of the people was created.

How the rights and immunities of citizenship or of membership in the people's domain evolved is the topic of T. H. Marshall's classic essay "Citizenship and Social Class." He describes the three major kinds of claims that citizenship or membership in the people's domain has come to represent historically in England. Each defines a prescribed area of rights which all citizens are presumed to share equally.

Marshall sees each component of citizenship as having developed at a different period of history. He assigns "the formative period in the life of each to a different century—civil rights to the eighteenth, political to the nineteenth and social to the twentieth." He goes on to say "These periods must, of course, be treated with reasonable elasticity, and there is some evident overlap, especially between the last two." (Marshall 1964:74).

The courts played a decisive role in elaborating on the civil and legal rights of the individual against the demands of the state and the powerful and in extending these rights to all citizens. One of the most important of these rights, according to Marshall, is the "right to work, that is to say, the right to follow the occupation of one's choice in the place of one's choice subject only to legitimate demands for preliminary technical training." Prior to this time, "this right had been denied by both statute and custom" (Marshall 1964:75). The universalization of these rights meant "'one law for all men.'" And "when freedom became universal, citizenship grew from a local into a national institution" (Marshall 1964:77).

"The story of political rights," according to Marshall, "is different both in time and in character" (Marshall 1964:77). At first the voting franchise was monopolized by a small group; no one could become a member of this group without permission from its existing members. The Act of 1832 opened up this monopoly by tying the franchise to property. As such "no sane and law-abiding citizen was debarred by personal status from acquiring and recording a vote. He was free to earn, to save, to buy property or to rent a house, and to enjoy whatever political rights were attached to these economic achievements. His civil rights entitled him, and electoral reform increasingly enabled him, to do this" (Marshall 1964:78). In this manner Marshall claims that political rights became a derivative of the person's civil rights. Not until the Act of 1918 were political rights made universal and thereby attached directly to citizenship.

Social rights also went through a series of stages before they too became part of the rights of citizenship. The structure of group obligation to the individual that characterized England in earlier days was virtually destroyed by the triumph of capitalism, which emphasized the right of the individual to sell his labor as he wishes, the limited obligation of the labor contract, and the competitive struggle of the individual against individual. The need to protect special groups of the population from the excesses of capitalism was recognized in the nineteenth century; accordingly protective legislation was enacted for the infirm, children, and women—individuals who were too weak to help themselves and were not part of the citizenry. As Marshall comments, "women were protected because they were not citizens, If they wished to enjoy full and responsible citizenship, they must forego protection" (Marshall 1964:81). This argument became moot as factory codes and protective legislation were enacted for all segments of the working-class population. From these beginnings in the early twentieth century, social legislation such as social security, health, and unemployment became part of the body politic and incorporated in the rights of citizenship. The elaboration and extension of these three types of rights have had a profound effect on the nation-state. First, they have enlarged membership in the national community; previously excluded groups have been granted the various rights of citizenship as in the case of the farming and working classes of England over the past century or so and in the case of the blacks in America of more recent history. Second, they have expanded the kinds of equalities citizens can expect to share. The civil and political rights presumably grant citizens equality of access and of "normative condition" in the legal and political systems and to a certain extent in the economic system as well. The social rights have placed an obligation on society to meet minimal health and social needs of its citizenry and have therefore introduced the right of citizens to at least minimal outcomes.

In general the development of the "equalities" have neither eliminated nor appreciably reduced inequality in the nation-state. Marshall raises this question early in his essay: "Is it still true that basic equality when enriched in substance and embodied in the formal rights of citizenship, is consistent with the inequalities of social class?" He answers that there is no contradiction between the two. He goes on to say "our society today assumes that the two are still compatible, so much so that citizenship has itself become, in certain respects, the architect of legitimate social inequality" (Marshall 1964:70). This is particularly true of the manner in which civil and political rights have operated in countries like England and the United States. They have "guaranteed" equality of access to major institutional environments, but not equality of outcome. In fact, they have encouraged the individual to strive to achieve what he can and have guaranteed him the right to keep what he gets. Lipset (1963) considers equality and achievement the two major values in American society. The result has been gross inequalities in the distribution of power, wealth, and privilege. The inequalities frequently feed back on the basic rights themselves. For the privileged are more likely to receive the maximum benefits from these rights than are the less privileged. Thus, they are able to obtain better results in the courts, in government, and in the economy. The net result is a further piling up of inequalities in the system.

The emergence of the social rights of citizenship has reversed somewhat the direction of this flow. They have granted the citizen the right to at least minimal outcomes such as stipulated in social security and health insurance legislation. This has reduced somewhat the inequality of outcome that might otherwise have prevailed and has opened the door to consideration of the policy of preferential inputs for certain groups to insure greater equality of outcome.

The Dominant Racial and Ethnic Group and the Nation-State

Although the development of the nation-state provides certain claims to equality for those who share citizenship or membership in the people's domain, the unequal distribution of power, wealth, and privilege is also a basic fact of life in the nation-state. Furthermore, the very character of the national community and the portrait of the people may reflect the imprint of one group much more than it does that of another. Scholars have generally agreed that the rise of the nation-state under capitalism was primarily the handiwork of the emerging bourgeoisie which in turn left its imprint on the character of the nation-state itself.

> With the rise of the middle classes to power, the nation and its welfare became the common denominator and the common end of thought and action. Through it the liberals of the eighteenth century, most of them of the middle classes, thought they could progress to the kind of society they desired and believed good for all men. Without conscious selfishness, and perhaps also sometimes without calculation, the middle classes conceived of themselves as the national societies and established national government which chiefly favored themselves. When they did, the highest and most prevalent political loyalty came to be that devotion to their *own* society and government which is called national patriotism (Shafer 1955:105).

However, according to Max Weber, the way of life and character of the bourgeoisie was itself a product of its religious and ethnic ties. In his book *The Protestant Ethic and the Spirit of Capitalism* (1930), Weber contends that values of Protestantism had so stamped the character and conduct of its adherents that it paved the way for their becoming the economic men of emerging capitalism. Though Tawney (1938) rejects this causal explanation, he accepts the compatibility between economic interests and religious values of the bourgeoisie and emphasizes the role that religious values played in legitimizing the activity of the bourgeoisie. However, whatever part political and economic interests and power may play in a group's getting into a position of dominance, once in that position the ethnicity of the dominant group plays an important part in shaping its conception of the national community, culture, and its definition of peoplehood. Wagley and Harris point to the crucial role that some ethnic groups may play in the very formulation and definition of the national culture and community:

> During the last few centuries, many conscious and unconscious efforts have ben made to achieve the ideal of a national state. In the process, the cultural traditions, the language, and physical type of one of the groups of a state society are proposed as the national language, the national culture, and the national physical type. Usually this dominant or "national" way of life is that of the numerical majority, and the strangers—the minority members—form smaller cultural and racial enclaves. But sometimes a handful of people have, through their superior economic, political, or military power, been able to impose their cultural and physical "ideal" of nationhood on the rest of the society (Wagley and Harris 1958:243).

Thus a dominant ethnic group not only seeks to monopolize the basic instruments of power of the state and of wealth of economy; it also seeks to put its distinctive stamp on the character and shape of the national culture and comunity with its people's domain. Accordingly it seeks to make its values and institutions the prevailing mold of the nation. Its language becomes the national language, its way of doing things become sanctified; and its standards of justice, virtue, and order become built into the very fabric of the community. It affects the basic definition and criteria of citizenship and membership in the people's domain, the allocation of rewards and power and the distribution of wealth and privilege. And it provides the models for major roles in the society and for the characterization and definition of the people. Thus various national cultures and communities can be distinguished by the stamp of dominant ethnic and racial groups. Wagley and Harris offer illustrations of the distinctive imprint of these dominant ethnic and racial groups on national communities:

> In the United States, the national ideal is English-speaking, Protestant, northern European in descent, and light Caucasoid in physical appearance. In Brazil, the national ideal is Portuguese-speaking (with a Brazilian accent), Catholic, Portuguese in descent and dark Caucasoid in physical appearance.

In Mexico, it is Spanish in language, Catholic in religion, Iberian with perhaps a distant Indian ancestor in descent, and mestizo (Caucasoid-Indian mixture) in physical appearance. In the French West Indies, the ideal is French in language, Catholic in religion, a descendant of an old plantation family, and Caucasoid in physical appearance. In Canada, despite the fact that the nation is officially a bicultural and bilingual state, the ideal is English-speaking, Protestant, northern European, and light Caucasoid (Wagley and Harris 1958:243–244).

The relative success of the dominant ethnic group in stamping the national culture and community depends in part on how large a proportion of the total population it comprises. Where the dominant group is numerically preponderant in society, it is better able to define the national culture and community on its own terms. A major case in point would be the imprint of the English, and later of the WASP on the American society from its beginning through the early part of the twentieth century. Not all members of the dominant ethnic group, however, become equally powerful and successful, but those who do become the principal interpreters of what is good for the ethnic group and for the nation. The less successful and less powerful of the dominant ethnic group become believers in the right of the powerful to wield authority and also in the truth, beauty, and virtue that the powerful dispense. In effect they share a common set of beliefs and values that are rooted in their common membership in both ethnic and national communities and in their participation in the peoples's domain of the latter. The two sets of loyalties are interchangeable. They define the ways in which people are equal in both communities, and sanction and legitimize the ways in which they are unequal. Thus the inequalities of power, privilege, and wealth become an acceptable part of the scheme of things.

While the overlap between the dominant ethnic and national communities reinforce each other in vital ways, rarely are their boundaries identical. Even South Africa which excludes all nonwhites from membership in the national community and from participation in its people's domain cannot overlook the various ethnic divisions within the white population. The national community primarily includes the Afrikaners, who comprise the dominant ethnic group, and the persons of English descent who have historically been in a competitive struggle with the Afrikaner for economic and political power. Thus, there is no ethnically homogeneous white national community but one riven by various nationality and religious cleavages. The strenuous efforts of Hitler to transform Germany into a racially pure Nordic community resulted in the expulsion of Jews, Gypsies, Slavs, and other pariah groups from membership in the national community; yet these efforts did not eliminate other kinds of nationality, religious, and other ethnic cleavages among the presumably Nordically pure population. These were obviously overlooked in promulgating and perpetuating the myth of racial purity. Hitler preferred the label "folk" to that of "people."

What is more the exclusion from being part of the people of ethnic and racial groups that differ from the dominant ethnic group does not reduce the significance of their presence within the boundaries of the nation-state. They may not be able to enjoy the rights and privileges of membership in the national community or of its people's domain but they occupy the attention of the state. In fact, they literally preempt the attention of the power wielders of the state who spend an increasing amount of time and energy in trying to find out more effective ways of controlling and exploiting them. Thus the presence of a large pariah and excluded group frequently gives the nation-state a schizoid character. On the one level we have the people who are part of the national community in which principles of equality and democracy may prevail despite unequal distribution of wealth, power, and privilege. On another level we have a set of excluded and pariah groups who become objects of control and exploitation and who are subject to the repressive powers of the state without the basic protection of citizenship. Nowhere is the contrast between the two levels more apparent than in the history of South Africa and of the United States, to which we shall shortly devote our attention.

More typical of the modern nation-state is the gradual inclusion within the national community of ethnic groups that differ from the dominant ethnic group and the gradual extension of the various rights of citizenship to them within the people's domain. Such rights do not in any way eliminate the disparity in power, wealth, and privilege between the groups, but they do mean that these ethnic minorities have gained some degree of access to significant institutional environments of the nation-state. Their disabilities are real and their struggle for position fierce, but they can wrap around themselves the same basic rights as those possessed by the dominant ethnic group. As the national community begins to include an increasing proportion of ethnically heterogeneous groups, and as these groups begin to challenge their subordinated position and move upward in the occupational and political systems then the very character of the national culture and community may undergo change. It may become less a mirror image of the dominant ethnic group and more a composite of the inputs of various groups. Members of the ethnically heterogeneous minorities tend to exaggerate the extent to which this happens; those from the dominant ethnic group, to minimize it.

5   The White European and Colonial Expansion and Settlement

Just as the history of the past several centuries has witnessed the rise and flowering of the nation-state, so have other kinds of political societies also emerged. These societies have been, by and large, the product of the conquest of overseas territories with their indigenous populations. In some of these conquered territories the white European also sought to establish a permanent settlement. The result was the formation of two different types of overseas societies: a colonial plural society and a "colonialist-colonist dual society." In this chapter we shall examine the distinctive imprint of the white European on each of these two types of society, the character of the racial segmentation in each, and the struggle of each for independence and nationhood.

First let us look at the colonial plural society that the white European built, and then we shall turn to the colonialist-colonist dual society.

The Colonial Plural Society

The white European as a sojourner elite

As we have already seen, the colonial expansion of the white European from the fifteenth century onward brought under his control vast areas and regions of the world that were comprised of racially different populations. In many of these areas he was merely interested in establishing the imperial control of the metropolitan country over the conquered land. In Chapter 3 we described the major structural characteristics of the kind of colonial plural society that he built. In this section we shall examine the role of the white European as a sojourner elite in these societies, the response of the colonialized, and finally at the latter's struggle for independence and nationhood.

In some of these conquered territories, such as in the Caribbean, the white European virtually exterminated the native population and brought in an enslaved labor supply for his plantations. In such areas he literally built a colonialist plural society from scratch. In other areas as in Africa and Southeast Asia, he subdued the native population, let most of them live, and superimposed a colonialist structure on the back of the traditional system. The form of colonial administration that he established to insure his control varied in part with the political style of the colonial power. For example, the British in Africa generally relied more heavily on the traditional system in the colony and on indirect rule than did the French who preferred their own direct rule. Perhaps of even greater importance in the colonialist's choice of administrative style was the state of political and social development of the conquered people. In Africa, for example, when the colonialists conquered a society with a developed set of governing institutions, they sought to coopt this structure of traditional authority and to harness it to their own purposes. Thus the British in northern Nigeria virtually perfected a model of indirect rule under the expert guidance of Sir Frederick Lugard.

> The British Resident, who acted as a sympathetic adviser and counsellor to native chiefs, was in charge of a province which contained several separate native administrations, whether they were Moslem Emirates or pagan communities. A British district officer was in charge of a division which might include one or more headmen's districts or more than one small Emirate or pagan tribe independent of other tribes. Although the Resident was not to interfere in such a manner as to lower the prestige of the native chief, the latter was required to follow the advice of the Resident. However, the native chief was permitted to issue his own instructions to his subordinate chiefs and district heads and was encouraged to work through his subordinates. The district officers supervised and assisted the district headmen, through whom they communicated instructions to the village headmen. Important orders emanated from the Emirs, whose messengers accompanied and acted as the mouthpiece of the district officers (Frazier 1957a:194).

Contrastingly, when the European colonialists conquered "stateless" African societies, they resorted to direct rule.

> At first they [the colonialists] chose as native administrative agents persons who were considered by Europeans to be the proper persons through whom they should administer. The persons chosen did not have the support of native peoples and very often they represented a violation of the traditional ideas and values of native peoples. The European bureaucratic system which came into existence as a part of a centralized administration was, in fact, a system of direct rule (Frazier 1957a:189–190).

No matter which mode of administrative control was exercised, the European colonialist stood at the pinnacle of power and privilege in these societies. He superimposed his own political, economic, and social institutions on whatever traditional base there was and retained in his own hands the ultimate instruments of coercion and power. He introduced and installed administrative and educational structures that enhanced his control. He created elite role models which were patterned in his image and style, and he introduced schemes of status evaluation with himself at the top.

In effect, much of his energies were devoted to securing and maintaining his political, economic, and socal dominance in the colony. As such he became obsessed with his elite status and where he could, as in the plantation colonies, he attempted to construct an aristocratic style of life with its elaborate codes of etiquette. As Freyre and Frazier state, the plantation house became the center of the life-style; and the development of the leisure class a la Thorstein Veblen, its hope. The style of life was modelled after that of the social elite in the metropolitan country, but in the colonies it became something different. It was characterized by a greater ostentatiousness, flamboyance, and display of wealth. This contrast in the use of wealth was made evident in the metropolitan country such as in England where some absentee owners of plantations set up residence. The colonial style of life was also characterized by a combination of fastidiousness and crudity and by a veneer of gentility over a foundation of cruelty. John Stedman graphically described these paradoxical features in his account of a planter's day in the eighteenth century (Stedman 1806:48–51).

The European elite in many of the colonies adopted what can best be described as a sojourner's philosophy. Even after generations in the colony, the elite professed a longing to return to the metropolitan country. As Eric Williams (1944) reported in his study of the British West Indies, the elite neither spiritually nor physically lost its ties with the home country. Whenever and wherever possible, they returned home for visits and retirement. As a result, members of the European elite frequently saw themselves as transients in the colony: someday they would leave. Mederic-Louis-Elie Moreau de Saint-Mery described in his eighteenth-century account of the French settler in Saint Dominique the pervasiveness of this attitude among the second-generation children of the original settlers. They had been sent back to the homeland for their education and were even more alienated from the colony after their return.

Memmi brought the special relationship between colonialist and home country into the twentieth century in his observations on the French in Algeria. He viewed the close identification with the homeland as an inextricable part of being a colonialist. "In order that he may subsist as a colonialist, it is necessary that the mother country eternally remain a mother country. To the extent that this depends upon him it is understandable if he uses all his energy to that end" (Memmi 1965:62). The mother country then helped him to establish his identity, to legitimize his privileged position in the colony. In effect, he sought the source of his grandeur in his connection with the mother country. He expressed an exaggerated patriotism for a mother country which he had transformed in his mind into a myth and an illusion.

> Having assigned to his homeland the burden of his own decaying grandeur he expects it to respond to his hopes. He wants it to merit his confidence, to reflect on him that image of itself which he desires (an ideal which is inaccessible to the colonized and a perfect justification for his own borrowed merits). Often, by dint of hoping, he ends up beginning to believe it. . . . The colonialist appears to have forgotten the living reality of his home country. Over the years he has sculptured, in opposition to the colony, such a monument of his homeland that the colony necessarily appears coarse and vulgar to the novitiate (Memmi 1965:59–60).

Memmi offered two major reasons for this glorification of homeland ties. First it reaffirmed the privileged position of the colonialist in the colony. Second, it further dissociated the colonialist from the colonialized by emphasizing a tie which the latter does not and cannot share.

This was but one way by which the colonialist sought to increase the gulf between himself and the colonialized. In word and deed, he widened this gap and avoided any kind of contact that might convey the notion of equality to the colonialized. His primary concern was to reaffirm his own superiority and the inferiority of the colonialized. As such, he virtually barricaded himself behind the boundaries of his own group and symbolically at least wrapped a mantle of invisibility around the colonialized so that his privileged position need not be disturbed. Despite his efforts to isolate himself, the colonialist nevertheless had to come to terms with his extreme dependence on the native population. Memmi believed that the colonialist only reluctantly faced the fact that his own fate was inextricably tied up with that of the colonialized.

According to Lowenthal (1972), the response of the colonialist as slavemaster in the British West Indies to this dependence was shame and tyranny. Memmi however went further. He was convinced that recognition of this dependence compelled the colonialist to degrade and to dehumanize the colonialized.

> With all his power he must disown the colonized while their existence is indispensable to his own ... . Having become aware of the unjust relationship which ties him to the colonized, he must continually attempt to absolve himself. He never forgets to make a public show of his own virtues, and will argue with vehemence to appear heroic and great. At the same time

his privileges arise just as much from his glory as from degrading the colonized. He will persist in degrading them, using the darkest colors to depict them. If need be, he will act to devalue them, annihilate them. But he can never escape this circle. The distance which colonization places between him and the colonized must be accounted for and, to justify himself, he increases this distance still further by placing the two figures irretrievably in opposition; his glorious position and the despicable one of the colonized (Memmi 1965:54–55).

The dual response of the colonialist to his homeland and to the colonialized reflected his limited commitment to the colony itself. Despite efforts through church missions, schools, and public media to diffuse his values and beliefs throughout the colony, the colonialist in most colonies did not see himself constructing anything resembling a national community within the colony. He did not view the colony as a collective entity toward which he had civic responsibilities and with which he could identify. In other words, he was not prepared to share certain kinds of ties and rights that such common membership might apply with the colonialized ". . . it would destroy the principle of his privileges" (Memmi 1965:69).

The response of the colonialized served to reinforce the segmentation of the colonial society. To the extent that they accepted the colonialist's definition of the situation to that extent they saw themselves as outsiders to the colonial society.

> The colonized enjoys none of the attributes of citizenship; neither his own, which is dependent, contested and smothered, nor that of the colonizer. He can hardly adhere to one or claim the other. Not having his just place in the community, not enjoying the rights of a modern citizen, not being subject to his normal duties, not voting, not bearing the burden of community affairs, he cannot feel like a true citizen. As a result of colonization, the colonized almost never experiences nationality and citizenship, except privately. Nationally and civically he is only what the colonizer is not (Memmi 1965:96).

The stigma of inferiority with which the colonialist has categorically branded the colonialized also served as a constant reminder to the colonialized that they were a group apart, that they did not belong to respectable society. (The extent to which the stigma permeated their definition of themselves is a matter of considerable debate.)

One of the ways the colonialized sought to protect themselves from the stigmatization and repression of the colonialist was to reduce contact with the colonialist and to stay among their own kind. As Fanon and others have shown, this was most feasible in the hinterland of colonies under indirect rule; however for the urbanized colonialized and for slave colonies, such isolation was difficult. Furnivall commented that under those circumstances the colonialized suffered from anomie, and Memmi stated that the older traditions become dessicated and petrified.

Another "solution" to use Memmi's term, was to cut themselves off from the colonialized by seeking to become assimilated into the ways of the colonialist. Certain strata of the colonialized were particularly responsive to this solution. In the Caribbean they included mulattos and the mestizos. Fanon insisted that the town residents, particularly those of the middle strata, were vulnerable to the values and life-styles of the colonialist. Further, the colonialist frequently favored certain tribal groups as in British Africa and brought them into school and church environments which served to acculturate them. However, the colonialized who were drawn into this way of life and were even recruited into lower level civil service and professional positions soon found that they faced a ceiling. They could only go so far and no further. They were finally not accepted by the colonialist. As such they became the marginal men in the tradition of Stonequist (1937) who were adrift between the world of the colonialist and the colonialized.

Some of these alienated but acculturated colonialized began to press for a third option: namely active opposition to the colonial system and to the driving out of the colonialist. A number of these persons were actually educated in the universities of the metropolitan country. These include such African nationalist leaders as Kenyatta of Kenya, Nkrumah of Ghana, Bourguiba of Tunisia, and Nyerere of Tanzania. Oxaal described this process as it affected students from Trinidad who were studying in England:

> Colonial university students in the metropolitan country were attracted by those social milieux which both stimulated and sympathized with their grievances against the colonial social and political order. These milieux and ideologies were not, however, homogeneous. Various radical and reformist social theories advanced competing ethical and actionist claims and the differential socialization of colonial students to such theories in the metropole laid the basis for the potential transfer of such issues to the emergent nationalist movements (Oxaal 1967:48).

In the developing nationalistic movement, a heroic past for the colonialized was "rediscovered"; religion and other traditional ways were revitalized and through it all ran a strain of xenophobia and racism, according to Memmi. Efforts were intensified to activate politically the various segments of the colonialized. Fanon claimed, as we shall discuss in the next chapter, that the struggle for independence could only succeed if the villagers, who were relatively uncontaminated by the colonial system, were politicized and brought into the nationalist movement. The goal of this movement was obviously the destruction of the colonial state and the establishment of the independent nation-state of the colonialized.

The colonialized and independence

In the last several decades a number of colonialized people have ousted the colonialist from political power through revolutionary or other means and have established the colony as an independent state; however, it has not been easy for these societies to expunge the influence of their colonial past. For example, the status and elite models of colonial days continue to guide the life-style of much of the new elite. In fact, in some British Caribbean countries membership in the social elite has not substantially changed though access to political power has. In these countries Braithwaite (1952) and Smith (1956) show that color gradations persist as a major dimension of status: being black still means being on the bottom of the social scale, being white is still associated with being at the top. In some African countries such as Sierra Leone, Senegal, and the Ivory Coast, the fastidiousness of the British and French colonial life still appeals to the new elite; they still seek to hold themselves aloof from the masses by staying primarily within the confines of their own exclusive social enclaves.

The colonialist has also bequeathed to the new state a bureaucratic and institutional structure that continues the imprint of the metropolitan country into the present. A basic expression of this is the system of education. The style and character of schooling frequently follows the model of the metropolitan society. Many students are being trained—that is if they return to the new society—for employment in an administrative structure that was patterned after that of the metropolitan country. The basic model for this structure is that of the Weberian rational bureaucracy with however distinctive stylistic features of the different metropolitan countries. This model has assumed an increased importance in those newly independent countries that have made modernization one of their major societal goals. These countries have expanded their civil service, have widely adopted the principles of the merit system as the basic criteria of selection and recruitment, and have expanded the realm of the technically efficient and competent. (In many respects the struggle over the preeminence of the traditional versus the rational bureaucratic systems had already been fought in the colonial days; the struggle after independence is over the pervasiveness of the latter's realm and who gets recruited to the bureaucracies.) In many respects the Western modes of administration have not only been retained but also expanded as governmental action and intervention has moved into an ever widening range of activities.

And finally the colonialist has bequeathed the new state an economic system that is still basically dependent on the metropolitan country. This dependence cannot be easily overcome given the kind of economic development that was encouraged in the colonial days. Accordingly, much of the economic destiny for the foreseeable future rests in the hands of groups within the metropolitan country. The goal of modernization moves the population increasingly away from traditional economic activities and places them at the mercy of the marketplace and of the economic development programs of the new government. The life circumstances of peoples and regions have become increasingly determined by governmental decisions where to locate development progams and the like.

These inheritances from the colonial days have complicated realization of one of the major goals that the new governing elite in these states has generally set for itself: namely, the transformation of the newly independent but segmented society into a nation. What has made this goal even more difficult to attain is the intensification of the competitive struggle among various ethnic and racial groups for power, position, and privilege in the new society. The stage on which this struggle is being played out can also be seen as part of the legacy from the colonial past. Colonial powers established the political boundaries that continue to define those of the new states. They did so on the basis of imperial design in the struggle with other colonial powers and paid little or no attention to the question of ethnic coherence. As a result, diverse ethnic groups were arbitrarily included within these boundaries. In addition, these boundaries all too frequently cut through ethnically homogeneous territories. They made those in one region subject to the rule of one colonial power and those in another region subject to the rule of a second. In colonies where indirect rule in particular was practiced, the colonialist power would seek to exacerbate the ethnic differences that existed. It would strive to divide and to conquer the established tribes by pitting one against the other, by awakening dormant ethnic and tribal ties and antagonisms, and by favoring certain tribes over others in granting access to schooling and to minor government positions. These favored tribes were frequently a mere minority among the colonial subjects.

The withdrawal of the colonial government opened up a wide range of opportunity for power, wealth, and privilege to the formerly colonialized ethnic and racial groups. In many respects the major arenas for these opportunities are in the bureaucratic structures of the new society. Thus ethnic and racial groups have been jockeying for more favorable allocation of power, position, and privilege in governmental bureaucracies including the civil service, the military, the police, education, and health and welfare. As a result, ethnic and racial interests, sentiments, and ties have become expressed more manifestly than ever within these environments and have become interwoven in varying degrees with the working of the bureaucratic enterprise itself. In some countries a virtual division of function has occurred, one ethnic group dominating one bureaucratic structure (civil service, for example) and a second dominating another structure (for example, the military). What has complicated the struggle in many of these countries is the competitive advantage enjoyed by minorities favored under colonialism. They tend to have the education and training to fill the various positions which the majority lack. As a result, this has become a significant source of conflict and strain. In some countries this struggle has erupted into open conflict and civil war as in the Ibo versus the Yoruba in Nigeria and the East Asian versus the African in Guyana. In other countries the property of the minority has been expropriated, and the minority itself sent into exile as in the case of the East Indian in Uganda. Much more frequent have been the efforts of the dominant group to redress the inequities inherited from the colonial past by pursuing policies of preferential treatment for these groups and of proportional representation of the disadvantaged in the better occupational and bureaucratic positions, as in the case of the Africanization program in Kenya.

In many of these countries, however, the dominant ethnic group has gone beyond merely seeking to redress the inequities of the colonial past. It has also sought to impose its stamp on the structure of the state and on the definition of the "nation". In some countries it has gained or seems to be gaining the legitimacy it is seeking. In many others ethnic minorities—whether favored in the colonial period or not—are opposing its efforts. This opposition is most pronounced where the dominant group has been charged with seeking to monopolize political power and with pursuing the policy of discriminatory allocation of scarce resources to its own people and to the regions where they live. As a result, the minorities challenge the authority of the dominant group and question the legitimacy of its rule. The result is that the kind of consensual framework that is necessary for the development of a nation-state is still missing. What remains is essentially a plural state society that is controlled by the dominant ethnic group through force and violence.

The Colonialist-Colonist Society: A Dual Legal-Political System

Pervasive as was the effort of the white European to conquer nonwhite races and to impose upon them a system of exploitation, in a number of conquered territories he did something more. He also assumed the role of colonist and founded a permanent settlement in which he created a society whose institutions were molded in his racial, religious, and national image and with which he closely identified. In those settings he dominated the colonial plural structure and defined his status as a permanently established, not as a sojourner, elite. At the same time he viewed himself as the people of the colonist society. His rights and immunities in both structures stood in sharp contrast with those of the racial groups that comprised the subjugated strata of his colonialist plural society. In effect he imprinted a duality on the society which persisted even as his "colonialist-colonist" society was transformed into an independent nation-state.

The earliest and perhaps most widespread historical export of duality happened during the conquest and settlement of the New World, first by the Spanish, then by the English, and finally by other Europeans. They built their dual societies in South America, Central America, and North America. They eventually lost them as these societies became independent nations still bearing the marks of their dualistic heritage.

By the time the white European moved onto the continents of Asia and Africa, he had become, by and large, a colonialist who was interested in building an imperial system for his home country. Accordingly he only constructed the kind of racially segmented plural society which we have just examined with himself perched at the top as a "sojourner elite." In some places, however, he settled permanently and evolved a colonist society too. As a result, duality resurfaced in such places as South Africa, Zimbabwe (Rhodesia), Australia, and New Zealand.

In Australia and New Zealand the white European overwhelmed an indigenous population that was pushed to the perimeters of the white society as a racial minority, much as the Indian was in the United States. In South Africa and Zimbabwe the situation was different. Whites built their own society as a small minority among a vast population of subjugated nonwhites. As might be expected, the dual structures built in these societies reflected the marked variations in population proportions of white and nonwhite as well as the different historical circumstances.

Let us now examine three examples of the duality imprinted by the white European: first that by the Spanish conquistador in the New World, then that by the English in Virginia and North America, and finally that by the Dutch and English in South Africa.

The Spanish Conquistador in the New World

Colonial exploitation and the encomienda

Within two decades after Columbus's discovery of the island of Hispaniola, the Spanish conquistador had not only wrested the land and its resources from the Indians, but had also imposed upon them a system of forced labor that was to remain in effect in the Spanish colonies for the next several centuries. Under this system of the encomienda, first elaborated and institutionalized by Governor Ovando, the successor to Columbus's successor as governor, Indians were parcelled out to Spaniards in numbers ranging from a few to several hundred. The number any Spaniard received depended on his status and his role in the conquest of Hispaniola. In the early days of Ovando's rule no Spaniard went without any Indians at all, for the governor had succeeded in extending the rule of Spain over the entire island and in bringing under Spanish control a large number of Indians, many after fierce battles.

Most of the Indians were employed in the mining of gold and of other precious ores; others, in cultivating foodstuffs for the Spanish conquistador. They had to endure backbreaking manual labor for long hours under intolerable conditions. For them the encomienda was a brutal and coercive system of labor control not unlike slavery. Thus was set in place a colonial system of political control and economic exploitation divided along racial lines.

So harsh were the working conditions that by the end of Ovando's governorship in 1509, the mortality rate among Indians had risen catastrophically. Some scholars have insisted that the rapid rise was not entirely due to the working conditions. They also attribute it to the Indians' vulnerability to the diseases brought to the island by the conquistador. But whatever the reason, many died. Others did not wait to die; they escaped into the wilderness or fled to nearby islands. As a result, by 1520 the Indian population had declined so markedly that it no longer functioned as an adequate labor supply for the island. Consequently, increasing numbers of Spaniards found themselves without any Indians and without any productive role to play on the island. To make matters worse, the mining industry was in a state of precipitous decline as sources of gold were being depleted.

Fortunately for the stability of the island, the surplus of Spaniards had begun to be drained off by 1520 as the conquest of New Spain got underway. In this fashion Hispaniola became a staging area for the conquest of the mainland; the surplus of Spaniards joined the bands of conquistadors in search of plunder and gold. In addition, the cultivation and milling of sugar cane had begun to challenge the ailing mining industry as the mainstay of the island's economy. The demand for labor for sugar plantations therefore intensified pressures for a new source of labor that would fill the gap created by the dwindling supply of Indians. Thus was erected another colonial edifice of exploitation: this time on the backs of the enslaved blacks.

Colonization and the aristocratic society

Most of the Spaniards in the early years did not expect to stay permanently in the New World. Instead they saw themselves as adventurers and conquerors who were out to win quick wealth and glory with which they would return home, set themselves up in hidalgo status, and live in a seignorial manner. Relatively few lived to realize these ambitions. Many more returned home disenchanted and penniless. Some, though, did stay, particularly after significant gold strikes had been made on Hispaniola and after Governor Ovando had formally established the encomienda and stabilized and extended the rule of the crown. They thereby became the first white European colonists in the New World. These early colonists included "the hidalgos, the peasants who aspired to become hidalgos, and the few letrados; [they] were the essential explorers, conquerors, and populators of Española." In their role as settlers, their goal was to recreate on the island an aristocratic way of life modelled after that in Spain. They disdained manual labor and "aspired to the seignorial status much admired in Spain; [accordingly] they desired a life surrounded by *criados* and serfs and slaves, the display of mansions and lands, and of silk and velvet" (Floyd 1973:69).

In addition, they glorified the role of the military hero and conquistador much as it had been glorified during the reunification and reconquest of Spain. Few colonists, however, were able to attain the wealth that would provide them with the Old World baroque splendor they sought. "These few were the actual founding fathers of Spanish civilization in the Caribbean. Some of these settlers came with Columbus on his second voyage; others came with Ovando or on some obscure intermediate voyage between these times or after, or on one of the many vessels carrying the Indies trade" (Floyd 1973:75). At the center of this nascent island aristocracy stood the members of the Columbus family: "they eventually had the most wealth, attained the highest social prestige, and boasted the greatest number of *criados*" (Floyd 1973:77).

The dual societal structures and their linkages

The entire aristocratic structure, though built by the colonists from their Old World antecedents, rested on the uniquely New World foundation of the colonial conquest of the Indians and the exploitation of their labor. This colonialist foundation to the aristocratic society was organized as a racially segmented plural society that reflected the raw exercise of power between conqueror and conquered and generated the labor energy needed to power the aristocratic society.

The Crown and the Laws of Burgos: A "Normative Umbrella" for the Peaceful Indians

The intervention of the Crown, in all likelihood, prevented the full realization of the brutalizing and dehumanizing potential inherent in the plural structure. From the earliest days of the encomienda the king and queen of Spain expressed a continuing concern about the treatment of the Indian. They deplored the excesses and brutalities of the system of forced labor, though they did not question the necessity for the system itself. (They even favored the enslavement of Indians who fought the conquistador.) The king finally gave legal expression to this concern with the enactment of the Laws of Burgos in 1512. In promulgating the Laws of Burgos, the king gave the system of encomienda as designed for the New World a legal standing it lacked before. It was now incorporated into the laws of the Spanish empire and was no longer merely a practice sanctioned by king and local authorities. In addition, the system's axiom that Indians had inherently evil and slothful inclinations which had to be remedied was adopted as a cardinal principle of the legislation itself. In legitimizing the system, the king also surrounded it with normative constraints that were meant to protect the Indians from its more coercive features. Furthermore, the encomendero was to assume the paternal-like obligations of civilizing and Christianizing the Indians so that they would not only lose their evil and slothful ways but would also in time become "free vassals" of the king.

By casting the encomienda in this normative mold, the king hoped to impose an organically interlocked status hierarchy, similar to the estate structure in Spain, upon what was essentially a dehumanized colonial system of racial exploitation and forced labor. In doing this, he was prepared to include the Indian in his hierarchic domain of subjects, though initially as wards of the Crown, just as the Church was prepared to include them in its hierarchic domain of souls.

Scholars have disagreed as to the extent the policy of the Crown did indeed shape the practice of the encomenderos. Some have continued to accept Las Casas's argument (1542) that the effect was minimal and that the sheer brutality of the system was primarily responsible for the rapid depletion of the Indian population in Hispaniola and in other parts of the Spanish Empire. While agreeing that the encomienda system was harsh, other scholars have insisted that the paternalistic features that it developed under the aegis of Crown and Church made it unlikely that it was the kind of graveyard postulated by Las Casas (1542). (As we have seen, these scholars attribute the population decline primarily to other causes.) The same concern was not expressed by the Crown, however, for those Indians who were enslaved, or later for the African slaves. Their fate was left primarily in the hands of their owners, although the Church retained a continuing interest in their souls.

The Spanish Conquistador and Indian Woman

Another link between the dual structures that the colonist forged almost from the moment that the first one set foot on the soil of Hispaniola was with the Indian woman. Primarily young and unattached, many of these men soon developed liaisons with the native women. According to Mörner, "in a way, the Spanish Conquest of the Americas was a conquest of women. The Spaniards obtained the Indian girls both by force and by peaceful means" (Mörner 1967:22). So widespread did this practice become that by 1501 the king and queen of Spain expressed concern in their instructions to Governor Ovando that Indian women were being forced into liaisons with Spanish men. They called upon the governor to send women back to their tribes and to permit only those liaisons to continue into which the woman entered voluntarily. Several years later they encouraged the governor to arrange a number of intermarriages for purposes of government policy, but few Spaniards sought to legitimize their relationships. As a result, interracial unions flourished but relatively few led to marriage.

Thus within two decades of the Spanish conquest of Hispaniola a generation of mestizos began to reach adolescence and early adulthood.

> As a rule the first generation of mestizos was accepted as "Spaniards." This is easy to understand for mestizos born in marriage, but, as we have pointed out, these were not at all frequent. On the other hand, during this early period many mestizos were recognized by their fathers. The process of legitimization seems to have been frequently used at this time both in Spain and Portugal (Mörner 1967:27).

Some of these mestizos, however, joined their maternal group, the Indians; a few even "led marginal existence between the two groups without being accepted by either. But this phenomenon was to occur on a large scale only later on" (Mörner 1967:29). In short, the mestizo as a distinctive racial category in a colonial status system was yet to emerge.

The sociedad de castas and the Creole elite

By the eighteenth century miscegenation in Spanish America had produced, according to various scholars, an elaborately refined, hierarchically arranged "Sociedad de Castas." In New Spain, for example, the nomenclatures of "castas" identified eighteen different categories; in

Peru, fourteen. They were based on the interracial unions of Spaniards, Indians, blacks, and their mixed offspring of varying racial combinations. The major divisions were "invested with different legal status as well as the strong element of corporative privileges" (Mörner 1967:54). According to another scholar, "there were in fact only three legally and socially definable groups: 'Spaniards,' 'castas,' and 'Indians'" (Mörner 1967:60). Mörner insisted that the legal status of five categories could be distinguished and ranked. At the top were the Spaniards; second, the Indians; third, the mestizos; fourth, the free negroes, mulattoes, zamboes; and last, the slaves. With reference to social status, Mörner retained the same rank order except for the Indians, whom he ranked last.

Thus by the eighteenth century the society which King Ferdinand had envisioned seemed to have materialized, but it was not merely a carbon copy of the society which the Crown and the colonists had sought to transport from Spain.

> [It was] a society *sui generis* . . . [crcated] by transferring to the New World the hierarchic, estate-based corporative society of late medieval Castile and imposing that society upon a multiracial colonial situation. This colonial reality was characterized, first, by the dichotomy between conquerors and conquered, masters and servants or slaves, and, second, by the miscegenation between these opposite groups (Mörner 1967:54).

In this manner the dual structures created by the forces of colonization and colonialization in Spanish America appeared to merge into a composite Sociedad de Castas. Its unifying external value framework was provided by the Crown and Church. Its internal system of stratification was organized around a "color" axis into what a Chilean scholar has called a "pigmentocracy." These colonial estate societies and their pigmentocratic status gradients were, however, less likely to emerge in those parts of Spanish America that lost their Indian labor force and had to depend upon black slave labor, as in the case of Hispaniola and other islands of the Caribbean. The racial segmentation of the latter plantation societies lacked the organic interconnectedness of the estate societies and resembled the more conflictual and coercive segmentation of the orthodox colonial plural society.

In effect, long before the Spanish colonists had gained their independence, their dual colonist and colonialist heritages seemed to have already joined to create a "novel," institutional, and stratificational framework that carried over into nationhood of each. At the same time there was built into the framework a basic cleavage within the Spanish elite that eventually became the axis around which the struggle for independence revolved.

Almost from the moment the first colonists settled in Hispaniola, conflicts of interest surfaced between the Crown and settlers. As we have already seen, the Crown disagreed with the colonists over their treatment of the Indians, but behind this particular disagreement loomed a fundamental concern of the Crown. It feared that the colonists intended to establish separate feudal-like fiefdoms in the New World, similar to those that King Ferdinand and Queen Isabella had to quash in Spain in order to unify their kingdom. Accordingly, the Crown sought to retain in its hands the reins of political power and authority. It did this by enveloping the colonists with an elaborate governmental and bureaucratic structure that allowed royal authority to reach into the local centers of residence in the New World. In doing this, the Crown coopted the early cabildos, the centers of local authority frequently established by the leading conquistadors, and made them part of the bureaucratic system. In addition, the Crown sent from Spain persons loyal to it to fill the high offices in the two structures and regularly replaced them with others from Spain so that none could build a private fiefdom in the colony; for a similar reason they denied the request of the colonists that the encomienda be made hereditary.

The colonists and their Creole progeny, however, were not without influence and power on the local level. On occasion, for example, they were able to thwart completely the implementation of royal policy. For example, their rebellious response to the New Laws of 1542 forced the king to withdraw his attempt to abolish the encomienda. He subsequently sought to dismantle it in piecemeal fashion; but what really dealt the system its mortal blow was the marked decline in the Indian population in virtually all of the Spanish empire.

In a more regular and routinized manner, the colonists infiltrated the lower and middle levels of the bureaucracy during the Hapsburg era and accordingly blunted the impact of royal policy it deemed contrary to their interests. Lang has offered other examples

> of the kind of *ad hoc* informal systems that emerged throughout the empire, linking together structures of local power and bureaucratic officials in an intricately layered network of cooptation and collusion which attained over the time the force of custom. Mediation between the content of directives and the reality of local conditions occurred at practically every level of bureaucratic administration. Cedulas directed toward the organization of Indian labor, the control of contraband trade, and the collection of taxes, . . . had to run the gauntlet of Creole influence. Bureaucratic structures were still crucial reference points for social organization. But this framework was susceptible to considerable manipulation by local interests (Lang 1975:45).

Despite the manipulative skill the local Creole elite developed in accommodating royal policy to local interest, the constant presence of officials from Spain, the Peninsulars, who monopolized bureaucratic and governmental power and who also viewed themselves as the font of respect and good taste, became a source of irritation and resentment. This resentment did not initially prevent the Creole from patterning his lifestyle after the Peninsular or from retaining his loyalty to the Crown. But in time his resentment became politicized and as he became alienated from the Crown, he formed the vanguard of the forces for liberation and separate nationhood.

The United States: Duality and the Creation of the "New Nation"

The English settler in Virginia

Seeking to duplicate the colonial success of the Spanish in the New World, the English finally succeeded, almost a century after Columbus's first voyage and after several abortive attempts, in establishing a settlement in Jamestown under a royal charter given to the Virginia Company of London. However, unlike the Spanish conquistadors, the English settlers did not try to achieve their economic goals on the backs of the Indian as a captive labor force. Instead they fought the Indian for his land and resources; and once they defeated him forced him to move beyond the perimeter of the settlement. They relied on their own labor at the beginning, and in the process they built a colonist society, first within the organizational framework of the Virginia Company and then as a distinctive territorial and political community under the Crown.

Under the Virginia Company, the colonist society underwent a marked transformation. After near collapse in the first several years, it was molded by the company into an authoritarian militarylike structure in which rigorous discipline was maintained to enforce the corporate economic arrangement. Approximately a decade later the company altered its policies dramatically and initiated a basic set of institutional reforms that carried over after the dissolution of the company six years later and profoundly affected the political, religious, and economic future of the colonist society.

At the heart of the political reform was the establishment by the company of a General Assembly in 1619 comprised of elected representatives that paralleled the legislative body already functioning in England. The assembly was set up to provide the company with a symmetrical design for governance of its operations and to give the colonists in Virginia a voice in the company's decision-making process. However, something more than an organizational mechanism was created in the governance plan for Virginia. It also gave the colonists an identity and sense of unity. Thus was created a primordial and politically generated consensual framework that bound the colonists to each other as a people and as a community, even as they still retained their organizational relationship to the company.

The political organization of the colonist's community barely survived the dissolution of the company in 1624. It continued to function on a de facto basis, but not until fifteen years later was it finally relegitimated by the Crown. The Crown's action meant to the colonists the reaffirmation of a structure that had already begun to be venerated as a sacred symbol of the people.

The company also bequeathed to the colonist society a moral and religious system that was closely linked to the secular and political structures of power and control. This linkage became even more manifest as the General Assembly assumed the role of the temporal governing body of the church in Virginia. Its enactments gave the religious and moral codes the force of civil law; they also empowered the selection of a vestry of laymen who would serve as the governing board of the local parish church and would also assume civic duties in the parish. The vestry, accordingly, connected the church to the local system of political control and was itself frequently at the vortex of power in the parish. What made this likely was the fact that the vestrymen were largely drawn from the socially established, the affluent, the landowners, and the influential. Many were also active in the larger political system of the colony. As a result, the vestry also became an important part of the total fabric of political control in the colonist society.

And finally the company bequeathed two policies that structured the economy of the colonist society and gave it its distinctive character during the first half century. One was the headright provision that granted 50 acres of land to anyone who paid his own way and 50 additional acres for each person whose transportation he paid. From this developed an economy "filled with little farms a few hundred acres in extent, owned and worked by a sturdy class of English farmers," whose primary crop was tobacco (Wertenbaker 1959:59). These yeoman farmers dominated the political and economic life of the colonist society for much of the seventeenth century.

The second policy inherited from the company was the system of indentured servitude. It had its origins in the earliest days of the settlement when the company underwrote the transportation and other expenses of planters who were then obliged to work on company land for a certain number of years. In this manner the company had hoped to meet the scarcity of labor that plagued it from its earliest days. And so too the yeoman planters relied on indentured servitude to meet their labor needs.

So widespread did this practice become that an estimated four out of five immigrants arrived in Virginia under terms of an indenture. From the very beginning, the servitude of the indentured white servant was defined as a contractual arrangement between two parties and of temporary duration. Further, the indentured white servant was assured of certain rights that cloaked him with some legal protection during his servitude; he could turn to the courts if he thought these rights were being violated. Upon completion of his indenture, the white servant was accorded full membership in the colonist community of the people and a claim for "freedom dues" to facilitate his transition to this status. Many became landowners and some even rose to positions of influence in the colonist society. Thus, according to Wertenbaker,". . . in the first half century of its existence Virginia was the land of opportunity. The poor man who came to her shores, whether under terms of indenture or as a freeman, found it possible to establish himself as a person of some property and consideration" (Wertenbaker 1959:71).

Even as the colonist society was being built under the yeoman planter, the foundations for a racially segmented colonialist plural society were also being laid. The arrival of a Dutch ship in 1619 marked the beginning of the involuntary flow of black slaves which grew only gradually during the next several decades. During this period their legal status was ambiguous; the nature of their servitude, unclear. Slowly through court decisions and finally through enactments of the Virginia legislature their servitude was defined as being in perpetuity and their legal status as being objects of ownership.

By the first decade of the eighteenth century black slaves had been completely dehumanized and transmuted into pieces of property. They were enmeshed in a web of legal and extralegal coercive constraints and oppressive controls that placed them completely at the mercy of their white masters. Their numbers had increased markedly by then. By mid-century the flow of black slaves reached flood proportions, just as the flow of white indentured servants had been reduced to a mere trickle. The result was the replacement of indentured white servants by black slaves as the major source of labor in Virginia. Their place of work, though, was not the small farm of the indentured servant but the large tobacco plantation of the white slave owner. And so a racially segmented colonial plural society reached maturity in Virginia that ended only with the Civil War.

Much of the clarification of the legal status of blacks however, took place under the political and economic hegemony of the small yeoman planters who still relied primarily on the white indentured servant. But by the end of the seventeenth century their fortunes declined precipitously and early in the next century they were replaced by the large slave-owning plantation owners as the elite of the colonist society. The influence of the plantation owners soon radiated into the major institutional arenas of the colonist society. They approached their political responsibilities in the manner of a religious calling and their religious responsibilities in the manner of a political calling even more than the yeoman elite had.

As members of the aristocratic elite, they espoused in the political arena of the colonist society the virtues of republicanism, self-government, and freedom in Virginia's relations with England. At the same time they stood as white masters atop a racially segmented colonial structure they had built on the backs of the enslaved blacks. Thus, by mid-eighteenth century the plantation elite presided over dual societal structures. One they inherited from the yeoman elite, the colonist; the other they had created, the colonialist plural. They saw no logical contradiction between the two; for in the colonist society they were dealing with the "people;" in the colonialist, with "things."

In the final analysis then, the English settler, unlike the Spanish conquistador, developed his racially segmented plural society much later chronologically than he did his colonist society. In addition, he also created an unbridgeable gulf between the two structures whereas the conquistador made some effort at the behest of the Crown and Church to develop normative links between the two in a kind of estate arrangement.

Duality and the transformation of the thirteen colonies into the "new nation"

Even as Virginia was solidifying its duality in the first half of the eighteenth century, the other twelve colonies were constructing theirs. All were affected in one way or another by the colonial conquest of the Indian and the legalization of black slavery. Accordingly, their racially segmented plural structures reflected these influences. All were also affected in one way or another by the processes of settlement that produced colonist societies. Each, however, reflected distinctive aspects of their British heritage and of the composition of their white population.

Perhaps the sharpest contrast to the duality imprinted in Virginia is that which developed in Massachusetts. The differences are evident in both the colonist and colonialist structures that were built. The colonist structure that the Puritans erected, for example, was built on a foundation different from that of the Virginia settler. Unlike the settlers in Virginia whose primordial sense of community and peoplehood was politically generated, the Puritans were originally a religious community. They built a political and civil society in the New World as an expression of their religious commitment. In time the white colonist society was transformed during the seventeenth and eighteenth centuries from a narrowly circumscribed religio-political community into a more broadly based people's domain in which most white inhabitants shared the rights of membership.

Similarly the colonialist plural society that eventually stamped Massachusetts toward the end of the eighteenth century seems to have departed significantly from that which characterized Virginia. Initially both plural structures were built on the foundations of the enslaved black. But slavery never constituted the major source of labor in Massachusetts as it did in Virginia, nor were slaves ever as significant a proportion of the total population. (Traffic in slaves, though, comprised a primary source of income for a significant segment of the colonist elite in Massachusetts.) Scholars agree that slavery was more benign in Massachusetts; manumission, more frequent; and antislavery sentiments, more widespread.

Even more striking is the evidence that the freed black replaced the enslaved black in the racially segmented plural structure that persisted in Massachusetts after the colonial period drew to an end. Seeds of this change were already evident early in the colonial history of Massachusetts. For example, the various restrictions imposed on the freed black by the Selectmen of Boston in 1723 at the behest of the white colonists seems to have been just part of the political, economic, and social proscriptions that he was to experience on a growing scale in the colony.

These versions of duality thrived and grew as the thirteen colonies prepared to oppose the rule of the British, and they survived the successful outcome of the War for Independence and the creation of the new nation. The colonist heritage, for example, found expression in the Declaration of Independence, in the Constitution, and finally in the Bill of Rights as the thirteen colonies were transformed into a federated nation-state: the United States of America.

To complete this transformation, however, several steps were required. The Constitution, for instance, sets forth a structure of governance for what its preamble identifies as "We the People," but few of the explicit rights of the people were spelled out in the document. This was a matter of considerable concern to a number of delegates, some of whom even refused to sign the Constitution for that reason. It was also a matter of considerable debate in a number of state conventions called to ratify the document.

And so the First Congress to meet after ratification continued the task begun in Philadelphia. (Interestingly, almost half of the delegates who signed the Constitution in Philadelphia were in attendance as either representatives or senators.) Within seven months of its opening session Congress rounded out the document with the first ten amendments, subsequently ratified by the states in 1791.

With the addition of the Bill of Rights, the Constitution truly came into being, and the colonist heritage fully realized. This Constitution not only designs a structure of governance for "We the People"; it also surrounds the people with a legal-normative shield that protects them against the arbitrary exercise of political power and authority from the very structure of governance it had created and that defines their rights and immunities within the communities they lived. In this manner a people's domain was constructed, and those within its boundaries were to have a number of clearly spelled out rights and immunities. (A more detailed description of these rights was offered in Chapter 4.)

Contrastingly, the colonialist heritage found expression in the same kind of structural arrangements that were already in existence. Its racially segmented plural societal form emerged unscathed with the writing of the Constitution—this despite the fact that nowhere in the Constitution is slavery explicitly mentioned or approved. It is through indirection that this reaffirmation and relegitimization takes place. This is evident in three sections of the Constitution.

The first instance has to do with the apportionment of representatives according to population numbers. Black slaves are to be counted as three-fifth's of a person; the reference though, is not to black slaves but to "all other persons." The second instance grants slave states the right to import slaves until 1808 without interference from the federal government. In this case too, slaves are not referred to directly; instead Article 1, Section 9 states "The migration or importation of such persons as any of the States now existing think proper to admit shall not be prohibited by the Congress prior to year one thousand eight hundred and eight." And finally Article 4, Section 2 Part (3) was written expressly for the return of fugitive slaves, but it made no direct reference to slaves. It says "No person held to service or labor in one State, under the laws thereof, escaping into another, shall in consequence of any law or regulation therein, be discharged from such service or labor, but shall be delivered up on claim of the party to whom such service or labor may be due."

The first two provisions were the subject of debate in which a number of delegates from the northern states participated. And yet in the final analysis these provisions seemed to require little from these delegates from the North, other than a willingness to accept a sectional compromise. Neither provision, for example, imposed any obligation on their home states to demonstrate active support for slavery. The provisions merely gave the stamp of constitutional legitimacy to the status of slavery as practiced within the borders of the various southern states.

The third provision, however, did impose such obligations on the northern states and in doing so gave "a nationwide sanction to property in slaves" (Robinson 1971:228). Yet on this provision the delegates from the northern states were curiously mute.

The joy with which the delegates from the southern states greeted this provision is evident in the words of the delegates from North Carolina. In their report to the governor of their state, they declared that "The Southern States have also a much better Security for the Return of Slaves who might endeavor to escape than they had under the original (Articles of) Confederation" (The Federal Convention of 1787 III:84).

The failure of any of the delegates from the northern states to object to this provision has puzzled scholars such as D. L. Robinson (1971). He takes it as evidence that blacks, even free blacks, had no spokesmen to represent their interests either in government or at the convention, and concludes that the white spokesmen were casually indifferent to their plight.

Robinson, we feel, fails to follow through on the logic of his own explanation. Blacks had no one to represent their interests not because "(white) Northerners cared only superficially" for their rights, but because these Northerners did not believe that blacks had any rights or should have any in the people's domain of the North. As such, we surmise, the northern delegates, much more through deliberate design than through casual indifference, were signalling to the blacks that they were not welcome in the North and that they were not to see the North as a haven of freedom. The inaction of these delegates suggests, in effect, that what we have earlier called the Massachusetts model of duality may have indeed become firmly imprinted in the North by the time of the Constitutional Convention.

What was implied in the body of the Constitution became explicitly articulated three years later by the First Congress to meet after its ratification. As we have already mentioned, one of the first orders of business of this Congress—with many of the Founding Fathers in attendance—was to fill in the content and meaning of the people's domain that had been merely sketched in the Constitutional Convention. On September 28, 1789, within seven months of its opening session, it completed its task and sent to the states the Bill of Rights.

Only six months later the same Congress let it be known in no uncertain terms that membership in the people's domain, which it had so carefully crafted, was to be confined to whites only. The Founding Fathers in Philadelphia, as we have seen, had already implied that this restriction was to apply for those who were already living within the boundaries of the United States, but the First Congress made this intention explicit when it turned to those who might be *coming* into this country. The matter-of-fact way in which this took place merits some comment.

In mid-January 1790 at the request of President Washington, who proposed it in his address at the opening of the second session of the First Congress, a committee of three was appointed in the House of Representatives to recommend a uniform rule of naturalization. Almost three weeks later the committee presented to the House the first clause of such a bill. It stipulated: "that all free white persons, who have, or shall migrate into the United States, and shall give satisfactory proof, before a magistrate, by oath, that they intend to reside therein, and shall take an oath of allegiance, *and shall have resided in the United States for one whole year* shall be entitled to all rights of citizenship ... " (US Congress 1790:1109).

In the ensuing two-day debate no argument arose over the racial restriction; the only topic that was debated was length of residence. This was precipitated by an amendment proposed by one of the committee members to delete the one-year requirement. By the second day sentiment for a residency requirement had grown sufficiently strong that the amendment was withdrawn by its author. Not even the one-year requirement seemed to satisfy the representatives. As a result, the bill was recommitted to a newly constituted committee of ten. Two weeks later a revised bill was reported that extended the residency requirement in the United States to two years, but only one year in a state.

The bill retained the racial restriction, though now it was worded, "that any alien, being a free white person, who shall have resided within the limits and under the jurisdiction of the United States for the term of two years, may be admitted to become a citizen thereof, on application to any common law court of record, in any one of the states wherein he shall have resided for the term of one year at least ..." (US Public Statutes at Large I:103). The applicant was also supposed to show that he was a "person of good character" and to take an oath supporting the Constitution.

The bill passed both houses and was signed into law on March 26, 1790. The phrase "white person" remained on the statute books for 162 years or until the McCarran Act of 1952. It survived an attempt to strike it from the naturalization laws during Reconstruction. As a concession to the spirit of the time, aliens of African nativity and descent were also made eligible for citizenship; immigrants from Asia were not. In this manner the very law of 1790 that guaranteed inclusion in the people's domain of white aliens whenever and from wherever they came was used almost 100 years later to deny membership in the people's domain first to the Chinese and then to the Japanese immigrant.

Almost 70 years after the enactment of the First Naturalization Law, the premise that was implied in the Constitutional Convention and that was later made explicit by the First Congress was elaborated into a full-fledged thesis of duality by Chief Justice Taney in the *Dred Scott* case of 1857.

In his suit instituted in a lower federal court, Dred Scott, a black slave, claimed that he and his family were entitled to their freedom on various grounds which he spelled out. The case eventually reached the Supreme Court. In his opinion for the court, the Chief Justice declared that even before any substantive issue could be decided, a prior question had to be answered by the Court. Did Scott have the right to bring suit in a court of the United States? He would have this right, the Chief Justice stated, if he were part of the people of the United States.

"The words 'people of the United States' and 'citizens' are synonymous terms, and mean the same thing. They both describe the political body who, according to our republican institutions, form the sovereignty, and who hold the power and conduct the Government through their representatives. They are what we familiarly call the 'sovereign people,' and every citizen is one of this people, and a constituent member of this sovereignty" (60 US 1857:404).

Thus, the fundamental question facing the Court, he argued, was whether Scott as a black man could become part of the people: "Can a negro, whose ancestors were imported into this country, and sold as slaves, become a member of the political community formed and brought into existence by the Constitution of the United States, and as such become entitled to all the rights, and privileges, and immunities, guarantied by that instrument to the citizen? One of which rights is the privilege of suing in a court of the United States in the cases specified in the Constitution" (60 US 1857:403).

The Chief Justice's answer to this more or less rhetorical question was that blacks—even if emancipated— cannot and do not "compose a portion of this people" nor are they "constituent members of this sovereignty." In other words, "they are not included, and were not intended to be included under the word 'citizens' in the Constitution, and can therefore claim none of the rights and privileges which that instrument provides for and secures to citizens of the United States" (60 US 1857:404).

He went on to enunciate the second component of a thesis of duality. He insisted that blacks were always meant to be under the control and domination of the white. "[T]hey were ... considered as a subordinate and inferior class of beings, who had been subjugated by the dominant race, and whether emancipated or not, yet remained subject to their authority, and had no rights or privileges but such as those who held the power and the Government might choose to grant them" (60 US 1857:404–405). In other words, according to Taney, freedom added little if anything to the legal and political status of the black. He was not under any circumstances meant to be one of the people. Instead he was still deemed a colonialized subject or thing in a legal and political system of repressive white control.

Chief Justice Taney then attempted to explain why the Founding Fathers were of this frame of mind. Their beliefs, he maintained, reflected the climate of opinion that prevailed among whites at that time in the colonies, England, and Western Europe generally. As further evidence of this, he pointed to the Constitution itself and to statutes passed by the First Congress. He also enumerated laws that were passed by states not only in the South but in the North as well during this and the colonial period.

And so it can be said that the Founding Fathers in writing the Constitution perpetuated and sanctified a Manichean dualism that had evolved from early in the history of the thirteen colonies. On a higher and more visible level, they transformed the white colonist America into a nation-state that was anchored in the rights and sovereignty of the people. On a lower and more invisible level they sanctified and perpetuated the stable plural society of a racially-segmented colonial America. They placed this society under the control of the political authority, primarily of the states but also of the federal government, but excluded it from the national community of the people. It was a society of the netherworld; it had a coherence and logic of its own, a dominant class of white masters and a subjugated class of slaves who were defined as "other persons" in the Constitution but as property in state law, though in neither instance were they presumably ever to be part of the people of the national community.

The two societal systems were set on parallel tracks, each evolving according to its own inner dynamics with its own creedal statement. Nevertheless, from the very beginning of the New Nation their coexistence was uneasy, for their fates were inextricably linked in several ways. The whites, for example, were the superordinate masters of the plural society, and the citizens and elected officials of the people's domain. In effect, they could move freely between the two systems and did so to protect their position, privilege, and property in both. The Southern white plantation owner, for instance, was particularly skilled in these maneuvers before the Civil War. He adroitly used his command of legal and extralegal resources and powers in both systems to keep the black in his "place" in the plural society.

In turn, the black, despite his position in this netherworld, was mindful of the universalistic language used by the Founding Fathers in writing the Constitution. As a result, from the beginning of the new nation blacks continually challenged the legitimacy of the plural society that prevented them from gaining access to the people's domain and/or from enjoying all its rights and immunities as guaranteed by the Constitution.

In sanctifying both models, the Founding Fathers set the stage for what turned out to be in succeeding generations a herculean struggle between the two for the control of the destiny of blacks and other racial minorities. And it is our basic contention that America's historic treatment of the blacks and its other racial minorities has been both an expression and product of the dialectical tension and struggle between these two models for ascendancy. (This will be further examined in Chapters 7, 8, and 9).

The American Indian and the frontier

Next in importance to the English settlers' encounter with the black in the development of the new nation's duality was their encounter with the first nonwhite they met when they reached the shores of the New World, the Indian. As a result, even before the duality based on the enslaved black was created in the institutional heart of the first colony, Virginia, another form was already in the making along its territorial frontier in the struggle between the white settler and the Indian. This struggle began from the moment the English settler pushed the Indian beyond the boundaries of Jamestown and continued elsewhere for almost 300 years, well beyond the transformation of the thirteen colonies into the new nation. So compelling was this conflict that it played a crucial role in the shaping of white America's frontier experience until late in the nineteenth century.

In the first half century or so, the Indians faced the white settlers as independent and sovereign nations with whom treaties were signed and between whom territorial boundaries were drawn. The initial encounter then was between two separate societies. Even as the power of the Indians waned and that of white America waxed along the frontier, the illusion of sovereign independence was maintained, though by early nineteenth century their claim to territorial autonomy and integrity was rejected by the United States government. They were tagged by Chief Justice Marshall of the Supreme Court with the ambiguous label of "domestic dependent nation" (30 US 1831:17). And when the last battle was finally fought along the frontier in the late nineteenth century, they became a conquered people and a racially distinctive segment in a structure of oppressive control under the administrative arm of the U.S. government. They had, in other words, become part of the duality internal to the American society much as the black already was.

South Africa: Apartheid and Duality

White dominance and conquest

Nowhere is the principle of duality more clearly etched than in South Africa. Whites comprise less than 20 percent of the population but to this day they are resisting fiercely any efforts to alter the duality that was imprinted over 350 years ago. From its earliest days, first as a colony of Holland and then of Britain, South Africa has followed a policy of white domination. The paternalism and miscegenation of the early Cape slave period soon gave way to the increasingly repressive and separationist policies as the Boers migrated into other areas, even as the British extended their control over these areas as well. The South Africa Act of 1909 not only created the Union of South Africa from the four territories of Cape, Natal, Orange Free State, and Transvaal as part of what has since become known as the British Commonwealth but also "extended and entrenched the long-standing British policy of granting to the White settlers the power to manage the affairs of the country without an effective participation, or even consultation of the majority of the population. Great Britain transferred, in effect, its prerogatives as a colonial power to the White-settler minority, giving rise to the dual nature of the South African government as 'mother country' and a colonial power" (van den Berghe 1967b:73).

By the turn of the twentieth century South Africa had indeed become a land dominated by the whites. The conquest of the blacks and the expropriation of their lands were virtually completed by 1910. By then 'the African chiefdoms were conquered and white settlement was extended to its present limits" (Thompson and Prior 1982:24). Once the blacks were subdued and the union estabished, all South African governments, according to van den Berghe, have followed a threefold racial policy.

1. The maintenance of paternalistic White domination.
2. Racial segregation and discrimination, wherever there was any threat of equality or competition between Whites and non-Whites.
3. The perpetual subjugation of non-Europeans, and particularly Africans, as a politically powerless and economically exploitable group (van den Berghe 1967b:110).

Apartheid and the homelands policy

Until 1948 these racial policies were expressed in a piecemeal fashion. With the victory of the Afrikaner National Party in the general election of that year, they became the cornerstone of an unfolding program of systematic racial subjugation, separation, surveillance, and coercion. Under the slogan *apartheid* this program developed an ideological coherence and efficiency of implementation over the decades of the continuing dominance of the National Party.

A major step in this direction was the enactment in 1950 of the Group

Areas Act which transformed the *native reserves* of earlier legislation into *homelands* "where each African 'nation' is to be given political and civic rights denied to it in the 'white areas' of the country" (Thompson and Prior 1982:92). In addition, other laws advanced the policy of separate development in the various institutional settings with the whites having monopolistic control over all.

Not until the late 1950s and early 1960s were the various strands brought together into a "unified" theory of apartheid. Its chief spokesman was Prime Minister Verwoerd who insisted that what was being done was for the benefit of all racial groups, the blacks in particular. They would be able to develop their cultural and national identities within the homelands without the unfair competition from the more advanced and "civilized" whites.

By the early 1970s the political fiction articulated by Verwoerd was given a legal definition. Blacks were no longer to be considered as having claims to citizenship in South Africa. Instead they were to be considered citizens of a homeland, "irrespective of whether he was born there or resides there or has ever been there" (Thompson and Prior 1982:92). In addition, a law was passed in 1971 that granted the South African government the power to bestow independence on any homeland.

For the next decade the South African government expended considerable energy and resources to make the legal fiction a reality. It succeeded in getting some homelands to declare their status as "independent nations" but failed to get the consent of most. However, despite its limited success, the government pressed ahead with a massive relocation and resettlement program that uprooted and forcibly moved blacks to the various homelands. These areas were barren wastelands— too small and unproductive to support the burgeoning populations. As a result, most residents had to travel for hours daily by bus to work in areas zoned for whites. Lelyveld (1985) describes in poignant detail the plight of these daily "commuters".

And so by the 1980s the apartheid policy had created a territorially segmented and racially divided society maintained by the white monopoly of instruments of coercion and by a government prepared to put down brutally any signs of resistance. Even so signs of increasing black resistance are widespread, and the future remains uncertain for continuing white control.

The Afrikaner and the English-speaking white

With their increasing political power, Afrikaners have sought to mold the national culture in their own image. They introduced compulsory instruction in the mother tongue (English is also considered an official language) and have in general sought to promote the symbols and history of the Boers and to generally establish the primacy of Boer and Afrikaner history. Efforts to endow the national culture with a uniquely Afrikaner stamp, however, have not been completely successful, for they have run up against a basic cleavage that has historically divided the white community: that between Afrikaner and English.

The struggle between the Boers and the British from the early colonial days on has left a bitter heritage between the descendants of the two. Even the spirit of compromise that pervaded Great Britain's approach to South Africa from 1909 to the birth of the republic in 1961, has not altered the Afrikaner memories of the past. It has merely shifted the setting of the struggle from external relations between the two countries to internal relations between the two populations. Interestingly, both national holidays and symbols are constant reminders to the Afrikaner of his historical opposition to both the British and to the black African. What contributes to the strain between the two white groups is the persisting class, cultural, and political differences. The English, though in a numerical minority, hold the economic power in the country. (The Afrikaners, however, have made significant inroads in recent years into the ranks of management in the private sector.) The Engish are in the better occupations, make more money, and control more wealth. As a result the English-speaking whites see themselves as the social elite whose life-style sets the example for the other strata, including the Afrikaner whom they define as their social inferiors.

Similarly the English define themselves as the cultural elite. They do so primarily because they are better educated than the Afrikaner. Further, they are also the ones who write and publish books, periodicals, and newspapers and who teach at the better schools and universities. The English see themselves as setting the cultural example for the country.

However, through the expansion of their control over governmental and other bureaucracies in the public sector, the Afrikaner has sought to remedy the situation. He has increasingly placed his stamp on the policies and personnel of these structures. "By 1980 over 80 percent of the civil servants were Afrikaners and the Afrikaans language prevails in the Union buildings to such an extent that it is surprising to hear English being spoken. This has vital political significance. The civil service has burgeoned since 1948, and by 1980 over 40 percent of employed Afrikaners were on the payroll of state or parastatal institutions" (Thompson and Prior 1982:133).

As a result, the Afrikaners seem increasingly to be bridging the gulf between the English-speaking whites and themselves. The English-speaking whites also seem to be accommodating themselves to this fact and to the rule of the Afrikaner. Traditionally, the English-speaking whites overwhelmingly supported the opposition party, but in recent years a significant minority has begun to vote for the National Party. Many still express an uneasiness over the extremism of Afrikaner nationalism and even disagree with the National Party on specific issues. But they do not basically question the legitimacy of the Afrikaner rule nor even more significantly do they question the fundamental premise upon which Afrikaner rule is based: the doctrine of white supremacy.

White supremacy: a basis for white consensus

In fact at this level there is a basic agreement between the two; van den Berghe comments on the basic acceptance by the English of the system:

> The English share all the privileges of the other Whites, and they do not want to change the existing system of White oppression. The dictatorial measures of the government do not effect the daily life of the English, as they are intended to suppress the non-White opposition. The government is prepared to tolerate the parliamentary White opposition because such opposition does not constitute a threat. At the same time, many English political and industrial leaders probably think that the Nationalists do a better job of keeping the Africans down than they themselves would. In order to maintain White supremacy and privileges, the mass of the English is willing to pay the price of increasing dictatorship, of gradual Afrikanerization, and of a measure of economic interference (van den Berge 1967b:106).

This drawing together has increased in the last several decades as blacks have reacted more negatively to the white racism.

> As racial tension between Whites and Africans mounted, and as non-White political consciousness increased, the Afrikaner-English conflict receded in importance. From that point of view, the Nationalists are correct when they claim to have contributed to White unity. They have achieved the union of practically all Europeans in a retrenched camp against the "sea of colour" (Van den Berghe 1967b:107).

Thus, white supremacy serves as the cornerstone of the consensual value scheme that unites English and Afrikaner despite other differences. It defines for both the identity of those who are to be treated as full-fledged members of the national community and of those who are to be treated as subjects and objects of that rule. What this means then is that the whites alone are viewed as South African nationals; the non-whites as something else. "When, for example, a White speaks or writes about 'people' and 'South Africans' he almost invariably means 'Whites'. Conversely, if he refers to non-Whites he will almost always use a racial label" (van den Berghe 1967b:238–239). Further on each side of the boundary a different set of values applies. Within the national community of whites, universalistic, egalitarian, achievement and democratic norms and values are the ideal; toward the excluded subject population of nonwhites particularly of the blacks, particularistic, discriminatory, ascriptive, and authoritarian norms are applied.

In effect, both English and Afrikaner have come increasingly to subscribe to a racially bifurcated society and to a dichotomized system of values. The net result is that they have built for 20 percent of the population a white Herrenvolk democracy to use van den Berghe's term; but for the overwhelming proportion of the population they have strengthened and elaborated the repressive racial plural society of colonialism.

However protected the White community may think it is from the repressive measures directed against the blacks, it nevertheless is proving increasingly vulnerable to the whittling away of certain of its rights and liberties. For in its ever increasing preoccupation with the regulation of the blacks, governmental authorities have expressed growing intolerance over expressions of disapproval of these regulations even from whites and have demanded maximum conformity to the dictates of the racial laws and regulations. As a result, governmental surveillance and arbitrary arrest have increased even among the whites.

> Since the Nationalist Party victory at the polls in 1948, there has been a slow but steady deterioration of civil liberties for everybody, including the Whites, to the point where the democratic facade has become empty of meaning even for the privileged race. Successive dictatorial measures have slowly transformed South Africa into an increasingly arbitrary police state. Book and film censorship; indefinite imprisonment without trial; house searches and dawn arrests without warrant for political offences; banning of newspapers, of political parties, and of practically all forms of protest, including orderly meetings and passive resistance; declarations of states of emergencies; telephone tapping and other forms of police spying; political indoctrination in the schools; arbitrary refusal of passports; and political extradition have become the order of the day during the last few years of South African history (van den Berghe 1967b:78).

6 Minority-Majority Relations Over Time

In the last chapter we examined the entry situation of those racial groups that come in at the top of a society, dominate it, and place their imprint upon its institutions. In this chapter we will first look at the entry situation of those that come in at lower levels.

What happens to a group over time once it enters the host society at the lower levels has attracted the attention of many sociologists. Some argue that an orderly sequence of events takes place and have accordingly developed ethnic and race relations cycles. Others have rejected this approach and have developed classification schemes depicting different kinds of majority and minority group orientations and adaptations. Examination of both approaches will be our second task in this chapter. We shall conclude with a reconceptualization of some of these classification schemes.

Initial Entry into the Societal System

It is fairly obvious that what happens to a racial-ethnic group over time depends in large measure upon the character and level of its initial entry into a given societal system. This approach is crucial to Lieberson's theory (1975) of the development of race and ethnic relations. He, accordingly, distinguishes between two major types of entry situations. One involves the entry of a migrant group which subordinates the indigenous population. Colonial conquests are prime examples of such a situation. The other involves the entry of a migrant group which is subordinated by the indigenous population. The history of the immigration of ethnic minorities from southern and eastern Europe and from non-Protestant countries into the United States exemplifies this type of situation. To Lieberson these two kinds of "entry situations" between migrant group and host society represent different kinds of experiences and have qualitatively different kinds of consequences for the unfolding relationships between the two and for the very restructuring of the internal character of the host society.

Entry at the top: a brief review

In the last chapter we examined the kind of entry at the top that has prevailed throughout the world for centuries and been dominated by the white European. Thus, we find that Columbus's first voyage to the New World in 1492 launched white Europeans on four and a half centuries of colonial conquest and expansion that eventually extended to all the continents of the world. From the Americas to Africa and Asia they conquered and subjugated nonwhite races and imposed upon each a system of exploitation for economic and political gain. In some instances, as in the Spanish conquest of New Spain and Peru, they took land and its resources away from the native populations and harnessed the native populations to this exploitative system as a labor force. In other instances, as in the English conquest of North America, they drove the native populations from their land and resources and then imported as a work force enslaved nonwhite populations from other lands. In each case the Europeans, beginning with the Spanish and English in the New World, through the force of arms created colonial "plural societies" hierarchically segmented along racial lines. They stood astride these societies as a colonialist elite, consolidated their hold on the channels of political and economic power, and monopolized the major instruments of control and coercion.

This description of the white European resonates throughout the literature on the plural society. Such resonance reflects the almost exclusive preoccupation of the scholars of the plural society with the white European as colonialist. They have failed, however, to give due weight to those historical situations of expansion and conquest where the white European did more than create a plural society on the shoulders of nonwhites who were either indigenous to or involuntarily imported into the territory.

In those areas, as we have seen in the last chapter, the white European also became a settler and colonist who was intent upon building a society whose membership was confined to his own kind. Thus, he presided over a dual societal system: one whose legal normative code reflected that he was part of a people and another whose legal normative code reflected that he was the ruler of racially "inferior" subjects or things.

Entry at lower levels: the subordinated racial and ethnic minorities

When we shift our attention from those racial and ethnic groups which enter society at the top to those which enter at lower levels, we find that their life circumstances and situations will vary according to such matters as (1) their level of entry; whether toward the middle or at the bottom of the occupational structure, (2) the character of their host society; whether it is a colonial type plural society, a dual colonist-colonialist society, or a competitive society, and (3) whether their migration is voluntary or involuntary.

The colonial expansion of the European countries frequently introduced new economic institutions and forces into the host society. Capitalist enterprise, a money economy, private property were superimposed upon what was essentially a self-subsistent barter economy governed by tradition and in the process disrupted, weakened, and often transformed this economy.

Under these transformed circumstances a variety of economic needs may develop and threaten to remain unfulfilled by the existing labor force within the society. As Lieberson comments, "In societies where the migrant population is superordinant, it is often necessary to introduce new immigrant groups to fill the niches created in the revised economy of the area. The subordinate and indigenous population frequently fails, at first, to participate in the new economic and political order introduced by migrants" (Lieberson 1975:49).

As a result, a new layer of alien "middlemen" is introduced to perform such roles as that of merchant, artisan, petty official, and professional. In medieval Europe, for example, Jews were given the protection of princes as they performed a number of these functions for the rulers. As Shibutani and Kwan say, "The rulers often left tasks requiring financial and administrative competence in Jewish hands, and some Jews became fiscal agents—the collectors of royal and municipal taxes, of tributes owed to lords and to military orders, and even of tithes for Christian church officials. During the early days of capitalism, when many merchants and princes found it necessary to borrow large sums of money, the Jews in many cases were the only people to whom they could turn" (Shibutani & Kwan 1965:191–192). Other groups have also performed such functions historically. Furnivall describes, for example, the middleman role of the East Indian in Burma and of the Chinese in The Netherland East Indies. Shibutani and Kwan offer an even wider range of examples.

> In Southeast Asia many of the merchants serving the natives, the doctors and lawyers, and the money-lenders are Chinese. In the early 1580's the Chinese in Manila were assigned a separate quarter, the Parian, which soon became

the center of the city's commercial life. The Chinese had a virtual monopoly over retail business and dominated the craft trades. In many parts of Africa people from the Middle East—Greeks, Syrians, and Lebanese—filled the gap between large European firms and petty African traders. In Indonesia Arab middlemen travelled from village to village to buy up surplus cash crops, to lend money, and to pay taxes for peasants; these traders often served as guides to the strange world beyond the village. Traders from India established themselves in East Africa even before the coming of the Portuguese in the fifteenth century, and toward the end of the nineteenth century Indian soldiers formed the backbone of the police and military forces (Shibutani and Kwan 1965: 192–193).

Within the colonial plural societies these middlemen ethnic groups became one more plural segment within the society, they lived within the confines of their own community monopolizing and dominating certain occupational functions. However, they remained a highly visible and vulnerable group whose fate and life circumstances were subject to contending forces. Blalock devotes considerable attention to the relative vulnerability of these middlemen ethnic groups. As he says,

> Often, although not always, the middleman minority is numerically small. Its power is largely dependent on the goodwill or tolerance of the power elite. As long as it is fulfilling its role successfully, but perhaps not too successfully, it will be protected by the elite. But although its power is weak, its general status and income are high relative to that of the subordinate masses. The middlemen minority is thus in a vulnerable position.
>
> In a very real sense, then, the middleman represents a barrier between the other two groups, serving as a buffer which can often absorb any major strains the system may undergo short of complete rebellion by the subordinate group. In many instances, the middleman minority actually mediates interaction between the other two groups, being the subordinate group's primary source of contact with the elite. The merchant, bargaining over prices, comes to symbolize the manufacturing elite; the overseer or tax collector, the large landholder or plantation owner, the small-time moneylender, the large financial interests. In times of prosperity and reduced class conflict, the middleman finds himself relatively secure under the protection of the elite group. In times of stress, however, he becomes a natural scapegoat.
>
> In effect, the price the minority pays for protection in times of minimal stress is to be placed on the front lines of battle in any showdown between the elite and peasant groups (Blalock 1967: 81–82).

Even more pressing within the colonial system was the need for a malleable but dependable supply of labor that could work the fields, dig the mines, construct the roads and railroads, and in general supply the brawn and brute energy for building an economy dominated by the superordinate migrant. The labor systems that developed varied but all were characterized by the central importance of coercion and force and varying degrees of unfreedom of the basic labor supply. In many instances drastic means were employed to enlist the subject population into the labor force. As discussed in Chapter 5, the Spanish organized labor in the 1500s around the encomienda in which the government distributed Indians as a workforce for the conquistador. This system was eventually outlawed and replaced by the repartimento—a system under which the native population could be called upon to do work which was in the public interest. And finally the system that the Spanish adopted for recruiting Indians into the labor force was that of debt peonage.

Frequently the supply of natives proved in time to be inadequate for the labor needs of the colonialists. Their numbers became so drastically depleted through disease, hunger, war, and escape that the colonialists had to turn to other sources of labor. One source was the importation of labor to supply their needs. The system that was most favored in a number of places was that which allowed maximum control over labor and its utilization, and that of course was the system of slavery. This system developed, according to Frazier, "primarily in response to the demand for cheap labor in a plantation system of agriculture which produced staples for export" (Frazier 1957a:110). Accordingly, the involuntary migration of the black slave became a major source of labor in the colonialized areas of the New World which produced agricultural products for sale and profit in the Caribbean areas, the southern United States, Brazil, and elsewhere.

In other parts of the colonial world—where slavery did not take hold or was abolished—the need for an enlarged labor supply also resulted in the importation of racial migrants as part of a "contract system of labor." This system, though ostensibly based on "free labor", took on many of the characteristics of an onerous indentured service in which the imported laborer was exploited and controlled by a powerful racially different employer. In this manner nonwhite migrants were recruited to serve the labor needs of the white colonialist. In Hawaii during the nineteenth century, for example, contract laborers from Asia—first from China, then from Japan, and later from the Philippines—worked on the sugar plantations owned and controlled by white Americans. In a similar manner East Indians were introduced after the demise of slavery in the Caribbean. They became the primary labor force on plantations in British Guyana, Trinidad, and elsewhere. They were also brought to South Africa as contract laborers to work on railways, mines, and plantations. And so the examples can be multiplied with different racial groups and different countries. In each of these countries the imported racial minorities performed the menial manual tasks. They lived in their own barracks or enclaves, functioned as either pariahs or outcasts, and lived in rigidly controlled environments much as they would under slavery.

On one level, the history of the importation of labor into the United States can be described in similar colonial terms. Thus, we find the coercion of the native Indians, the reliance on and frequent harsh treatment of the black as slave, and the building of a plantation economy in the South literally on the back of the forced labor of the black.

At another level, the American experience represents one of history's most remarkable examples of the mass voluntary migration of a formally "free labor supply" seeking to gain the benefits of real and perceived opportunities in an expanding economy of an open competitive society. Wave after wave of immigrants, first from northern Europe and then from southern and eastern Europe crested in the late nineteenth century and early twentieth century and provided much of the basic brawn and energy for the expanding American economy. Selected parts of their occupational history will be discussed later. For the present all that need be noted is that most entered at the bottom of the occupational structure and their movement up the occupational ladder comprises a major part of the dramatic development of the American society. Thus, America is the product of the overlay of two systems of labor: one forced and slave and the other free.

Ethnic and Race Relations Cycles

Many sociologists have been intrigued by what happens to an ethnic or racial group once it enters a societal system. Some have been convinced that an orderly progression of events follows entry. According to Berry and Tischler, these sociologists,

> Deny that each situation where unlike groups come together is a law unto itself, but insist that there are recurring phenomena that have a natural, chronological relationship. They maintain that there is a succession of events or processes, a series of steps or stages, certain uniformities and similarities in all situations where the races have met. They have expressed their generalizations in a form of a *race relations cycle*. We must bear in mind that cycles these scholars have constructed are not the products of wild speculation, but were developed from observation and analysis of many concrete situations (Berry and Tischler 1978:149–150).

However, despite the attempts to bring into a single conceptual framework a variety of ethnic and racial situations, these generalizations are nevertheless based upon a limited number of observations within a given temporal and spatial framework. Accordingly, none of these efforts can truly do justice to the wide range of variations and as Lieberson comments, "... the sharp contrast between relatively harmonious race relations in Brazil and Hawaii and the current racial turmoil in South

Africa and Indonesia serve to illustrate the difficulty in stating—to say nothing of interpreting—an inevitable 'natural history' of race and ethnic relations" (Lieberson 1975:45).

However, despite the limited validity of such formulations they do indeed have a heuristic value, for they alert the observer to the need to view unfolding race and ethnic relations within a temporal framework and to consider their sequential character. Accordingly, we propose to examine some of these "cycles" and to identify the societal conditions to which they seem to apply.

Park: the "natural history" of race relations

Perhaps the earliest attempt to formulate a "natural history" of race relations was done by Professor Robert E. Park of the University of Chicago. Park spent much of his early career in moving back and forth between the academic world and the world of action and reform. He was a journalist for a number of years; of particular interest are his first-hand reports on the Belgians' exploitation of the natives of the Congo. His interest in race and ethnic relations began relatively early. Through the influence of Booker T. Washington he became concerned with the plight of the black in America. Then later he became interested in the immigrant, particularly with the loyalty of the immigrant population during and after World War I. Finally he became involved in observations and studies of the Orient. As such he traveled extensively around the world and wrote prolifically. In many respects Park was less a specialist in race relations and more a sociologist. He and Ernest W. Burgess developed a conceptual scheme built around the four basic social processes: competition, conflict, accommodation and assimilation.

In 1926 Park wrote an article, "Our Racial Frontier on The Pacific," in which he set this conceptual scheme into a temporal framework and characterized it as expressing the natural sequence of events in race relations. As he says, "In the relations of races there is a cycle of events which tends everywhere to repeat itself." He then goes on to say, "The race relations cycle which takes the form, to state it abstractly, of contacts, competition, accommodation and eventual assimilation, is apparently progressive and irreversible. Customs regulations, immigration restrictions and racial barriers may slacken the tempo of the movement; may perhaps halt it altogether for a time; but cannot change its direction; cannot at any rate, reverse it" (Park 1950:150).

In effect, Park concluded that relations between ethnic and racial groups which may start with conflict and competition eventually result in the amalgamation of the groups into a newly constituted society. In this formulation Park does not seem to make any distinction between colonial plural type societies or the open class, competitive type society. To him results seem to be the same irrespective of the specific societal structure.

Other sociologists, however, in seeking to formulate stages or cycles of race and ethnic relations either implicitly or explicitly direct their attention to one or the other type of society. The progression of events in colonial societies seems to have captured the imagination of several sociological observers. Perhaps one of the most striking features of these attempts is the extent to which conflict and tension are treated as essential features of these unfolding relations. This is evident in the writings of W. O. Brown.

Brown: the colonial situation and race conflict

In 1934, Brown brought together his studies of racial conflict, particularly those of countries which were invaded by an imperialist power seeking to take over political and economic control of the nation. However, he did not confine his observations to such countries, he also included America and its relations with the black. Basically though, his formulation of "natural history of race conflict" applied more to the imperialist situation. As he says, "The typical race-conflict situation described suggest a certain cycle of development in race conflict. It appears to have a natural history, the stages of which will be briefly outlined, though we recognize that not all cases of race conflict fit the pattern" (Brown 1934:40).

According to Brown, contacts at first rarely involve open conflict. "These first contacts tend to be of the symbiotic, categoric sort, involving a minimum of overt hostility but accompanied by some uncertainty, fear, and probably curiosity" (Brown 1934:40). In short, there may be some exchange of goods and services, in what has been called a silent trade. However, conflicts of interest tend to emerge in short order. Such conflicts are likely to focus on "land, resources, and physical survival rather than status" (Brown 1934:41). At this juncture, open warfare breaks out between the two groups, each viewing itself as a distinctive societal entity with primary claims to the matters under dispute.

The struggle can lead to the destruction of the weaker indigenous group, but rarely does this happen, according to Brown. Instead the defeated group comes to terms with its conquerors "preferring subordination to destruction or even accepting isolation and at times enslavement" (Brown 1934:41). As such, the "weaker race" becomes incorporated as a subordinated part of a society dominated by the conquering invader.

According to Brown, if the conquered group is numerically small, it may be absorbed into the class system of the dominant society, and as such the "race-relations cycle" will end at this point. Much more frequently the "weaker race" remains relatively intact and soon the accommodations that ended the war begin to wear thin. Brown claims that this is likely to happen if "the weaker race is potentially or actually menacing and the mores of the dominant race resist fusion." As such, accommodations break down and a struggle ensues over "questions of rights, status, and social systems." As a result, "the end of racial war apparently means the beginning of another sort of race conflict" (Brown 1934:41), which is focused on a "struggle for status" and for place in the societal order (Brown 1934:42).

Brown sees several things happening at this stage of the race relations cycle that "give content and intensity to race conflict" (Brown 1934:42). First, the traditional system of the weaker race begins to break down. The life circumstances and needs of this indigenous population increasingly require that the native comes to terms with the "civilization of the stronger people" (Brown 1934:42) and enters into the struggle over the allocation of resources and over his rights in the various arenas of society. "Need and human nature have forced him to become a competitor in the economic system and to become conscious of his rights in the social order." The European, however, "prefers the native to remain native;" he "wants the services of the native but resents him as a coparticipant in a social order." The European wants the native to remain in his subordinated position within his own native enclave. Thus the stage is set for a collision between the two groups. "Out of this struggle for existence and status within the framework of a social system considered by the white man to be uniquely his own, race conflict has naturally emerged" (Brown 1934:43).

Brown discusses this primarily in terms of the distinct integration of the cultural system of the weaker race and its assimilation into the dominant culture. However, what he is really talking about is not so much a struggle over competing value systems but more a struggle over the distribution of power and the recognition by the subordinated group that its fate depends upon gaining rights and access to the various sources of power and privilege in the society. The extent to which his own cultural and value system disintegrates becomes an empirical question.

A second factor, according to Brown, at this stage of race conflict is the "rise of the 'marginal' man". The person "who first loses his traditional culture orientation and assimilates the culture of the stronger group" but is not accepted by it (Brown 1934:44). Such persons, according to Brown, come to resent their treatment by the dominant group and may turn back toward their own group and become its leaders in a developing race consciousness and expressed hostility toward the dominant group. As the stage is set for the struggle, both dominant and subordinate groups mobilize their energies and resources. "As the conflict situation develops the dominant race formulates supporting ideologies and myths justifying its dominance and designs repressive policies and programs to secure it. Such myths as racial inequality and the menace of race mixture do yeoman service. Repressive programs halt, at least temporarily, the advance of the rising race. Race becomes an obsession, an eternally present issue in political policy" (Brown 1934:45).

In turn, the subordinated group also mobilizes its resources. It develops a race consciousness which finds expression in nationalistic and race movements. "These movements aim to secure status and human rights as defined in the ideology of the stronger race. Race prejudice and race consciousness operative on both sides mobilize the races for struggle, define issues, and create an impasse which cannot easily be broken. In the meantime the weaker race is forced to take what it can get, while the stronger race is determined to give nothing that is fundamental" (Brown 1934:45–46).

Such conflict should ultimately be able to be resolved. "Abstractly, there are probably three possible ways out." One is isolation which is never quite possible; for as Brown says, "The existence of race conflict implies that the races are involved in the same social order. Attempted isolation menaces the interest of the stronger race and arouses the ire of the weaker. Conflict typically emerges because of the breakdown of isolation, and social processes are no more reversible in race relations than in any other type of social contact." Another possibility is continued subordination. "This again represents a reversal of the process by which the races became entangled. Race conflict usually indicates the breakdown, or at least the challenge, of accommodations based upon inequality of placement." According to Brown, the only long term permanent solution for race conflict is "the complete absorption and assimilation of the races in a common culture and social order" (Brown 1934:46). Brown is pessimistic about this happening in the foreseeable future. Accordingly, he predicts as of 1934 that "race problems will continue to harass mankind and intrigue sociologists" (Brown 1934:47).

Frantz Fanon: the colonial situation and revolutionary change

An even more pessimistic view about the possible peaceful amalgamation of the races in the colonial situation was expressed three decades later by Frantz Fanon who, as we have seen, developed his own version of "ethno-Marxism." He accepted Marx's thesis that the inevitable result of the growing antagonism and disenchantment of the subordinated groups to the rule of the elite under capitalism was an eventual drive for revolutionary change. In fact, Fanon insisted that conditions were even riper for such change in the colonial society. He also agreed with Marx that this drive would be spearheaded by some—not by all—segments of the subordinated groups, but he differed in his choice of the revolutionary vanguard. Marx had insisted, for example, that the vanguard was to consist of that particular class of dispossessed who bore a special relationship to the unfolding technology of society; under capitalism, it would be the industrial proletariat. Fanon however located his vanguard elsewhere. He was convinced that virtually all of the occupational strata in the towns and cities had been contaminated by the colonialist. They had accepted "economic crumbs" from the table of the colonialist, had sought to adopt his values, and had become soft on the issue of colonialist rule. Even the proletariat occupied a favored position under colonialism and had identified its interests too closely with those of the colonialist. Fanon exempted the town lumpenproletariat from this contaminating influence and considered it one of the major allies of the vanguard. (Marx had contemptuously dismissed the lumpenproletariat as having any effective role in the revolution.) The vanguard itself, according to Fanon, was the peasantry who lived in the hinterland under a traditional system of authority far from the "siren song" of the colonialist way of life.

The peasantry, Fanon opined, did not automatically develop revolutionary ardor. For this to happen the peasants had to go through stages similar to those posited by Marx for the proletariat. According to Marx, in the early stages of the introduction of machinery into the factory system, members of the proletariat—egged on by the capitalist—fought among themselves as they competed for the scarce jobs. Similarly, Fanon argued, rivalry and dissension rent the ranks of the peasantry along ethnic and tribal lines as they were encouraged by the colonialist to fight among themselves in their struggle for survival and as they began to displace aggression built up by the exploitative colonial system onto other peasants. In time, Marx postulated, members of the proletariat would stop fighting among themselves as they came to recognize their common interests and needs, and from this would develop a class consciousness and solidarity. The peasantry, according to Fanon, was also destined to attain a similar level of cohesion, but unlike the proletariat of Marx, its solidarity was to be organized around a collective identification with emergent nationalism and not around an emergent class consciousness. Finally, both proletariat and peasantry would be ready for being molded, through effective political leadership, into an organized and disciplined vanguard of the revolution.

Fanon recognized that for Marx, passage from one stage to the next was inextricably linked to the elaborating technological changes and processes of capital accumulation within the capitalistic economy. These changes, according to Marx, exacerbated relations between the various classes with the capitalist class growing ever more powerful though declining in size and the proletariat becoming ever more powerless and propertyless though expanding in size. Thus according to Marx, the objective conditions of the classes generated the tensions and strains which literally forced the members of the proletariat to become subjectively aware of their situation, and as their class consciousness grew they became increasingly convinced that the future was theirs. Revolution involved cognitive and rational processes that made the exploited class subjectively aware of the nature of its rational interest; revolution was a rational outcome to an organic process which literally "compelled" the exploited to act against the exploiter. It was in effect the product of a dynamic set of forces internal to the economic-technological system and the end result of a summatory and cumulative process.

The colonial society, Fanon acknowledged, had neither the technological nor the industrial development of the capitalist society which could generate the kind of internal dynamic that Marx postulated linked one stage to the next. It was instead a society whose elite was externally imposed and for whom political instruments of control were uppermost. Therefore Fanon was obliged to view the revolutionary process as the unfolding of political processes in which stages could be identified but which lacked any propelling force that provided the momentum for the next stage.

In the absence of a Marxian dynamic in the institutional system of the colonial society, Fanon found in the psychoanalytic theories of Freud a functionally equivalent "psychic" dynamic.* According to Fanon, the collective psychic and libidinal energies of the peasantry became transformed under the repressive rule of the colonialist into a seething volcano of violent emotions and action that under appropriate political channeling propelled the revolutionary process from one stage to another.

The primordial response of the peasant to the violently repressive, dehumanizing colonial system was anger, resentment, and hatred of the colonialist: "The settler keeps alive in the native an anger. . . ." But in its initial stages, "the native is trapped in the tight links of the chains of colonialism," and was accordingly deprived of an outlet for his mounting anger against the colonialist. In short, fear of violent retribution prevented the native from expressing his anger openly and directly against the white colonialist (Fanon 1968:54).

Unable to direct his anger against the "real" target of his oppression, the native, Fanon insisted, displaced his anger onto his fellow natives.

---

*Marx was not Fanon's only inspirational model. As a practicing pyschiatrist, he was also greatly influenced by the work of Freud. Pivotal features of Fanon's theory show this influence.

The native also deflected his anger from the colonialist by concentrating on a magical and mythological superstructure populated by malevolent spirits of frightening proportions. "The supernatural, magical powers reveal themselves as essentially personal; the settler's powers are infinitely shrunken, stamped with their alien origin. We no longer really need to fight against them since what counts is the frightening enemy created by myths. We perceive that all is settled by a permanent confrontation on the phantasmic plane" (Fanon 1968:56).

Periodically, Fanon argued, the natives sought to exorcise the evil spirits and to relieve themselves of the mounting internal pressures of unrelieved violence and anger through dance and community rituals. However, despite these various efforts to drain off this molten core of suppressed libidinal energies the brutal repressions of the colonialist regime continually refueled it so that it retained, if not expanded, its potential for volcanic violence. The arrival among the peasantry of radicalized and politicized nationalists from the town who were seeking to escape the dragnet of the colonial police set the stage for the next phase of the revolutionary process.

> From the beginning, the peasantry closes in around them and protects them from being pursued by the police. The militant nationalist who decides to throw in his lot with the country people instead of playing at hide-and-seek with the police in urban centers will lose nothing. The peasant's cloak will wrap him around with a gentleness and firmness that he never suspected. ... [in this way] the men coming from the towns learn their lessons in the hard school of the people; and at the same time these men open classes for the people in military and political education. The people furbish up their weapons; but in fact the classes do not last long, for the masses come to know once again the strength of their own muscles, and push the leaders on to prompt action. The armed struggle has begun (Fanon 1968:126–127).

In sum, Fanon insisted, "... the meeting between these militants with the police on their track and these mettlesome masses of people, who are rebels by instinct, ... produce an explosive mixture of unusual potentiality" (Fanon 1968:127). In this fashion the natives become politicized and shift their attention from parochial concerns onto a growing national consciousness in which they join with others of their own kind. And the volcanic libidinal energies they had previously displaced on scapegoats now become channeled into sluices of revolutionary action and political violence against the colonialist oppressor. The revolutionary ardor soon spreads to the lumpenproletariat in the towns and the stage is set for the final assault on the colonialist.

Bogardus: host society's reactions to racial immigration

Another sociologist who developed a race relations cycle was Emory S. Bogardus who published it in an article in the *American Journal of Sociology* in 1930. Unlike Brown or Fanon, Bogardus did not focus on the sequence of occurrences that characterize the colonial conquest by an invading ethnic migrant. Instead he confined his observations to the response of the dominant indigenous population to a racial minority as it entered and sought to make its way into the society. In effect, the racial immigrant entered not as a conqueror but as a supplicant. In this, Bogardus made clear that his cycle was based on his observations of the experience of certain minorities in America and not elsewhere. However, his subjects were Chinese, Japanese, Philippinos, and Mexicans—essentially racial minorities who have experienced a level of hostility and legal and other institutional discrimination that has resembled the experience of the black in America more than that of the white European immigrant. Bogardus emphasizes the hostility that greet these minorities as they move through certain stages of his cycle. Unfortunately he failed to recognize the continuing importance of this hostility in the later stages.

Bogardus's cycle contains seven stages; each is described briefly below: (1) Curiosity: The first immigrants become objects of curiosity; they arouse attention because of their strange customs and habits. The response of the dominant group tends to be fairly sympathetic because the immigrants seem to be "a lone stranger far away from his home." Furthermore, they are relatively few in number which makes them seem helpless and nonthreatening. (2) Economic welcome: The pervasive need for cheap labor makes the immigrant especially attractive to employers who are quick to take advantage of this new source of labor. The immigrants are even encouraged to send for their relatives. (3) Industrial and social antagonism: At some point soon, however, there develops a spontaneous reaction against the immigrants for which they are not prepared. These outbursts of prejudice eventually give way to organized movements. According to Bogardus, "At the time these immigrants seemed to be getting a footing and to be reaching a degree of economic independence for which Americans are noted, they have heard the roar of an oncoming storm" (Bogardus 1930:614). Thus, organized labor comes to fear the competition of these immigrants; labor leaders and leaders of patriotic societies head the opposition forces. The organized opposition gains increasing momentum because of the spreading fear among the native population of being overrun by the immigrants. This fear is not only confined to the worry about jobs, but a special type of antagonism develops as neighborhoods seem to be invaded by these foreigners. (4) Legislative antagonism: So widespread does opposition become that bills are introduced into legislature and into Congress. A massive campaign is organized against the "undesirable" immigrants who are openly, publicly, and viciously denounced. Politicans play on these fears against the foreigners who lack the vote* and who therefore have little muscle that the politician needs fear. "The legislative phase" according to Bogardus, "gains momentum until its objective is reached or until the threatened danger is past" (Bogardus 1930:616). (5) Fair-play tendencies: In time, a movement for "fair-play" develops. According to Bogardus, "Broadminded Americans initiate a countermovement, not only because of friendship for the immigrants but because the latter are being attacked unjustly. This counterphase operates under serious handicaps. It is usually not well organized, is lacking in financial support, is not steadily aggressive, is hampered by the zealots and dreamers among its numbers to bring it into disrepute. It is, however, a source of comfort and understanding to many of the immigrants in question. It helps them to retain confidence in American life and principles. It holds somewhat in check the antirace reactions and prevents the race antagonists from going to ultimate extremes. It serves as a balance wheel to an otherwise one-sided mechanism. It maintains the idealistic reputation of the nation in the eyes of the world" (Bogardus 1930:616). (6) Quiescence: Once the restrictive legislation is obtained, antagonism diminishes. Even the antagonistic organizations may modify their attitudes as they consider the danger to have passed; they start to talk in terms of tolerance and sympathy and to espouse "justice" for their foes. According to Bogardus, this stage has been reached in both the Chinese and Japanese race cycles; however, at the time of his writing, he says neither the Mexican nor Philippino race cycles have attained this stage. (7) Second-generation difficulties: Finally the problems of the second generation emerge as the native born children of the immigrants start to respond to their marginal situation. This marginal generation finds itself out of touch with the culture and way of life of their parents but without acceptance by the Americans. As a result, it becomes a resentful and insecure generation.

Bogardus's cycle is, in the final analysis, of limited value in understanding the treatment of the immigrant from Asia up to and including the time about which he wrote. Its major defect is Bogardus's failure to recognize the continuing importance of the statutory constraints of stage 4 that prevented the Asian immigrant from becoming a citizen which in turn played a crucial part in the incarceration of the Japanese immigrant and his children in World War II. As a result, his stages 5 and

---

*Bogardus should have said *cannot* vote because they were unable to become citizens because of the 1790 statute that confined naturalization to whites only.

6 reflect a temporary equilibrium which may have prevailed during the time he wrote but which collapsed by the mid-1930s and early 1940s. More about the experience of the immigrant from Asia later in this book.

Gordon: the assimilation sequence

Conflict and antagonism are not the central themes of sociologists who seek to apply a cycle theory to the experience of white European immigrants in America; instead accommodation and assimilation are featured. Thus, the cycle frequently describes the sequence by which the ethnic immigrant takes on the characteristics of the dominant society and becomes increasingly identified with and accepted by it.

One of the more significant statements of this approach is to be found in Milton Gordon's *Assimilation in American Life* (1964). Though Gordon does not manifestly set for himself the task of developing a cycle theory, he does refer to sequential stages in the "assimilation process." Each stage represents the working out of a distinctive subprocess. The four of greatest interest to us are labeled by Gordon as 'cultural or behavioral assimilation," "structural assimilation," "marital assimilation," and "identificational assimilation." The first refers to the subprocess by which members of an ethnic group take on more and more of the cultural characteristics and patterns of the host society. "Structural assimilation" refers to "large-scale entrance into cliques, clubs, and institutions of host society, on primary group level." "Marital assimilation" refers to "large-scale intermarriage;" and "identificational assimilation" is defined as "the development of a sense of peoplehood based exclusively on host society" (Gordon 1964:71).

For Gordon total assimilation into the host society can only occur if members of an ethnic group go through these subprocesses or stages. The sequence begins with acculturation or cultural assimilation; it may also end there. As Gordon says, "Cultural assimilation, or acculturation, of the minority group may take place even when none of the other types of assimilation occurs simultaneously or later, and this condition of 'acculturation only' may continue indefinitely" (Gordon 1964:77).

However, Gordon considers the dynamics of the process will generally lead from cultural to structural assimilation. He does not view the latter as necessarily the next stage, but he does view it as the key to the whole process. As he says, "Once structural assimilation has occurred, either simultaneously with or subsequent to acculturation, all of the other types of assimilation will naturally follow" (Gordon 1964:81).

Accordingly, he notes an

> indissoluble connection, in the time order indicated, between structural assimilation and marital assimilation. That is, entrance of the minority group into the social cliques, clubs and institutions of the core of society at the primary group level inevitably will lead to a substantial amount of intermarriage. If children of different ethnic backgrounds belong to the same play-group, later the same adolescent cliques, and at college the same fraternities and sororities; if the parents belong to the same country club and invite each other to their homes for dinner; it is completely unrealistic not to expect these children, now grown, to love and to marry each other blithely oblivious to previous ethnic extraction (Gordon 1964:80).

Finally, should marital assimilation take place, then, according to Gordon, identificational assimilation is likely to follow. As he says, "If marital assimilation, an inevitable by-product of structural assimilation, takes place fully, the minority group loses its ethnic identity in the larger host or core society, and identificational assimilation takes place" (Gordon 1964:80). At this juncture the ethnic group will disappear as a distinctive entity; its members absorbed into the dominant society.

Gordon, however, has something else to say. He recognizes that the assimilative process tells us what happens to the ethnic minority in its relation to the host society, but he also recognizes that the host society— that to which the ethnic group is assimilating—may be characterized by more than one model for assimilation. Accordingly, he adopts the 'three historic principles" or ideals that the Coles had articulated earlier in their book *Minorities and the American Promise: The Conflict of Principle and Practice* (1954). The three that they had identified as being idealized expressions of the American society past and present are Anglo-conformity, melting pot, and cultural pluralism. However, in their book the Coles merely describe the workings of these principles and on occasion resort to the Myrdallian approach of examining the disparity or conflict between principle and practice.

Gordon goes well beyond this level of description. He incorporates the three "principles" into his theoretic framework for the analysis of assimilation. They become in effect the "goal-systems" that have been used to define what the host society is or should become. They are, in other words, the 'three main axes" around which the processes of assimilation have grouped themselves historically in the American experience; each has provided a distinctive normative model for this experience.

> In preliminary fashion, we may say that the "Anglo-conformity" theory demanded the complete renunciation of the immigrant's ancestral culture in favor of the behavior and values of the Anglo-Saxon core group; the

"melting pot" idea envisioned a biological merger of the Anglo-Saxon peoples with other immigrant groups and a blending of their respective cultures into a new indigenous American type; and "cultural pluralism" postulated the preservation of the communal life and significant portions of the culture of the later immigrant groups within the context of American citizenship and political and economic integration into American society" (Gordon 1964:85).

Gordon's assimilation cycle fits quite well his "melting pot" and "Anglo-conformity" models, but he has considerable difficulty in its application to the "cultural pluralist" model of society. In addition, even within the framework of these models, Gordon oversimplifies the assimilative process, neglects the role of conflict and tension, and too narrowly defines the concept "structural assimilation."

Classifications of Minority-Majority Situations

Interesting as these race cycles may be, Lieberson and others have criticized them as trying to generalize beyond the relatively narrow range of racial and ethnic experiences to which they may actually apply. Other sociologists have eschewed this approach and have instead sought to develop classification schemes which could serve as a broad conceptual framework for subsuming a wide variety of different kinds of ethnic situations. Among the most interesting are those that employ a "normative frame of reference" for distinguishing among the various ethnic situations. As such they view either the minority or dominant group as an active agent and they seek to identify its definition of the situation and the goals and policies it self-consciously pursues. In this manner, a classification scheme is built from the different perception and definition each of the various groups has of a desired present or future state of affairs.

Wirth: a "normative" typology of minority groups

One of the most provocative attempts to follow this approach in distinguishing minority group situations is that of Louis Wirth who published his classification scheme in the 1940s. In that essay, Wirth addresses himself to problems in constructing an adequate typology of minorities which he says must be able to "take account of the general types of situations in which minorities find themselves and must seek to comprehend the *modus vivendi* that has grown up between the segments of those societies in which minority problems exist" (Wirth 1945:352).

After describing a number of "axes" around which a typology could be built such as "number and size of distinct minorities in the society in question," he selects as the most fruitful axis: "the goals toward which the minority and dominant groups are striving in quest of a new and more satisfactory equilibrium" (Wirth 1945:352). He does so because he believes that "analyzing the major goals toward which the ideas, the sentiments, and the actions of minority groups are directed" comes closest to helping us understand "the actual minority problems that plague the modern world" (Wirth 1945:354). Accordingly, he distinguishes four types of minority groups: (1) pluralistic, (2) assimilationist, (3) secessionist, and (4) militant. Interestingly his examples for all but the assimilationist are drawn primarily from Europe; those for the assimilationist are drawn primarily from the United States.

According to Wirth, a pluralistic minority seeks to maintain its distinctive identity and to gain toleration of its distinctiveness from the dominant society. Initially its goals may be quite limited. It may merely seek freedom to practice a dissenting religion as was the case of the Jews in Medieval Europe or the Protestants in predominantly Catholic countries; or to attain cultural autonomy as a first step as was the case of the nationalities in Europe which subsequently pursued national independence during the nineteenth and twentieth century. "It would be an error, however, to infer that the claims for cultural autonomy are generally pursued independently of other interests. Coupled with the demand, and often precedent to it there proceeds the struggle for economic and political equality or at least equalization of opportunity. Although the pluralistic minority does not wish to merge its total life with the larger society, it does demand for its members a greater measure of economic and political freedom if not outright civic equality" (Wirth 1945:356).

Wirth concludes that the final aim of the pluralistic minority is obtained only "when it has succeeded in wresting from the dominant group the fullest measure of equality in all things economic and political and the right to be left alone in all things cultural" (Wirth 1945:357). Wirth's formulation suggests that he includes in his concept pluralistic minority the kinds of ethnic-racial segments of Furnivall's plural society. In fact much of what he says would also apply to the "partial ethnic community" of American cultural pluralism.

The goal of assimilation to Wirth obviously places the minority in quite a different relationship to the dominant society.

> Unlike the pluralistic minority, which is content with toleration and the upper limit of whose aspiration is cultural autonomy, the assimilationist minority craves the fullest opportunity for participation in life of the larger society with a view to uncoerced incorporation in that society. It seeks to lose itself in the larger whole by opening up to its members the greatest possibilities for their individual self-development. Rather than toleration and autonomy,

which is the goal of the pluralistic minority, the assimilationist minority works toward complete acceptance by the dominant group and a merger with the larger society (Wirth 1945:357–358).

In effect the ultimate goal of the assimilationist minority is its complete disappearance as a distinctive group and the full acceptance of its members in the larger society. Wirth views the experience of religious and nationality groups in America as basically reflecting the power of assimilationist tendencies. The major impediments to assimilation, according to Wirth, are the barriers imposed by the larger society. He is convinced that with the breaching of these barriers, the power of assimilation will become the dominant process in the American society, even for the Jews whom Wirth recognizes as having a strong inclination towards retaining their separate identity.

The secessionist minority, his third type,

> repudiates assimilation on the one hand, and is not content with mere toleration or cultural autonomy on the other. The principal and ultimate objective of such a minority is to achieve political as well as cultural independence from the dominant group. If such a group has had statehood at an earlier period in its career, the demand for recognition of its national sovereignty may be based upon the cultivation among its members of the romantic sentiments associated—even if only in the imagination—with its former freedom, power and glory. In such a case the minority's cultural monuments and survivals, its language, lore, literature, and ceremonial institutions, no matter how archaic or reminiscent of the epoch of the group's independence, are revivified and built up into moving symbols of national grandeur.
>
> The Irish, Czech, Polish, Lithuanian, Esthonian, Latvian and Finnish nationalistic movements culminating in the achievement of independent statehood at the end of the first World War were examples of secessionist minority groups. The case of the Jews may also be used to illustrate this type of minority. Zionism in its political, as distinquished from its cultural variety, has acquired considerable support as a result of the resurgence of organized anti-Semitic movements. (Wirth 1945:361).

According to Wirth, "The protest against the dominant group, however, does not always take the form of separatism and secessionism. It may, under certain circumstances express itself in movements to get out from under the yoke of a dominant group in order to join a group with whom there exists a closer historical and cultural affinity. This is particularly true of minorities located near national frontiers" (Wirth 1945:361–362).

Here again Wirth has in mind a number of ethnic enclaves near national boundaries in Europe such as the Sudetenland in Czecho-slovakia, Alsace, and Lorraine which was lost to the Germans in 1871 and which constantly retained a longing to be rejoined with France. According to Wirth, "And when these same provinces were lost to Germany at the end of the first World War, a similar propaganda wave on the German side was set in motion. When the Nazis came to power and embarked upon their imperialistic adventures they made the 'reunion with the Fatherland' of such territories as the Saar, Alsace, Lorraine, Eupen-et-Malmédy, Sudetenland and the Danzig Corridor an object of frenzied agitation" (Wirth 1945:362).

For Wirth, the goal of the fourth type of minority, the militant, "reaches far beyond toleration, assimilation and even cultural and political autonomy. The militant minority has set domination over others as its goal. Far from suffering from feelings of inferiority, it is convinced of its own superiority and inspired by the lust for conquest. While the initial claims of minority movements are generally modest, like all accessions of power, they feed upon their own success and often culminate in delusions of grandeur" (Wirth 1945:362–363). Here again, Wirth's examples are in Europe. He mentions the push of the Sudetenland Germans not only to alter their minority status in Czechoslovakia but also to assume control over the country itself. He also alludes to the Hindu majority under British domination which sought to take over power in India and dominate the country as well as the Moslems. It is quite apparent, however, that his militant label has much more applicability to what has happened in colonial situations such as the overthrow of the French in Algeria, British in Nigeria and Kenya, and so on.

Wirth comments further on the value of his typology. "The justification for singling out the four types of minorities described above for special delineation lies in the fact that each of them exhibits a characteristic set of collective goals among historical and contemporary minority groups and a corresponding set of motives activating the conduct of its members. These four types point to significant differences between actual minority movements" (Wirth 1945: 363–364). However, Wirth cannot resist the temptation to convert this typology into a statement of temporal sequence for he feels that his various types may also mark the successive stages in the life cycle of minorities generally.

The initial goal of an emerging minority group, as it becomes aware of its ethnic identity, is to seek toleration for its cultural differences. By virtue of this striving it constitutes a pluralistic minority. If sufficient toleration and autonomy is attained the pluralistic minority advances to the assimilationist stage, characterized by the desire for acceptance by and incorporation into the dominant group. Frustration of this desire for full participation is likely to produce (1) secessionist tendencies which may take the form either of the complete separation from the dominant group and the establishment of sovereign nationhood, or (2) the drive to become incorporated into another state with which there exists close cultural or historical identification. Progress in either of these directions may in turn lead to the goal of domination over others and the resort to militant methods of achieving that objective. If this goal is actually reached the group sheds the distinctive characteristics of a minority.

For our purposes, however, the value of Wirth's contribution is not in its description of a cycle of inevitable occurrences, for serious questions can be raised about the adequacy of his typology as a statement of the natural history of minority groups. Instead it provides us with a heuristic device for examining different kinds of minority situations according to the collective goals of these minorities.

Simpson and Yinger: policies of the dominant society

Standing between the minority group and the achievement of its goals are the power and policies of the dominant society which may actively support, oppose, or be indifferent to the attainment of these goals. Which option the policy pursues varies significantly with the country, the specific minority group, and time and place. Simpson and Yinger have constructed a typology of these varying policy situations. However, they do not consider these types as merely expressing official or governmental policies; they also view them as describing a "normative model" that members of the dominant society feel should govern relations between society and its minority groups. "Some are conscious long-run plans; some are *ad hoc* adjustments to specific situations; some are the by-products (perhaps unintended) of other policies. In some instances they are the official actions of majority-group leaders; in others they are the day-by-day responses of individual members of the dominant group" (Simpson and Yinger 1965:25).

In addition, Simpson and Yinger assert that several such policy models may be present and practiced at the same time in the dominant society though only one may be the primary model. They distinguish six types of dominant group policies; most of them are mirror images of the types of minority group goals which we have just discussed, though in a given society, societal policy and minority goal need not correspond.

The first type of policy is assimilation. Many societies, according to Simpson and Yinger, seek to encourage the disappearance of the ethnic minority as a distinctive group, they seek to absorb its members into the larger society. However, the way this is done varies significantly. Some societies, such as czarist Russia and Nazi Germany, sought to accomplish this through brutal and coercive means; they denied minorities "the right to practice their own religion, speak their own language, follow their own customs." In other words, they resorted to forced assimilation (Simpson and Yinger 1965:20). Other societies have pursued a more peaceful course. They have fostered acculturation, promoted legal and normative models of equalitarianism, dangled the rewards of power and privilege for those who assimilated, and in general created an atmosphere that everyone benefits if the minority group gives up its distinctive ways and identity. Such an atmosphere is obviously attractive for the minority group whose goal is assimilation; it creates problems for the minority group that seeks to maintain its identity. Further even the minority that accepts the dominant society's "offer" finds the road to acceptance difficult and some barriers almost insurmountable to breach. Examples of such a relatively benign assimilationist environment are to be found in Brazil's treatment of virtually all of its minorities and in the United States treatment of its national and religious minorities though not of its racial minorities.

The second type of policy is pluralism. A number of societies are willing to grant the right to an ethnic group to exist as a distinctive entity within its borders; they vary though according to the extent to which they permit the ethnic minority to pursue its own distinctive way of life. Invariably there are limits beyond which the dominant society will not allow the ethnic minority to go in developing its own way: particularly in the area of self-government and self-policing.

Beyond the common denominator of legitimating the right of the distinctive ethnic minority to exist, pluralistic policies also vary according to the extent to which they allow the minority to gain access to significant sources of power and privilege in the larger society. These policies range between two extremes: those that seek to perpetuate a given stage of subjugation of the minority to those that insure equality, acceptance, and full membership in society of the racial or ethnic group in all its distinctiveness. Examples of the former are easy to find: caste, colonial, and Furnivall's plural societies; the latter are easier to find in theory than in practice. Examples of such theoretical statements would be the constitution of the Soviet Union, the American ideology of cultural pluralism. In practice, perhaps Switzerland—if we exclude its treatment of "guest workers"— comes closest to the "ideal"; its French, German, and Italian enclaves seem to enjoy a political and economic equality as well as harmonious relations. Other countries fall in between; their pluralistic policies reflect neither a state of complete inequality nor complete equality between the ethnic segments. The actual situation as in the case of Central Europe, Soviet Union, United States, and others depends in large measure upon the "negotiating" strength of the ethnic minority itself.

A third type of policy is legal protection of minorities. Simpson and

Yinger consider this policy as "closely related to pluralism, or a subdivision of it" (Simpson and Yinger 1965:23). Certainly such a policy is a necessary condition for the formulation of any kind of a pluralistic policy by the dominant society. But a policy of legal protection is also a necessary condition for the fulfillment of assimilationist policies in a society as well. It provides access to the legal and political systems of society for immigrants whose initial entry into the society is that of culturally and institutionally distinctive aliens.

In effect, the policy of legal protection is the cornerstone for both pluralistic and assimilationist policies of the dominant society. It operates from the basic premise that despite racial or ethnic variations, all persons within the political boundaries of the nation share that characteristic in common and therefore have the right to be certified as legitimate members of that body politic through gaining access to citizenship, to equal treatment before the law and courts, and even to the voting franchise.

The fourth major policy is that of population transfer. Throughout history dominant societies have periodically sought to deal with their minority problems by relocating the minority within the nation. When this happens, it is likely to involve minorities in border regions whose national loyalties are viewed as dubious by the dominant society. At other times the dominant society has expelled these minorities from the nation itself. On occasion these transfers have been peaceful, particularly if they correspond to the secessionist aspirations of the minority group itself as happened in the relatively successful exchange of minorities among Greece, Turkey, and Bulgaria in the early 1920s.

Much more frequently population transfer has been forced upon the minority group which has literally been pushed out of the place it wanted to stay. As such these transfers express hostility and discrimination on the part of the dominant society. As Simpson and Yinger comment

> the transfer can be of two types—direct and indirect. In the former, the minority involved is specifically required and forced to leave. Many nations and cities drove out Jews in the late medieval period; the United States drove the Indians out of area after area; the British kept the Irish beyond the Pale; the Soviet Union deported millions of her citizens, members of religious and national minorities, during World War II; and Nazi Germany followed a relentless policy that sought for a homogenous nation by forcibly transferring large numbers of persons of many minorities. The indirect policy is to make life so unbearable for members of the minority that they "choose" to migrate. Thus czarist Russia drove out millions of Jews. This was also part of Germany's policy (Simpson and Yinger 1965:24).

The fifth policy is continued subjugation. Such a policy obviously becomes the driving force in those societies that are literally based on the exploitation of racial and ethnic minorities as in colonial societies, South Africa, and even in America in its treatment of the blacks. The major differences between such societies is the extent to which coercion and force is an essential ingredient in maintaining the subservience of the exploited group. At the one extreme are the plural colonial societies of Furnivall and Rex where coercive compliance is their central feature. At the other extreme is the caste system, such as in India, where the subservient groups presumably accept their low status. In other societies discriminatory policies also play a significant role, but these become subject to challenge as the minority groups gain strength.

Oppressive and brutal as the policy of continued subjugation may be its coercive character is limited by the fact that the dominant society "needs" the services of the exploited group. This no longer applies to the sixth type of policy: extermination. As Simpson and Yinger state, "Conflict between groups sometimes becomes so severe that physical destruction of one by the other becomes an accepted goal. This may have been true of some ancient tribal contacts; modern history gives many examples. The United States destroyed perhaps two-thirds of the Indian population before her policy changed. The small Tasmanian population was completely wiped out by the British (and by the civilized diseases that they brought to the island). The Boers of South Africa looked upon the Hottentots as scarcely more than animals of the jungle and hunted them ruthlessly. And Germany, between 1933 and 1945, murdered six million people" (Simpson and Yinger 1965:25).

Reconceptualizing the Typologies

The parallelism between the types of minority group goals that Wirth identifies and the majority group policies of Simpson and Yinger is too obvious to require much comment. Both specifically include assimilationist and pluralist categories. Both also include categories that reflect willful withdrawal from the other, such as Wirth's secessionist type and Simpson and Yinger's population transfer. In addition, there are categories built around the continuing exercise of force such as continued subjugation for Simpson and Yinger and militancy for Wirth. Only the categories of extermination and legal protection of minorities from Simpson and Yinger find no exact counterpart in Wirth. However, as we have already mentioned the latter functions as a basic ingredient in both the assimilationist and pluralist approach.

Beyond their manifest content, however, it is evident that these two typologies are constructed in large measure from two different sets of variables: each set describes a different kind of actual or potential relation between the minority and the dominant society. The more obvious of the two can be called the "dominance-equality" set. Wirth and Simpson and Yinger are fully aware that in many societies racial and ethnic minorities occupy the lowest rung of the stratificational structure; they are powerless, propertyless, and without prestige. Simpson and Yinger recognize that the dominant group in a society frequently seeks to perpetuate this state of affairs as in slavery, colonialism, etc. It therefore promotes policies to keep ethnic minorities relatively powerless and in a state of marked subjugation or to render them helpless either by removing them physically from the scene or from life itself. Such policies serve to define what may be called the situation of maximal subordination for a minority.

However, other policies that Simpson and Yinger allude to are not predicated on subjugation of the minority; instead they express a toleration of and even a granting of various rights to the minority. Such policies may lessen though not completely eliminate the disabilities under which a minority may function in society. Several types of policies—such as assimilation and pluralism— may even go beyond that and provide recognition for full acceptance and equality. Whether such policies do indeed lead to that becomes a matter of empirical fact, but at the least the potential is there.

No such ambiguities characterize Wirth's typology of minority goals and aspirations. It rejects a subordinated status and envisions at the least some future state of equality for the minority group. (One of his types goes even further and would substitute a dominant for a subordinate position for the minority.) Thus, equality is the underlying premise of the various group goals that Wirth describes. What distinguishes the goals of the minorities is the character of the equality to which they aspire. At the one extreme is the kind of equality that would lead to full membership, acceptance, and absorption by the host society (assimilation). At the other extreme would be literal independence from the dominant society in the form of secession and independent nationhood. In between would be some type of pluralism; the minority would remain within the framework of the larger society but as a distinctive entity. Wirth, however, fails to distinguish clearly between various forms of pluralism. For example, the kind of pluralism that Furnivall and Smith talk about in reference to the plural society is obviously quite different from the kind of pluralism that Gordon (1964) and Kallen (1924) talk about in referring to the American society. It is evident that the former involves a much greater isolation and divorce from institutions and life of the larger society than does the latter. For want of a better way of saying it, we can label the former pluralistic autonomy (van den Berghe calls it social pluralism) and the latter integrative pluralism (Gordon (1964) and Kallen (1924) call it cultural pluralism).

Thus, we have been able to identify four types of equality toward which minority groups aspire; they differ according to the degree to which the minority group seeks association with or separation from the dominant society. This is illustrated in the following diagram:

Secession (independent nationhood)	Pluralistic Autonomy	Integrative Pluralism	Assimilation

← Dissociation from larger society   Association with larger society →

Accordingly we find that the second variable around which the typologies of Wirth and to a lesser extent of Simpson and Yinger are built is the "associative-dissociative" character of the actual or potential relations between minority group and dominant society.

A third variable is less obvious. Its presence in the typologies is barely revealed; but its significance increases as we shift from a static to dynamic view of relations between minority and dominant society. For example, Simpson and Yinger indicate that some policies, such as forced assimilation, continued subjugation, and population transfer, may require the exercise of coercion by the dominant society for their implementation; others may be implemented through peaceful means. Wirth does not particularly dwell on the employment of peaceful or forceful means by the minority group in the achievement of its goals, although he does identify the militant minority as one of his types. He leaves unspecified how the minority will attain its goal, but he does expect them to try, thereby challenging their present status. Thus the stage may be set for a struggle between minority and dominant society which may be expressed in overt conflict between the two. And yet such a struggle is not inevitable at any given time or place. For the minority may not seek to challenge its subordinated status, and the dominant society may not resort to force. Thus relations between the two may range from relative harmony to open warfare. This then provides the basis for identifying an 'accommodative-confict" component as our third variable.

As we have already seen this variable plays an important role in cyclical theories of race relations; it presumably describes a basic process that supposedly has the following almost invariable sequence. From an initial stage of conflict and competition relations between groups eventually move to a stage of harmony and accommodation. Several theorists, most notably Park, go so far as to combine in their cyclical theory this variable with the 'associative-dissociative" variable we discussed above. As such they view the final outcome as not only culminating in harmonious relations between minority members and society but also as resulting in the complete amalgamation of the minority group with the larger society.

Our contention is that accommodative and conflictual tendencies are neither irreversible nor inextricably tied up with only one kind of normative or structural outcome. Instead we view them as problematic features in time and space of relations between groups whether these groups are pursuing separatist or amalgamative goals and policies or whether they stand in positions of marked inequality or near equality to each other.

Obviously the incidence and balance of these accommodative and conflictual tendencies can be expected to vary significantly in different societal contexts. As we have already noted, theorists of the colonial situation emphasize the coercive and conflictual character of minority and dominant group relations. Theorists of the American scene have tended to emphasize the assimilative and accommodative tendencies. And yet in each, contrary tendencies can and do occur at various levels and at different times.

For example, even under the colonial system, castelike paternalistic relations may develop between the lowest racial strata and their overlords which mitigate the coercive and exploitative character of the system. In time, such accommodative relations may break down between certain strata of the subjugated population; they may be renewed or take a new mode of expression among others. In like manner in America, the relatively quiescent state of relations between the new and impoverished European immigrant and the dominant society has in the past often given way to conflict and stress as the immigrant has sought to challenge his subordinated status and to move up; this pattern may continue to be repeated at various levels and situations. In effect the history of relations between minority and dominant groups has been a history of shifting balances of accommodative and conflictual tendencies as these relations become subject to change and to challenge.

Now that we have identified three basic variables that have been explicitly or implicitly used to construct the various typologies and cycles, let us see if we can put them together into a general temporal-spatial framework which would prove useful in examining a variety of ethnic and racial situations. Let us assume that we are dealing with a racial or ethnic minority that enters the societal system at its bottom rung. It may have arrived there through voluntary immigration as in the case of the European immigrant in America, through involuntary migration as in the case of the black slave, or even through being subjugated within its own territory as in the colonial situation. At this juncture it occupies a situation of maximal subordination which can be represented by a vertical line with the dominant group at the top and the racial or ethnic minority at the bottom.

```
         D
         |
         S
```

Even at this juncture, relations between the two do not operate in a vacuum. They become increasingly surrounded by a normative environment comprised primarily of policies and expectations of the dominant group as to how the minority should behave and what its future may be like. In the case of the colonial situation such a view of life may focus primarily on continued subjugation of the minority; in the competitive class society, it may incude eventual assimilation. Whichever the emphasis, relations between the two tend to be incorporated within a system of what should be as well as what is.

Either at this junction or later, most minorities contribute to this normative environment by spelling out their own view of the future. Some may be resigned to their station in life and see the future in some worldly release. Many others may aspire to a better position for themselves in this world. And as we have already seen through Wirth's typology this version of the future describes either explicitly or implicitly a future state of equality. This goal can be represented by a horizontal line which touches the vertical line at mid point . . .

```
                        D
E _____|_____ E
                        |
                        |
                        |
                        |
                        |
                        S
```

The history of many minorities is told in their efforts to move from the vertical axis of subordination toward the horizontal axis of equality. The direction of their movement though varies. Some view the future in terms of becoming one with the dominant society and as such their movement is toward greater incorporation within the society. Others view the future as involving greater and greater separation from the dominant society. These opposing tendencies can be illustrated in the diagram by labeling the horizontal axis to the right of the vertical axis as toward association with the society; the one to the left as greater dissociation from society;

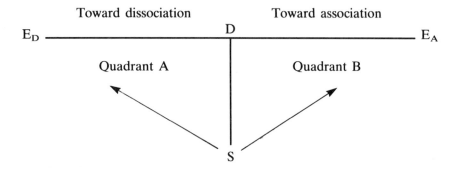

In this manner, we are able to represent diagrammatically two of the major variables in the various typologies. For the sake of convenience we can label the area bounded by the vertical axis and the horizontal axis to its left as Quadrant A; the other area as Quadrant B. Each area represents the spatial distance that the minority must travel to reach its version of equality.

Traversing this distance involves the minority in some sort of struggle with the dominant society. As we shall see, the intensity and scope of this struggle varies with the quadrant in which it takes place. Just as conflict and strain are built-in features of the struggle, so should it be recognized are certain accommodative tendencies. For example, relations between minority and dominant society may become stabilized somewhere between equality and subordination in either quadrant and these may be accompanied by live-and-let-live policies.

The minority may accept something less than full equality in exchange for tolerance of its differences. Such a state of affairs may even characterize the position of the minority at the point of maximal subordination. Van den Berghe describes a castelike etiquette that may unfold which regularizes and "normalizes" relations. Thus "accommodative-conflict" tendencies become problematic features at the various stages of these relations.

It is evident though from our earlier discussions of the various theorists that certain societal situations are more likely to be characterized by one or the other tendencies. We can now locate these societies within the context of our diagram. For example, Furnivall, Smith, Rex, and Brown's discussions of the colonial societies clearly belong in Quadrant A. Such societies are clearly built on racial segmentation. The racial groups live almost exclusively in their own enclaves and have at best only tenuous relations with the larger society. These arrangements though may become stabilized into a castelike structure and reflect relatively peaceful accommodation and harmony. More frequently, the coercive character of the system become evident and the repressive machinery of the dominant group keeps the system in a state of tension and strain. Should the minority seek to challenge its status, the struggle frequently takes on a nationalistic and politically revolutionary character as it finds its path blocked by the resistance of the ruling group. In effect, such societies have a chronic state of tension built into them unless they are able to stabilize into secure castelike structures.

Other examples of Quadrant A would be many of the pluralistic arrangements in Europe and the Ottoman Empire. The dominant societies' policies of legal protection of the rights of minorities provided an environment in which plural communities could survive, though not as equals. As such accommodative arrangements would develop, particularly if they were part of a set of symbiotic relations between the various racial-ethnic groups. But even in this setting, tension and conflict would erupt along the boundaries of the groups; and more frequently than not a sense of armed truce prevails.

Gordon and Lieberson's description of the assimilative character of the American society, particularly as experienced by the European immigrant, belongs in Quadrant B. In their view, movement out of the lowest rungs is facilitated by an acculturative process that brings the ethnic minority into closer union with the larger society, by a normative environment that supports such a movement, and by channels of upward mobility which ostensibly reward individual merit and achievement through impersonal mechanisms of evaluation. As such the appearance is that of a harmoniously functioning system which results in peaceful amalgamation of its minorities.

What is missing from such a portrayal is frank recognition that struggle, conflict, and stress have been integral parts of the experience of European immigrants in America as they have sought to move out of their subordinate status. At each step important segments of the dominant society have resisted their challenge, despite the presence of a normative environment that seems to have supported their challenge. Again, a balance of conflictual and accommodative tendencies are to be found, but this time the normative and institutional environment may lend itself to a more peaceful accommodation of the struggle than is true of Quadrant A.

Thus far we have implicitly assumed the compatibility in minority group goals and dominant society policies in our discusssion for Quadrant A and B. Obviously, the potential for conflict increases where these diverge, as for example, a secessionistically inclined minority or even a pluralistically inclined one within an assimilatively inclined dominant society. Or a pluralistically inclined minority intent upon equality or becoming dominant in a plural society that may tolerate differences but not permit equality.

To complicate matters still more, the same group may simultaneously hold incompatible goals and policies. For example, the American society—long the purveyor of an assimilative policy—has had recently to come to terms with a pluralistic approach to white ethnic groups. In addition, for much of America's history the dominant society has sought to exclude racial minorities from being assimilated into its people's domain. Instead it has treated them as though they were segments of a plural society and objects of continued subjugation.

7 The New Nation and the Black Encounter with Its Duality

When it comes to examining the experience and treatment of racial minorities in the United States, it is apparent from text in Chapter 5 that the three-variable set of Chapter 6 cannot be applied simply and readily.

Whereas it can be argued that the experience of white immigrants falls exclusively in Quadrant B, that of racial minorities is quite different. The duality that confronts them as elaborated in Chapter 5 makes their experience and treatment overlap both Quadrants A and B. Historically the dominant society has sought to exclude them from Quadrant B and its people's domain, but in time constitutional and statutory pressures were brought to bear to allow them to gain access. In turn, the response of the racial minorities has also been mixed. The quest for entry into and for acceptance and equality in Quadrant B has also been countered by a drive for separaton and by the nationalistic aspirations of Quadrant A.

We have already analyzed how the dual character of the dominant society's treatment of racial minorities, specifically blacks and Indians, was imprinted in the formation of the United States and its Constitution. In the next two chapters we shall examine how this duality was reaffirmed throughout much of the subsequent history of America. We shall in this chapter study its effects on the blacks from the period of the Constitution onward; in the next chapter we shall analyze its effects on the immigrants from Asia and Puerto Rico.

From Slavery to the First Period of Reconstruction

Nowhere and at no time in American history was the Manichean dualism that was sanctified and stabilized by the Constitution more in evidence than in the antebellum South. On the one side stood a fully elaborated plural societal structure whose racial segmentation was built on slavery, organized around the plantation, and governed by black codes and a racial creed. On the other side stood the people's domain whose sovereignty was guaranteed by the supreme law of the land under a creed derived from the Declaration of Independence but whose rights and immunities applied to whites only. The linchpin between the two structures was a planter elite who dominated both and who also succeeded in clamping its values and interests on the two. Thus white supremacy and control came to be the leitmotif not only of the plural structure but of the people's domain as well. In this manner the fates of the two systems were seen as inextricably linked: survival of the one required survival of the other.

In the North, slavery had been disavowed by the early nineteenth century, but its heritage of black subordination and inferiority indelibly stamped the plural edifice of racial segmentation, discrimination, and exclusion that was then justified on more purely racial and racist grounds. This edifice, though, never attained the closure of the plural structure of the South. As a result, blacks were not as completely locked out of the people's domain of the North as the enslaved blacks were in the South; they were able to drive a slim wedge into the domain even though most whites treated them as intruders who did not belong in the company of the people.

America's first major confrontation with its duality occurred during the first period of Reconstruction following the Civil War. With the enactment of the Thirteenth, Fourteenth, Fifteenth Amendments and of other reconstruction legislaton, America seemed to be reshaping its duality into a single domain of the people in which the blacks would gain full rights of access and membership.

The Dual Plural Societies: Jim Crowism in the South and Racial Segmentation in the North

This effort collapsed in what is called the first period of Redemption, and by the turn of the twentieth century a new version of a racially segmented plural society was constructed in the South that stamped black-white relations for the next half century. This version was built on legal and institutional grounds that differed significantly from those of the older slavery version. And it required a series of decisions by the Supreme Court to reconcile these grounds with the great Reconstruction Amendments and to establish thereby the legitimacy of the new plural society.

For example, in its *Plessy-Ferguson* decision of 1896, the Court carved out of the domain of the people a large institutional area of behavior and practice in which the guarantees of the Constitution and the American creed no longer automatically applied and a smaller institutional area in which they did. It identified the former as the realm of the "social"; and the latter, as the realm of the legal-political. The Court however did more than create a legal vacuum for the social realm. It accepted as constitutional the doctrine of "separate but equal" and accorded local and state governments the right to enact statutes in this realm which legalized and enforced the racial cleavages and discriminatory practices of the community. In this manner the Supreme Court virtually neutralized the effects of the Fourteenth Amendment and incorporated into the supreme law of the land the principle of racial differences and separation as a legitimate basis for the enactment of state legislation and for the perpetuation of customary practices in the private and social realms of the community.

By accepting the principle of racial difference and "social inequality" as part of the supreme law of the people's domain, the Supreme Court in effect endowed the racial beliefs of the white man with a respectability and legitimacy that they did not have before. During the period of radical Reconstruction, only the American creed served as the basis for the legal-normative code of the people's domain. Racial beliefs were popularly expressed and widely held, but as Myrdal maintains they were transmuted into presumptive statements of fact and were not part of the legal-normative code of the people (Myrdal 1944). Even prior to Reconstruction, the American creed was the sole basis for the legal-normative code of the people; the racial beliefs and values that were expressed in law and through decisions of the Supreme Court applied to a category of beings who were excluded from the domain of the people and treated as chattels or nonpersons subject to the authority of the state. The language of the *Dred Scott* decision indicated that the blacks were viewed as inferior beings close to savagery and in need of the "protecton" of the whites. This judicial legitimation of racist beliefs reinforced the conception of the black as unfit for citizenship and therefore ineligible to receive the privileges and immunities of the American creed. Thus the racist creed was viewed as dealing with a lower order of beings; and the American creed, with a higher order of people in the American society.

The relegitimation of the racial creed during the post-Reconstruction period was different for it now applied to blacks who had gained membership in the higher order of the people and who were presumably to be governed as were the whites by the tenets of the American creed. Thus, the new racial doctrine, which was a thinly disguised version of the old racial creed, gained a level of respectability that it had not had before. Supported by the legal and moral authority of the Supreme Court and Constitution, it became a part of the legal-normative framework of the people and as such could compete on relatively equal terms with the American creed as a guideline for policies on and treatment of the "Negro problem."

The history of the American society from the post-Reconstruction period until recently witnessed the dynamic tension between the two creeds, as adherents of each sought to foster and to enact policies and legislation that bore the stamp of their creed. In no instance, however, was either able to eradicate completely the presence of the opposing principle.

In the South, for example, the racial creed gained preeminence during this period, for most southern states quickly realized the significance of the Supreme Court decisions. They sought to extend the social realm into as many reaches of society as they could so that the racial doctrine of separateness could be applied without breaching the limit defined by the Supreme Court as the realm of the political and legal which was still protected by the American creed. Some states breached this limit frontally and were set back by adverse court rulings. Others discovered bypasses to this realm by such devices as "literacy" and "understanding" clauses which succeeded in once again pushing the blacks out of the people's domain. But these successes proved vulnerable in time as the Supreme Court never quite abandoned the principle which for a period seemed more fictional than real, that the blacks had become part of the people through the Fourteenth and Fifteenth Amendments and that at least in theory their political and legal rights were to be protected by the American creed.

In the North the struggle between the two creeds was much more complex and complicated. On the surface the American creed seemed to be the dominant force as Myrdal implies, but in many ways the racial creed also made its presence felt. Although the whites in the North did not enact the Jim Crow laws of the South, they were also not prepared to accord the blacks full membership in the social realm nor allow them to compete equally with whites for privilege, power, and position in this realm, despite the laws on public accommodation. In fact, they treated the blacks as a pariah group and relied heavily on their control of the social realm for effectively curbing the black as a competitive threat for these resources. They did this in large measure by superimposing the creed of racial differentiation and segmentation on the workings of the allocative machinery in society and thereby reaffirming their historic claim that blacks were unworthy of full and equal membership in the social and economic domain of the people. In short, the whites carved up the marketplace for jobs and residence into plural segments and forced the blacks to compete primarily in those segments of the market which could only lead to inferior jobs and residences, the more desirable segments being more or less for the whites.

What gave legitimacy to the northern whites "pluralization" of the marketplace was the legal framework created by the Supreme Court.

Particularly important were its decisions on *United States v. Cruikshank* in 1876, the civil rights cases in 1883, and *Corrigan v. Buckley* in 1926. Through decisions such as these, the Court provided a protective shield for the kind of de facto plural society that the northern whites had been creating since Reconstruction. The Court, in effect, carved out a private sector from the people's domain in which whites had the right to pursue policies and practices of discrimination and exclusion—both severally and collectively. Thus, blacks could lawfully be kept out of the "private" environments of work and residence of the whites. The Supreme Court even placed the local courts at the disposal of the whites to enforce their various private exclusionary agreements, such as restrictive covenants.

The mass movement of blacks northward during and after World War I solidified this plural structure. And with the hardening of the dual structures in the North and South an atmosphere of fear and tension was generated between the races. The blacks expressed resentment at the dilution and loss of their rights to and in the people's domain that they had won during Reconstruction. They also balked at the dictates of the reconstituted plural societies with their racial creed. As a result, whites in the South resorted to legal and extralegal repression and "pogromlike" violence to keep blacks in line that exceeded the level reached during slavery. In the North, tension between the races erupted into violence and riots and kept the relations between the two in a chronic state of rawness. However, the increasing separation of the races in places of work and residence minimized direct contact and kept overt conflict within certain bounds.

The Supreme Court and the Delegitimation of the Racial Creed

Reaffirming and extending the rights of blacks in the legal-political realm

Even as the Supreme Court was bestowing legitimacy on the new plural society being constructed in the social realm by the southern states, it was prepared to place limits on what whites could constitutionally do to deprive the blacks of benefits from the Reconstruction Amendments in the legal-political realm of the people's domain. For years, though, these limits were defined by the Court in a very narrow and literal fashion. They were viewed as beng exceeded only if a state passed statutes which explicitly and directly violated the legal and political rights of the black as in the case of *Strauder v. West Virginia* (1880) or if a state approved legislation whose particularistic and discriminatory character was so immediately transparent that its racist purpose could not be disguised, despite claims of universal applicability as in the case of the grandfather clauses.

Only since the third and fourth decades of the twentieth century has the Court been prepared to move more decisively into the thicket of actions by the state which have discriminatory consequences but no professed legislative intent to produce these consequences. For example, the Court's rulings on jury service over the past half century have increasingly eschewed manifest legislative intent and treated as prima facie evidence of state discrimination any continuous history of exclusion or marked underrepresentation of the black. Further, the Court has expressed greater willingness to curb the power of the state in areas which were formerly deemed its sacrosanct bailiwick. Thus in decisions in the white primary cases, the Court not only entered an area of state jurisdiction that it had always treated gingerly but it also extended its rulings to include all elections and primaries and not merely those conducted for federal office.

Even more significantly, the Court extended the scope of state responsibility for eliminating overt and covert discriminatory practices and policies within the legal and political domain. As early as 1880, the Court refused to confine its standard of state responsibility merely to explicit legislative enactments that were discriminatory in character. It also insisted that discriminatory actions of state officials were not to be treated as those of private individuals and citizens which are excluded from constitutional constraint, but were instead to be treated as behaviors of agents of the state and therefore subject to constitutional control.

Years later the Court expanded the concept of agent or agency of the state to include political parties and voluntary associations that had been charged with electoral responsibilities by the state. In this manner, the Court countered effectively the efforts of various states to evade their constitutional responsibilities to blacks in the legal-political realm by transferring some of its functions and activities to the private realm and private organizations that are free from such constitutional constraints. In the process, the Court sharpened the distinction between private and state spheres of action while broadening the concept of state accountability.

Yet, despite the increased resolve of the Supreme Court during the 1940s, its decisions were of a patchwork nature and only of limited effect, particularly in the South. They pushed back the more extreme encroachments on the legal and political rights of the blacks, but left virtually untouched the underlying normative base that legitimized the unequal treatment of blacks and anchored them to an inferior and subordinated status. In other words, even as the Court was seeking to apply nondiscriminatory and universal standards in the legal-political domain, it still accepted as the law of the land racial segmentation in the other major institutional environments of the social realm. As a result, the Court could not treat decisively or even effectively with the massive and continuing flow of racial inequities in the legal-political domain as long as it was not prepared to root out their generating sources in the social realm.

Desegregating the social realm

Having adopted in 1896 the Plessy-Ferguson Doctrine as the law of the land, the Supreme Court, in effect, provided whites, particularly in the South, with a legal-normative foundation and scaffolding for legitimizing their racial creed and for constructing a plural society in which races were to be kept apart in the various institutional environments of the social realm. And yet in promulgating the doctrine, the Supreme Court attached an important condition: the segmentation of the social realm must be based on equal availability of public resources and facilities to each race. For the next half century, though, the whites in the South conveniently ignored the *equal* part of the "separate but equal" doctrine and concentrated all their energies on the *separation* of the races. Even the Supreme Court seemed more intent in the first several decades after the decision on reaffirming and amplifying the principle of racial separation; it paid little attention to the question of equal facilities

By the late 1930s and early 1940s the Court began to probe into the equal part of the doctrine and let it be known that failure of the state to meet the standard of equity could serve as grounds for the Court's breaching the walls of separateness. And in a series of decisions over more than a decade, it required the admission of black students into white law schools in Missouri and Texas and into a graduate school of education in Oklahoma. Over the period the Court moved from focusing on the tangible facets of equality to the more intangible, such as reputation of school and faculty, but it continued to refuse to question directly the separate part of the Plessy-Ferguson principle.

The final assault on the "separate but equal" doctrine came in 1954 when Chief Justice Warren speaking for a unanimous Court declared that separate was inherently unequal and therefore the Plessy-Ferguson principle as it applied to the school cases before it was unconstitutional. With this *Brown* decision, the Court shook the foundations of the "Jim Crow" plural society in the South and began the rapid process of stripping the racial creed of its constitutional mantle. The *Brown* ruling soon became the touchstone for a series of other court decisions that extended the delegitimation of the racial creed and of state-imposed racial segmentation to all the major institutional environments of the social realm from public transportation to public recreation.

In addition, the Court completed with its *Brown* decision what it had started with its *Shelley v. Kraemer* decision in 1948. It withdrew the machinery of government and of the state from support of the private sphere of discrimination. By driving an ever expanding wedge between the two, the Court deprived the private sphere of discrimination of access to courts and instruments of legal coercion and police control that it had been able to rely upon in the past. The full significance of this became evident in the "sit-in cases" that flooded the courts of the South in the early 1960s.

The Resurgent Plural Society and the White Southerner

The reaction of the southern white to the *Brown* decision was quick, intense, and widespread. While officials in some border states took almost immediate steps to comply at least in part with the desegregation ruling, most other white southerners, particularly in the Deep South— from elected state and local government officials to private citizens— expressed their determination to resist and to defeat the court ruling.

The stage was, accordingly, set for the first serious confrontation over the racial issue between the two sovereignties—state and federal—since the Civil War and Reconstruction. Each sovereignty represented more clearly than ever a different facet of the duality America had precariously balanced for much of its history. The state governments of the Deep South championed a plural society and its racial creed; the federal government through its agency, the Supreme Court, championed the people's domain and the American creed.

The confrontation grew in scope and intensity for more than a decade as the court extended its delegitimation of the racial creed into the various institutional recesses of the social realm and into the deeper reaches of the South. The southern whites, in turn, mounted massive resistance along a broad front. They denounced the Supreme Court for its alleged usurpation of power and for its betrayal of the Founding Fathers' vision of a dual society. Accordingly, they resurrected the doctrines of interposition and nullification, but not to the extent of threatening actual secession from the Union as they had in fact done one hundred years before. The Little Rock encounter convinced many that none of the southern states, alone or in unison, could match the force that the federal government could bring to bear if it so wished. But Little Rock also convinced them that the executive was in league with the judicial branch of the federal government in persecuting them. Legislature after legislature censured the president; the Georgia legislature, for example, condemned him for "his arbitrary and illegal action unprecedented in the annals of history" (Race Relations Law Reporter April 1958:357). The Florida legislature decried the "brute force" and the "high handed tactics reminiscent of Hitler's storm troopers" that the citizenry of the South were being subjected to (Race Relations Law Reporter December 1957:1172).

Convinced therefore that the federal government had abandoned the rule of constitutional law, the white southerners believed that they were the sole defenders of the faith. Self-righteously they defied the Supreme Court's edicts, breathed fresh life into their plural society and remolded it deliberately in the image of the golden age of the Confederacy. Phoenixlike, the symbols and rhetoric of the antebellum days blossomed. Almost over night the present had become the legendary past in which black and white presumably lived in contentment and harmony.

Throughout this period of consolidation, white southerners reassured themselves that their struggle was entirely with forces and enemies external to their society: the Supreme Court, the presidency, NAACP, northern blacks, and white liberals. They were confident that most southern blacks were not part of this cabal. They firmly believed that these blacks were still content with their lot and still accepted the basic values of the plural society. Consequently the whites justified much of their counteraction to *Brown* as an effort to restore the racial tranquility and harmony of the past and to prevent contamination of the "innocent" southern blacks from outside agitation. Even as the southern blacks began to stir against the reinforced and renewed constraints of the plural society, southern whites persisted in the myth of the outsider and only belatedly realized that southern blacks had become the energizing source for the assault on the plural society.

Dr. King and the "Black Revolution" in the South

In 1955 the southern blacks made their collective presence felt for the first time in the boycott of segregated buses they successfully conducted in Montgomery, Alabama. This prologue to the civil rights drama that was soon to unfold brought to the fore Dr. Martin Luther King, Jr. Under his charismatic leadership a "hammer-anvil" strategy was forged in the crucible of protest. It was based on the premise that black pressure alone was no match for the consolidated strength of southern white resistance just as the Supreme Court alone also proved no match for this resistance in the Deep South in the years immediately following the *Brown* decision. Together, it was felt, some dent could be made in the wall of white resistance in the Deep South.

As the civil rights movement spread and pressure was stepped up, including sit-ins against the Deep South citadel of the resurgent plural society, it became increasingly evident that even with the support of the Supreme Court no more than modest wedges could be driven into the wall of resistance and no more than local victories—spectacular though some might be—could be won. What was needed was the full measure of federal authority, not merely of its judicial branch.

Accordingly the hammer-anvil strategy was revamped' and spelled out in even more sweeping and bolder terms than before. The legal-institutional fabric of the resurgent plural society had to be forced against the anvil of federal authority generally by a hammer whose toughness and strength would be tempered through the heat of increased demonstrations by the blacks and also through the forging of a national coalition with the northern white liberals.

Birmingham proved to be the turning point. It galvanized the formation of the coalition which peaked a year later in the march on Washington and brought President Kennedy more actively into the fray. The extent to which he had shed his role as neutral spectator was revealed several weeks later in his confrontation with the governor of Alabama over a court order to admit two black students to the state university. The president overwhelmed the governor's defiance of the order through a show of federal force. That night he also delivered before a nationwide television audience his most dramatic and far ranging attack on racial injustice, segregation, and discrimination and committed himself openly to strong and comprehensive legislation on civil rights. One week later he spelled out his legislative proposals in a special message to Congress and reaffirmed his determination to see the matter through. Thus was the omnibus civil rights act of 1964 truly born; ironically Kennedy's own death provided the final impetus for its early passage in 1964.

Somewhat more than a year later President Johnson was himself caught in the middle of a voter registration drive begun by Dr. King in Selma, Alabama. Johnson intervened personally as the brutality and violence of the police elicited cries of indignation throughout the nation. A week later the president announced at a televised news conference that he would submit a voting rights bill to Congress that would have the teeth absent from all earlier voting rights laws. He also provided troop protection for the celebrated second march from Selma to Montgomery. Thus, the passage of the two most important civil rights acts of the twentieth century can be directly linked to the pressures of the civil rights movement and its interracial coalition and to a nationwide revulsion against the legally constituted authority in the Deep South. The hammer-anvil strategy had finally succeeded and had broken the back of the resurgent plural society in the South.

These laws plus the Fair Housing Act of 1968 completed the delegitimization of the racial creed and the dismantling of the lawful basis for America's duality that had begun with the Supreme Court's *Brown* decision of 1954. They mandated that all the major institutional environments of the people's domain were to be governed under a common legal-normative framework based on nondiscrimination and equality of access and opportunity. Thus, the normative task begun in the first period of Reconstruction seemed finally to have come to fruition almost one hundred years later.

The De Facto Plural Society in the North: Black Militance and the Colonial Analogy

Even as these laws were being enacted, the fuse that Dr. King had lighted in Birmingham detonated explosions in cities of the West and North as increasing numbers of blacks began to take to the streets in spontaneous protests. Within a few years the full fury of these riots and disturbances sent shock waves that disrupted the civic and the political fabric of the American society. They stripped away the optimism of the liberal and the veneer of racial equality with which the legal codes of many of the states in these regions had just been coated. They laid bare the ossified structure of racial segmentation and white dominance that had long been embedded in the major institutional environments of the social realm. This northern version of a plural society had frozen most blacks to the bottom of the occupational ladder and had confined them to the black ghettos in slum areas. Long nourished and legitimized by the racial creed, "separate but equal" and "private sector" doctrines of the Supreme Court, the plural structure had lost its quasi de jure status by the mid-1960s with the delegitimation of the creed and doctrine in 1954 and with the passage of state laws on nondiscrimination and racial equality, but it still seemed as viable as ever as a de facto plural system of racial segmentation and inequality.

The urban riots, however, did more than make visible the underlying de facto plural structure; they also energized, politicized, and radicalized the ensuing black challenge to this structure. In this manner a political rhetoric was articulated by the more militant of the black leaders. Its ideological themes were black nationalism, black separatism, and black power. Its axiomatic foundation was the premise that blacks had never had and never would have the benefits and protection of the American creed, Declaration of Independence, or Constitution. As a result they were doomed to be perpetual victims of dehumanizing racism and to continued exploitation as a subordinated and segmented racial group in white America.

These ideologists then likened the fate of blacks and other nonwhite minorities in America to the colonialized people of the Third World who had been subjugated by the whites but had never accepted the legitimacy of their subjugation. In sum, the colonial analogy surfaced in the ideological heat of the 1960s as the rallying cry for Malcolm X, Carmichael, and the Black Panthers. The analogy also caught the imagination and attention of some scholars such as Blauner, Allen, and Tabb who sought to apply it to a reexamination of the black experience in America, thereby bestowing upon it a respectability it lacked while still a product of the streets. From the ferment of the 1960s, then, emerged an alternative perspective and model for viewing the historical encounters of blacks and other nonwhite minorities with the American society.

Any literal application of the analogy to the American experience exposes basic flaws and inadequacies in the analogy. However, despite these flaws, the proponents of the analogy have made a contribution to the study of the racial situation in America. They have insisted that the encounter of racial minorities in America is qualitatively different from that of the white immigrant, and they have attempted to apply a qualitatively different conceptual scheme in dealing with this difference. But in the process they have exchanged one oversimplified conceptual scheme for another. They have tried to do what they have justifiably complained that the advocates of the immigrationist model had done earlier: to reduce the singularly complex racial experience in America into a linear and overly simple conceptual framework. To do this, they have tried to apply a conceptual scheme which was adequate for one set of societal conditions onto another which was similar to the former in some respects and not similar in others. Instead of sorting out those features of the American racial experience that resemble the colonial and those that do not, they have staked out the monopolistic claim that their framework accounts for the total character of the racial experience in America.

As we have made eminently clear, one of the major conceptual frameworks we have employed in our analysis of the racial situation in America derives from this colonial perspective. This is evident in the terms that have proved basic to our analysis—plural society and plural segmentation—terms that were first used by Furnivall in his study of tropical dependencies. However, we have seen it neither necessary to transport the entire vocabulary of colonialism nor to transplant its baggage of details onto the American scene. We have defined our problem as understanding the complex character of the American racial encounter and not as reducing it to a carbon copy of a racial encounter in another societal context which bears some but not complete resemblance to the American. Accordingly, we have insisted that America's encounter with its blacks and other racial minorities can only be understood by examining the duality imprinted from its colonist and colonialist past that was legitimated with the formation of the new nation. (For a fuller treatment of this thesis, see Ringer 1983.)

The Policies of Nondiscrimination and Affirmative Action and the Middle-Class Black

Just as the proponents of the colonial analogy and its neocolonialist offshoot have overstated the contemporary role of racism and the heritage of continuing racial inequities from the past, so have those who subscribe to the "black-as-latter-day immigrant" thesis* been too quick to dismiss them as having any continuing relevance today. They insist that the civil rights legislation of the 1960s created at long last a color-blind people's domain with the American creed as its legal-normative code and nondiscrimination as its sole policy.

To the "immigrant theorists" the effective implementation of the color-blind policy has virtually wiped out the vestiges of America's racist history. As a result, they have looked with abhorrence at the surfacing of such race-conscious government policies as affirmative action. They view affirmative action, for example, as an illegitmate and retrogressive product of arbitrary government action and as being a perversion of the color-blind civil rights laws of the 1960s. In Chapter 9 we shall examine in detail their response to these policies and the controversy that exploded over them. In the meantime, though, let's look at the historical connection between the policies of nondiscrimination and affirmative action that has either been lost sight of or never considered in the swirling dispute over the matter.

Affirmative action originated some four decades ago as an abstract policy of nondiscrimination that President Roosevelt established through executive order for government defense contracts. Part of the order stipulated that "all contracting agencies of the Government of the United States shall include in all defense contracts hereafter negotiated by them a provision obligating the contractor not to discriminate against any worker because of race, creed, color or national origin" (Executive Order 8802 1941).

Ten years later President Truman sought to infuse some life into the policy which in practice had been dormant from the moment of its birth. He issued Executive Order 10308 in 1951 that established the Committee on Government Contract Compliance. The committee's major accomplishment was the series of recommendations it made near the end of its term of office. It offered a design and blueprint for the future that would presumably transform the policy into an effective instrument of action and control. The committee however was unable to take even a small step in this direction during its lifetime, for it had been merely set up as an advisory body without any authority or functional responsibilities.

---

*This thesis will be examined in depth in Chapter 9.

In 1953 President Eisenhower reaffirmed the policy of nondiscrimination with Executive Order 10479. This order replaced that of Truman and substituted a committee of his own making and choosing for that of Truman. He even shortened its name to Committee on Government Contracts. In addition, his committee, unlike Truman's, assumed certain limited functions such as reviewing (but without authority for changing) the actions and decisions of contracting agencies. Though operationally more active, the committee did not strike out in new directions nor pioneer new initiatives from those already mapped out in the blueprint of the Truman committee. Instead it merely followed the latter's lead and sought to implement some of its recommendations, such as revising the nondiscrimination clause in government contracts.

As Eisenhower had done before him, President Kennedy replaced his predecessor's executive order with one of his own. But unlike Eisenhower, he did not merely reaffirm the policy of his predecessor; he fundamentally reshaped it. Specifically Kennedy's Executive Order 10925 issued in 1961 had the government do more than eliminate policies and practices of discrimination. It also had the "plain and positive obligation to insure equal opportunity for all qualified persons without regard to race, creed, color, or national origin." Kennedy demanded "affirmative actions" from both government and contractors. Thus, was introduced into the vocabulary of the government contract program the phrase that subsequently became its label.

Having broadened the normative scope and purpose of the program, Kennedy made this redefinition visible by naming his committee the President's Committee on Equal Employment Opportunity and by endowing it with an authority that none of the earlier committees came close to having. His committee succeeded in devising a set of rules and in constructing an administrative apparatus for the processing of individual complaints of discrimination. This apparatus operated relatively effectively and efficiently and produced results far beyond those realized by any of the earlier committees. In the area of compliance review, though, which the committee agreed was potentially of even greater importance than complaint processing, the committee merely took a first step. It mandated the filing by contractors and subcontractors of annual compliance reports. Data on the proportionate distribution of various racial minorities in the contractor's work force at each job level were to be included in these reports. However, the committee faltered and equivocated in constructing the kind of evaluational and enforcement machinery that could use the data from the reporting system effectively. In addition, the committee failed to come to grips operationally or otherwise with what it meant precisely by the requirement of "affirmative action" for contractors. As the phrase came to be used by the

Committee, it applied more to its exhortations to government agencies to do a better job in carrying out the program than to its demands on contractors.

As his predecessors had done before him, President Johnson sought to place his own stamp on the government contract program by issuing soon after his election Executive Order 11246 that replaced all earlier ones on the subject. Again, similar to theirs, his order reaffirmed important features of the past programs but also introduced significant new changes. Thus, Johnson's order retained the normative framework that Kennedy had articulated; the goal of the program was to be equal employment opportunity through affirmative action and not merely the absence of discrimination. To realize this goal however, Johnson introduced a major structural innovation. He scrapped the notion of a committee as the focal administrative organ for the program. Instead, he placed authority for the program in the hands of an established component of the administrative mainstream of the executive branch of government, the Department of Labor. By doing this, Johnson brought to fruition what Truman's committee had recommended fifteen years earlier as a basic requirement for a successful program: centralization of authority within an integral part of the bureaucratic system of government. Within a month after issuance of the order, the Office of Federal Contract Compliance was established in the Department of Labor.

Not until the last year of his administration, however, did some of the major ramifications of this structural change become manifest as the first comprehensive code of rules and regulations under the Johnson order was finally issued by the OFCC. The new code reflected a profound shift in priorities. It deemphasized the processing of complaints, retaining intact most of Kennedy's version, and stressed the development of procedures for compliance reviews. In this it built on the rudimentary foundation laid by Kennedy. For example, the new code did not basically alter the compliance reporting procedure of the Kennedy Committee; it merely added a number of significant details. This new code also put contractors on notice that henceforth the compliance review would become a routinized and integral part of the program and the results of these reviews would be fed regularly into a strengthened and invigorated apparatus of enforcement which would no longer follow the lax proceedings of the past but would be prepared to apply sanctions and penalties when needed.

Perhaps the most significant contribution of the new code was the groundwork that it laid for translating the generalized commitment to affirmative action that Kennedy had been the first to espouse into a distinctive set of demands on and requirements for contractors. Contractors were to conduct utilization analyses of minorities in their work forces and correct any deficiencies exposed through the analyses by setting up specific goals and timetables for final realization of full and equal employment opportunities for their minorities.

The code however, failed to provide contractors with guidelines or criteria that would enable them to ascertain the extent to which their utilization of minorities was inadequate or deficient. That was left undetermined. Nevertheless, in doing what it did, the Johnson administration had taken an important step; it had set the basic direction and design for transforming Kennedy's vague and general normative goal of affirmative action into an operational set of procedures and processes.

Departing from the practice of the past five administrations, President Nixon merely modified the executive order of his predecessor without replacing it entirely with one of his own. As a result, the heritage of the past was much more inviolately transmitted from the Johnson to the Nixon administration than it had been between any of the earlier administrations. However, the Nixon administration soon went far beyond the rudimentary procedural engineering of the past and honed a comprehensive yet precise set of bureaucratic instrumentalities and regulations that was better able to effectuate the goals and design of the past than could any of the earlier efforts.

This was immediately evident in the fall of 1969 when the OFCC launched major programmatic and procedural initiatives that added a key element to the design for affirmative action that the office had been evolving: that of external standards onto which contractors could peg the goals of their affirmative action programs. The pioneering venture in the forging of this key element was the Philadelphia Plan for the employment of minorities in construction trades. But its major formulation awaited another programmatic initiative launched in the late fall of 1969 by the OFCC which finally emerged as Revised Order Number 4 in 1971.

This order not only adopted some of the features and approaches of the Philadelphia Plan but it also built on the foundation laid in the Johnson code of 1968. The order, for example, retained the requirement that contractors conduct a utilization analysis of minorities and women in the various job categories, one of the major innovations of the 1968 code. But unlike the earlier code, which stopped with this internal analysis, the revised order went on as the Philadelphia Plan had already done before to require that the contractor evaluate the results of his utilization analysis by matching them against an external standard: the availability of minorities and women for the various job categories in the relevant labor markets that served the contractor. (Availability was operationally defined by eight measurable components.) Through this comparison, then, the contractor was to locate objectively and systematically any "underutilization" or deficiency in his employment of minorities and women. His affirmative action program was to spell out in detail goals and timetables for remedying any deficiencies that were uncovered, and at the least, the contractor was to engage in "good faith" efforts to fulfill his affirmative action commitments. Soon the OFCC also set forth detailed procedures and processes for regular compliance reviews of contractors (Revised Order Number 14).

In general then it took approximately 30 years for the policy of nondiscrimination in government contracts, as first enunciated by President Roosevelt, to develop the kind of administrative machinery and procedural codification that enabled it to become something more than an abstract normative statement. This 30-year evolution cut across six presidential administrations, Republican and Democrat alike, but it made a difference which party was in power. For example, normative formulations and reformulations took place primarily during Democratic administrations as in the case of Roosevelt's and Truman's first enunciation of the nondiscrimination policy and Kennedy's transformation of the policy into equal employment opportunity and affirmative action. Also basic structural foundations were laid while the Democrats were in power as in the case of Roosevelt's and Truman's first use of a committee as the focal organ of the program and of Johnson's subsequent locating the program in the Department of Labor. By contrast, Republican administrations increased the effectiveness of the procedural machinery that was devised to function within the normative and structural framework inherited from the Democrats, as in the case of Eisenhower's giving his committee more authority than Truman had given his and of Nixon's honing an effective bureaucratic apparatus within the normative parameters of Kennedy and structural parameters of Johnson. Thus, Republican presidents implemented more effectively than did Democratic presidents what the latter had in fact initiated, until Reagan, that is. He has attempted to dismantle the program and has even threatened to rescind Johnson's Executive Order 11246. To date this has not come to pass.

Overall progress toward an effective administrative instrumentality was snail-like, and the cumulative effects of the actions of the various administrations were modest for most of the policy's history. Even Kennedy's normative reformulation of the policy from nondiscrimination to affirmative action and Johnson's structural transformation did not initially speed up the process. They served though as blueprint and generating source for the burst of energy that propelled the program into the 1970s. With the addition of key procedural elements under the Nixon administration, the blueprint became fully operational and a bureaucratic machine was perfected. The machine subsequently developed an almost inexorable momentum of its own—despite the ideological opposition of

President Nixon—and implemented with a marked degree of success the policy first enunciated three decades before.

Even the Equal Employment Opportunity Commission, despite its origin as the administrative arm for the implementation of the nondiscriminatory provisions of Title VII of the Civil Rights Act of 1964, moved in the same direction. Its guidelines on testing and examinations reflected its growing preoccupation with the lingering consequences of past discrimination irrespective of present intent. And with legal challenges of the OFCC's and the EOCC's actions and policies, the United States Supreme Court has also become involved in the matter. In a case-by-case approach, it has shown a measured willingness to affirm the race-conscious policy of affirmative action as a constitutionally lawful way of redressing the continuing effects of racially discriminatory practices and policies of the past.

Despite the claim of critics who say that it would have happened anyway, affirmative action policies have facilitated the development of a new black middle class that differs strikingly from the old middle class that Frazier wrote about in 1957. Then it consisted largely of teachers, nurses, social workers, small shopkeepers, and the like. Today it consists primarily of those who have gained access to the mainstream of the corporate, academic, and public sectors of the economy. They are employed at the managerial and professional levels. Their numbers are still relatively small; the obstacles to further advancement, formidable, but they are there—the pioneers who are opening up new job possibilities for blacks. How long these policies will have to remain in effect to undo the fossilized inequities of the past is open to question.

The Black Masses and the Reordering of National Priorities

The black masses, however, have remained far removed from the workings of the American creed and have been only indirectly touched by the policies of equal employment opportunity and affirmative action. They have continued to be locked behind the historically frozen walls of poverty and discrimination. If anything their lot is worsening as advancing technology and automation make their unskilled labor service obsolete and cause an increasing number to swell the ranks of the unemployed and unemployable. They clearly comprise the kind of unassimilable and alienated Lumpenproletariat about whom Newton (1972) wrote. Their concentration in the harsh and impoverished environment of the black ghetto lends credence to that part of the colonial analogy which maintains that they are an oppressed people who have been cordoned off from the dominant white society and are subject to its oppressive control.

To deal frontally with the basic problems of the black masses will require more than mere implementation of a government policy that opens up doors to various institutional environments such as Affirmative Action. It will also require coming to grips with the fundamental problems of poverty and unemployment. This will in turn necessitate a basic reordering of priorities in the allocation of resources and funds in the system and a greater dependence on government intervention and planning than on the workings of the marketplace.

Whether such a fundamental challenge can finally be met by a capitalist society, no matter how egalitarian its legal-normative code, remains to be seen. But failure to meet this challenge will mean the persistence of a molten core of anger, hatred, and frustration in the very heart of many American cities—a molten core that will grow ever larger as the inner city expands in scope and size. Periodically the combustible forces in this molten core may explode in riots and mass looting as they have in the past. Perhaps the siphoning off of any emerging leaders into the new black middle class by the working of the American creed and its capillary process will prevent the molten mass from developing a sustained and disciplined revolutionary direction and focus.

But what may well happen should such violence erupt with any frequency and should the molten mass expand dramatically is that the dominant white society may expend ever more resources and manpower on securing and patrolling the boundaries between itself and the ghetto. And in the name of law and order create an even more insidious and terrible version of the plural society than in the past. This version might eventually gobble up the American creed and the people's domain, and America would then become what Newton and the Black Panthers have said it already is, a fascist society. But even if this nightmare fails to materialize, the fact nevertheless exists that as long as the smoldering mass remains, it will perpetuate the North's heritage as a de facto plural society, even as a small segment of blacks become absorbed into the major institutional environment of the people's domain.

8   Duality and Other Racial Minorities

After its transformation into a federated nation-state under the Constitution, the United States extended the principle of duality to governmental policies dealing with the entry of people into the country and with the acquisition of new territory to the United States—areas that were not officially imprinted with this duality prior to the establishment of the New Nation.

In the first part of this chapter we shall look at the extension of duality to immigrants from Asia, first from China and then from Japan. In the last section of this chapter we shall examine the imprinting of duality on Puerto Rico, the first newly acquired land to be stamped in this manner since the writing of the Constitution.

The Chinese-American and the Boundaries of the Plural Terrain

In 1790, two years after the formation of the new nation, the First Congress encompassed the immigrant within the sway of America's duality. As we have already mentioned in an earlier chapter, it stipulated in its first naturalization act that only the white alien could become a citizen and gain access to membership in the people's domain. The nonwhite foreign-born was to remain in the then undefined role of alien under the direct administrative control of the federal government. Within this unchartered plural terrain, he was to carve out his way of life as a permanent stranger in the land.

Almost one hundred years elapsed before the full impact of this racial restriction was felt on the flow of immigration. Implementation of this restriction revitalized America's historical duality at a time when the vestigial effects of the first period of Reconstruction were still muting it. It spun a web of duality around a new category of nonwhites—the immigrant from China and later from Japan—a web from which he escaped only recently.

California and the Chinese immigrant

The drama began in the frontierlike atmosphere of California. It had just become a state in the Union in 1850 and was in the throes of an explosive population growth as hordes of white Americans and foreign migrants, including the first wave from Asia, the Chinese, poured into the state in search of opportunity and gold. The structure of discrimination and exclusion that eventually engulfed the immigrants from Asia was built upon the foundations of a plural arrangement and racial creed that was articulated against the black and the Indian at the Constitutional Convention of 1849. However, in less than a decade, a structure had evolved explicitly directed against the Chinese.

Not content with quarantining him behind the walls of this plural structure, the Californians mounted an increasingly strident campaign to drive him out of the various labor markets. The campaign reached such an intensity in the constitutional convention of 1879 that it threatened to deprive the Chinese immigrant of even the most rudimentary means of making a livelihood. It also threatened to strip him of all rights of property and of any protection of the law. Its central demand was an end to any further migration of Chinese into the state. The legislative result of this campaign, however, bumped up against judicial constraints that threw out key elements as unconstitutional. Finally, the people and elected officials of California reluctantly conceded that they had reached the limits of their authority to deal with the Chinese immigrant. And so they turned more than ever to Washington to solve the "problem."

The federal government, China, and the exclusion acts

The reticence of the federal government to come immediately to the aid of California as it began to clamor increasingly for assistance had little to do with any sympathy for the Chinese immigrant. Instead it had to do with the imperial interests of the federal government that collided at that moment of history with the interests of the state of California.

For 30 years the U.S. government had been endeavoring to open China to commerce. By the 1860s it had succeeded in gaining significant trade concessions and imposing extraterritorial rights on a weak Chinese government. What compounded its reluctance to aid California was the signing of the Burlingame Treaty in 1868. While reaffirming the unequal treaties of the past, it also provided for the right of free and voluntary access to each country and for the protection of the immigrant from

171

discriminatory treatment in either country. The Senate, though, limited the scope and meaning of these provisions by adding the stipulation that naturalization was not to be conferred on the immigrants to either country. (The treaty was written by two Americans, one of whom represented China, and reflected in part the liberal glow of the early Reconstruction period.)

Before the ink dried, disenchantment with the treaty had already surfaced in California, and in time the East Coast also began to have second thoughts as some Chinese immigrants began to appear there and as turmoil increased in China. Thus, by the mid-1870s the national climate had changed, and with the encouragement of the California delegation, pressure began to mount inexorably on Congress to abrogate the immigration provisions of the treaty. The stark picture was drawn of the Chinese immigrant as an unassimilable alien who was building his own quasi-political plural community which was threatening the stability of the people's domain and the well-being of the white American. The fear was expressed that this community would destroy the white man's institutions through numbers and through competitive advantage in the labor markets and would, accordingly, take over the Pacific Coast in time.

Congress soon passed a bill on the matter, only to have it vetoed by President Hayes. However, within months after the veto, the president began to press China to reopen negotiations on the immigration provisions of the Burlingame Treaty. China finally gave its grudging consent to an article which would permit the United States to regulate, limit, or suspend the immigration of laborers including artisans. Almost immediately California congressmen pounced on this provision and pushed through an exclusion act in Congress that would suspend the immigration of Chinese laborers. Their first version would suspend immigration for twenty years, but they reduced it to ten years after another presidential veto. And so in 1882 a legislative process began that increasingly cut back on the flow of Chinese immigration. In 1888, the ban was extended to the return of any Chinese laborer who may have gone back to China and now wished to come back to the United States. Even Chinese who had earlier received bona fide certificates of return were included in the ban. Four years later an entirely new dimension was added to the legislation. Chinese immigrants who were already in the United States were required to register or face the threat of deportation. The next year the deadline was extended because the U.S. government faced the prospect of having to deport almost half of the Chinese population in America at overwhelming expense.

By the end of the century, Congress added nothing further of substance to the legislation, but it increased the authority of the Treasury

Department in handling Chinese immigration. This proved to be a fateful decision, for the department interpreted the various laws so narrowly and so literally that even the most exclusionist of California congressmen could find no fault. The most flagrant example was the administrative ruling of the secretary of treasury in 1898 that reduced the size of the exempted class only to those who were explicitly mentioned in the Treaty of 1894; namely, officials, teachers, students, merchants or travelers for curiosity or pleasure. All other gainfully employed Chinese, even though they were not of the laboring class, were henceforth denied admission. This meant that Chinese in such prestigious occupations as physicians, managers, scientists, and the like could no longer enter the United States.

This drastic shift to a denotative definition of the exempted class was justified by the secretary as being in accord with the true intent of Congress. Thus in one fell swoop an administrative decision transformed the category of the excluded from Chinese laborers to all Chinese but those in a limited number of occupational and avocational categories. In effect what Geary had sought to attain in the original version of his act six years earlier was now attained by administrative fiat.

The Chinese government was outraged by this decision, and sought as it had in the past to persuade the U.S. government to change the policy, but as in the past it failed. Four years later the Chinese government made one last effort to blunt the increasingly repressive administrative controls and to head off the threat of another extension of the exclusion laws. In a carefully drawn and documented report, the highly respected Chinese ambassador reviewed the history of America's flagrant abandonment of the ideals of the Burlingame Treaty. He recounted the hardships imposed on the laborers and with special bitterness described the difficulties and degradations experienced by the privileged classes. He argued that despite these controls America had gained little for its domestic economy and had in turn lost ground in its commercial relations with China.

The ambassador's entreaties were to no avail, and within a year the exclusion acts were extended. Two years later the Chinese government abandoned the hope that anything would ever be done by the U.S. government to remedy the iniquitous treatment afforded the privileged and laboring classes of Chinese in America. In 1904 China decided to withdraw the aura of legitimacy that the Treaty of 1894 seemingly bestowed on this treatment and formally announced its intention to terminate the treaty.

Congress responded by transferring the Bureau of Immigration from the Treasury Department to the newly created Department of Commerce and Labor and by giving the commissioner-general of immigration even greater control than in the past over the personnel and the machinery of enforcement. But even as the bureaucratic behemoth was being created over the years to control and to exclude the Chinese, it began to have less and less human fodder to feed its maw as the flow of immigrants declined by 1910 and the total number grew ever smaller.

Boundaries and the ambiguous legal status of the Chinese immigrant

The various exclusion acts etched in bold legal detail two major boundaries of and in the American society that the emigrant from China was to find increasingly difficult if not impossible to cross. The first boundary defined the territorial limits of America, and as time went on fewer and fewer Chinese were able to cross it lawfully. Initially, for example, only laborers—skilled and unskilled—were prevented from doing so; by 1888 even those laborers who had once been allowed in were forbidden from entering a second time despite the fact that they may have had legal certification to do so. By 1898 the pool of the banned was further enlarged to include most of the privileged nonmanual occupational classes. Thus by the early twentieth century, the Chinese were barred from America to an extent and in a manner that no other immigrant had to face until then.

Even if they managed to cross the territorial boundary, Chinese immigrants were still unable to move about freely in the institutional life of the American society. They faced yet another formidable boundary which none were allowed to cross because all were categorically denied the privilege of naturalization and citizenship. As a result, they could neither gain access to nor participate in the people's domain as full-fledged members of the American society. In general then, most Chinese found themselves uneasily ensconced between one boundary they could not cross even if they wanted to and another they might not be allowed to recross once they crossed. Thus, many resigned themselves to settling permanently in the plural terrain between these boundaries as alien residents, only to discover with the passage of the Geary Act in 1892 that just as they had no vested right to return to the plural terrain once they left the country, so they also had no vested right to stay there, even if they never left.

In key decisions, particularly the one that upheld the Geary Act, (*Fong Yue Ting v. United States*), the Supreme Court confimed the inherently unstable and ambiguous legal status created for Chinese immigrants by the various exclusion laws. It cast their permanent status in the constitutional mold of transient aliens who had no vested rights of domicile and could be deported at the pleasure of the government, no matter how long they had resided in this country. The Court had also determined previously that the immigrants had no vested right of return once they left the plural terrain. In this manner, the Court branded constitutionally the Chinese immigrants as perennial sojourners, at a time when most of them had given up any sojourning inclinations and had sunk their roots into the American society.

However, even as the Court carved out this transient alien status for the Chinese immigrants, it reaffirmed its earlier ruling in the *Yick Wo* case that as long as the Chinese resided in this country, they would come under the mantle of the equal protection and due process clauses of the Fourteenth Amendment. In explaining its stand, the Court insisted in the later *Fong Yue Ting* ruling that "the question there (in the *Yick Wo* case) was of the power of a State over aliens continuing to reside within its jurisdiction, not of the power of the United States to put an end to their residence in the country" as in the present case (149 US 1893:725).

Subsequent decisions of the Court solidified this dualism in the treatment of the Chinese. The *Ting* principle was extended in rulings that enhanced the power of immigration officials in deportation proceedings and constricted the rights of the alien to fight the proceedings. In turn the *Yick Wo* principle was extended to protect the Chinese alien from being held "to answer for a capital or other infamous crime, unless on a presentment or indictment of a grand jury," or from being "deprived of life, liberty, or property without due process of law" (163 US 1896:238).

This dualism continued to plague the fate of the Chinese for the next half century and symbolized still another manifestation of the bifurcated character of America's response to its racial minorities. For example, the *Ting* principle reflected the further corrosion of the status of a nonwhite minority in the plural terrain of America. Its first-generation settlers could not even claim the right to stay permanently there no matter how long they were in the country. By contrast, the *Yick Wo* principle permitted some of the rights and immunities of the people's domain to spill over to the Chinese as long as they were ensconced in the plural terrain. And finally, under the *Wong Kim Ark* ruling in 1898, the second-generation Chinese could shed their Transient Alien status in the plural terrain for the status of "citizen" in the people's domain by virtue of birth in this country.

The Japanese–American: From the Plural Terrain and Concentration Camps to the People's Domain

Early days in California and the school board crisis

Even though the Chinese were the manifest target of the restrictive and exclusionary policies and practices first adopted by the state of California and then by the nation as a whole, the plural structure that was thereby created had an inherently flexible design and a generic mold that allowed it in time to be applied to the Japanese and other immigrants from Asia.

Through the early 1880s, however, there were too few Japanese immigrants in California to collide head-on with this latent plural structure. As the numbers began to increase by the turn of the century, anti-Japanese sentiments began to surface. At first they were closely linked to the anti-Chinese agitation that was once again in ascendance as the expiration date for the various acts of exclusion was drawing near. Congress' extension of these acts did much to mute the clamor against the Chinese whose immigration had by then been reduced to a trickle. However, Congress' failure to extend the ban to the Japanese forced the issue of their immigration to the center stage of public concern. The visibility of this issue was enhanced by an annual flow of approximately 8,000. In this way the Japanese, no longer in the shadows of the "Chinese problem," by 1905 became the primary lightning rod for opposition to the "Oriental invasion" and became the heirs to the stereotypic baggage that was bestowed earlier on the Chinese.

A year later the San Francisco School Board joined the growing anti-Japanese movement. It decided to segregate Japanese, Chinese, and other Asian children in a newly established Oriental public school. Almost immediately the local action of the board blossomed into an issue of international import. The Japanese ambassador, for example, informed the secretary of state in Washington of his government's displeasure with the board's action and of the widespread anti-American agitation that had exploded among the people and the press of Japan.

Disturbed by the outbursts in Japan, the U.S. government sought to reassure the Japanese government even before the meeting with the ambassador. It conveyed its friendliness through the American ambassador in Tokyo, pledged equitable treatment for Japanese subjects in America, and promised a full investigation of the school board incident. President Theodore Roosevelt kept this promise. A day after the meeting with the Japanese ambassador, he announced that his secretary of commerce would leave immediately for San Francisco to investigate the school incident. The lengths to which the president and the secretary of state went to mollify the Japanese government indicated the stature that Japan had achieved in world affairs with its victory over Russia the year before. The concern of the U.S. government contrasted strikingly with the contemptuous manner it was even then treating the protests of the Chinese government over the treatment of the Chinese immigrants in America. It had no fear of China, but it had developed respect and fear of Japan. Within weeks of the school board crisis, President Roosevelt conveyed these sentiments in a letter to a senator. In it, he expressed respect for the "formidable character" of the Japanese armed forces, and fear that the incident could lead to war between the United States and Japan or at the least to the United States being substituted for Russia as the national enemy of Japan. To avoid this he resolved to defuse the dangerous potential of the incident.

Having committed himself to this course of action, the president replaced the Japanese as the primary target for the spleen of the Californians. He nevertheless pressed ahead on several fronts and obtained the reluctant consent of the school board to rescind its order. In turn he withdrew the law suit instituted by the federal government against the school board and entered into active negotiations with the Japanese government for a treaty that would put an end to the immigration of the Japanese laborer to the mainland—an objective with which he agreed personally despite his stand on the school board issue.

The Gentlemen's Agreement of 1907

After months of fruitless negotiations, Japan decided to control unilaterally the emigration of Japanese laborers to the United States. To this end, it worked out a set of procedures in consultation with the U.S. government that it would follow in issuing passports, but these procedures were not to be codified as part of a treaty. In this manner the Gentlemen's Agreement of 1907 was promulgated and put into effect the next year. Under the terms of the agreement, the Japanese government would issue passports to nonlaborers and only to those of the laboring class who were "former residents of the United States," "parents, wives or children of residents," and "settled agriculturists." In return for this action, the Japanese government expected the U.S. government to refrain from enacting any discriminatory legislation against the Japanese.

The response of the U.S. government to the working of the agreement during the first three years was highly favorable. The U.S. commissioner-general of immigration, for example, praised Japan for its vigilance in issuing passports. What pleased him even more was the fact that total Japanese immigration had dropped dramatically to only a fraction of what it had been previously.

In scrupulously abiding by the agreement, the Japanese government was not only prepared to deny passports to its laborers, but it was equally determined to issue passports to those who were entitled to them under the agreement. Its protection of the rights of the "exempted classes" contrasted strongly with the dramatic whittling away of these rights of the exempted classes among the Chinese through legal and administrative action by the U.S. government. For example, the Japanese government consistently protected the rights of Japanese laborers and nonlaborers alike to return to the United States if they had established residence here prior to the date of the agreement.

Another distinctive feature of Japan's performance throughout the duration of the agreement was the relatively unchanging character of the occupational criteria it used in defining the "nonlaboring classes" to whom passports of entry and re-entry could be issued under the original terms of the agreement. Japan rejected the kind of redefinition that American officials had imposed upon the Chinese in 1898 that reduced the category to only those explicitly mentioned in the Treaty of 1894. The Japanese government refused during the first decade of the agreement to exclude women whose marital status American authorities questioned, the so-called "picture brides," from the category of "parents, wives or children of residents."

As a result of the Japanese government's consistent and even-handed implementation of the Gentlemen's Agreement, immigration which had declined for the first several years, began to rise markedly during the second decade of the twentieth century. The effusive enthusiasm that U.S. officials expressed during the first few years of the agreement began to curdle by the fourth year. And increasingly the "picture bride" became the target of the growing disenchantment with the agreement. By 1919, the issue had become so alive that it was at the center of the mounting anti-Japanese campaign in California. In an attempt to short-circuit this campaign, Japan finally acceded to the request of the U.S. government that it stop granting passports to "picture brides."

Though the flow of these brides came to a halt by late 1920 it had already done much, along with the influx of other women, to alter the sex ratio of Japanese in America for the decade from 1910 to 1920. Women comprised well over one-third of the total Japanese population by 1920; in 1910 they were only one-eighth. Among the Chinese, their percentage never exceeded one-eighth, given the stringent controls exercised by the U.S. immigration authorities.

Thus by 1920 the different immigration policies and controls had clearly and decisively etched their imprint on the character of the Japanese and Chinese populations. The Chinese, for example, constituted by and large a declining and aging population of single men; few, in short, had any chance for a relatively normal family life. In sharp contrast, the Japanese comprised an expanding younger population in which women were becoming an increasingly significant part. As a result a substantial number of Japanese men—albeit still a minority—were able to establish and to live relatively normal family lives.

California and the antialien land laws

The San Francisco school crisis had hardly been resolved and the final touches put on the Gentlemen's Agreement when rumblings in California threatened to undo what President Roosevelt had worked out with the

Japanese government. Pressure from Roosevelt and later from President Taft kept at bay the legislative assault of anti-Japanese forces. But with the election of Wilson, who supported exclusion during the campaign, the anti-Japanese forces regrouped and moved in a direction that reflected the extent to which the Japanese immigrant had become involved in agriculture. They pushed for a law forbidding the ownership of land by aliens ineligible to citizenship.

As the legislative drama unfolded in California from the opening gavel of the 1913 session, the Japanese government expressed to the U.S. government an ever increasing concern about the proceedings. Only a few days after President Wilson had taken office, the Japanese ambassador had already conveyed an urgent request that he do something about what was going on in the California legislature. Wilson, who found that as president he could not treat the Japanese immigrant issue as casually as he did as a candidate, assured the ambassador that he would intervene within the limits of the constitutional separation of state and federal governments.

Other than amending their bill to permit the leasing of land by aliens not eligible to citizenship, the authors of the bill stood firm against the president's pressure; the bill was passed early in May. This convinced the Japanese government that stronger measures were needed, a week later its first formal protest was lodged with the U.S. government. So began an exchange between the governments that continued for almost a year. In this exchange, Japan charged that the law was "intentionally racially discriminatory" and violated the Treaty of 1911.

The U.S. government denied both charges. The U.S. secretary of state insisted, for example, that economics, not race, motivated the California legislature. He admitted though that the two factors might have become intertwined. In explaining what he meant, he offered what can be labeled as a "quasi-Marxist" theory of plural societies in which the economic struggle for survival generates conflict and antagonism between racial groups which can neither amalgamate with nor assimilate to each other but must remain separate and distinctive entities, segments or societies. The secretary repeated this thesis throughout the year's exchanges, just as Japan continually reaffirmed its position.

Agitation for further legislative action against the Japanese resumed in California immediately after the end of World War I. It was deflected for a year by pressure from the State Department then in the midst of negotiations at the Peace Conference in Versailles. The legislature though requested the State Board of Control to investigate thoroughly the land situation in California and to prepare a comprehensive report based on its findings. Even before the state board formally submitted its report, an initiative petition was circulating in California to remedy the defects of the 1913 law. It won overwhelmingly and eventually resulted in a bill eliminating the leasing provision of the earlier law. Two years later the law was amended to curtail further any other abiding tie between the Japanese who engaged in farming and the land they cultivated.

By the mid-1920s Japanese aliens who engaged in farming but did not own their own land were forced to become a rural proletariat that sold its labor services to Japanese and American farmers. Once again the Japanese government pressed the U.S. government to take forceful action against the increasingly oppressive land restrictions. It was even prepared to negotiate a treaty in which further immigration of Japanese would be virtually cut off. In turn, it wanted the U.S. government to confer on the Japanese already in the United States the same property rights as were conferred on other aliens. The proposed treaty never got beyond the draft stage. Pressure from the senators from California prevented it from ever reaching the Senate for consideration. Had it been enacted, it would have voided the California land laws.

The double-edged yellow peril: Japan and the Japanese immigrant

The care and restraint with which the three presidents and their secretaries of states engaged in diplomatic conversations and conducted negotiations with Japan during this entire period was a constant reminder of Japan's status in world affairs. It had become respected as a military power and its expressions of national concern, whether about its subjects in the United States or its national interests in the Far East, could not be lightly dismissed or cavalierly rebuffed by the U.S. government as often happened in its response to China. However, with this growing respect, the attitude of the U.S. government underwent a significant change. From the friendly benevolence that characterized its treatment of Japan throughout the latter part of the nineteenth century once it had forcibly breached Japan's wall of seclusion, the U.S. government became suspicious and distrustful as Japan staked its claim to equality, began to compete with the United States in the Far East, and openly expressed its concern over treatment of its nationals in America. Japan too expressed its growing wariness of America's national aims and purposes. As a result, with each instance of acute tension and strain, fears mounted that relations between the two countries were about to deteriorate to the point of open hostilities.

Alarmed at the military prowess of Japan in its victory over Russia, the California press—the Hearst newspapers in particular—resurrected the theme of yellow peril which originally had been used in the late 1800s to describe the competitive economic threat of the Chinese "invasion" of California. Now it was to be used to alert America to the dangers of

Japan as a military threat to the national interests and aims of the United States. The theme took on a special prominence in the press with the war scares generated first by the school board crisis and then by other incidents in San Francisco. In addition, the Hearst newspapers turned its focus inward toward the Japanese immigrants and developed a fifth column version of the theme. The newspapers insisted that the imigrants were in fact military men in disguise who were awaiting orders from the emperor.

Thus was set in place the two edges of the yellow peril theme. For the next decade they came alive in the fictional accounts of an Armageddon-like collision between Japan and the United States fantasized by such writers as Fitzpatrick and Welles. The Magdalena Bay affair of 1912 and 1913 seemed to give the threat of the yellow peril a touch of reality, but it soon became evident that the alleged threat had been primarily a product of the overwrought and overactive imaginations of Senator Lodge and of Hearst. But during this period a number of military officers, particularly in the Navy, became literally obsessed, according to Daniels (1944), with the threat of the yellow peril. Even Franklin D. Roosevelt, then a newly appointed assistant secretary of the Navy shared this conviction. According to Roosevelt, it was a "perfectly natural attitude of Army and Navy officers whose duty it has been in the past to prepare the country against the most probable enemy" to single out Japan as their target (Neumann 1953:150).

With Japan actively on the side of the Allies, World War I served to mute the yellow peril theme despite the efforts of the German propaganda machine and of Hearst. However the collision of national interests and policies after the war breathed new life into the theme and molded it into an even more threatening version of Japan as a fearsome and formidable military power. Japan had become, in the eyes of one of the leading ideologues of the yellow peril theme, "the Germany of Asia" (McClatchy 1920). So ideally did this label seem to fit the Japan of the renascent yellow peril threat that it was soon widely adopted and used with increasing frequency in the revitalized campaign against Japan and the Japanese. Under this version of the theme, Japan threatened more than the national interests of the United States in Asia; it also threatened the very survival of the United States. It intended to gain control of this country by placing an unlimited number of its surplus population here through peaceful penetration. This "lebensraum" thesis provided an important ideological bridge for linking the national policy of Japan to the Japanese immigrants in a domestic variant of the yellow peril theme. In this manner the ideologues defined the Japanese immigrants as tools for a national policy of lebensraum imperialism. No longer, however, were they necessarily military men in disguise as in the prewar image;

instead they were just ordinary tillers of the soil or hewers of wood who never gave up their ties to Japan.

Accordingly, the loyalty of the average Japanese in America became an increasing preoccupation of yellow peril ideologues by the end of the war. Earlier in the century the question had little relevance for virtually all of the Japanese had been born and reared in Japan. They had not been allowed to become naturalized citizens of the United States and were therefore expected to view themselves as loyal subjects of the emperor. By the end of the second decade though an increasing number of Japanese were born in America and were therefore entitled to U.S. citizenship. Accordingly, the question of their continuing ties to Japan became a focal concern of these ideologues.

The ideologues made much of the fact that under Japanese law, children of a Japanese father are considered to be Japanese, no matter where their birth may have taken place. As such they were subject to all the rights and obligations of Japanese citizenship, including military service. They made even more of the fact that few American-born Japanese had taken advantage of the Law of Expatriation passed by the Japanese government in 1916 that slightly modified this provision. It allowed foreign-born Japanese, domiciled in a foreign country, to drop their Japanese citizenship under certain conditions.

The yellow peril ideologues saw behind all this a sinister plot by the Japanese government to retain the loyalty and devotion of its subjects, even the American-born. They viewed the small number of applications for expatriation as evidence of how successful the government was. These results, the ideologues claimed, were not accidental; the Japanese government, they insisted, had spread its tentacles into the Japanese-American communities and had brought even the American-born Japanese into the orbit of its control. As a result, they concluded, the Nisei who presumably were American citizens, had in fact rejected becoming Americanized and an active part of the American society and its people's domain: instead they had opted for remaining loyal subjects of the emperor.

In elaborating the postwar version of the yellow peril threat, a number of these ideologues had little difficulty in linking it with the call for tighter controls on acquisition of land by first- (Issei) or even second-generation (Nisei) Japanese. But unlike other supporters of such legislation, they did not base their approval merely on the grounds that continued acquisition of land by Japanese posed a serious competitive economic threat to white farmers. Instead they opposed acquisition primarily on the grounds that it threatened the political survival of California and other states of the Pacific slope. They were convinced that such acquisition was part of a diabolical scheme by the Japanese government to gain indirect control of the wealth and resources of the various Pacific states for future conquest.

The Immigration Act of 1924 and the end of the gentlemen's agreement

By the early 1920s the leaders of the anti-Japanese coalition in California and their yellow peril ideologues were prepared to press their cause onto the national stage. They had just succeeded in cutting the last viable tie to Japanese land ownership in California and now they wanted to put an end to the Gentlemen's Agreement and to ban any further immigration of Japanese into the country. Only governmental action on the federal level could do that.

The Supreme Court's decision in 1922 on the *Ozawa* case that reaffirmed the law of 1790 and legitimized the exclusion of Japanese from citizenship and from the people's domain gave them the tag line they needed. No longer did they have to name the Japanese immigrant or even the Gentlemen's Agreement as their target; instead they could say that they were merely against immigration for those who were ineligible to become citizens.

By 1924 they had no difficulty in getting the House of Representatives to include a clause in the immigration bill then under consideration that would bar admission of such immigrants. They had greater difficulty in the Senate, but they were able to exploit the unfortunate phrase "grave consequences" that was used by the Japanese ambassador in an otherwise friendly attempt to rally support for the agreement and against the exclusion clause. And so in a flag-waving mood the Senate also passed the exclusion clause and later the entire immigration bill.

Overall the Immigration Act of 1924 represented the complete triumph of the racial creed as the regnant legal-normative code for controlling entry of aliens into territorial United States and into its institutional domains. Until then Congress relied on the creed from the days of the Founding Fathers to determine which aliens could become naturalized and gain membership in the people's domain. In 1924, Congress decided to extend the reach of the racial creed still further. It would not merely bar entry of nonwhite aliens into the people's domain but would also bar their entry into the territory of the United States itself. The particular target was the Japanese alien; all other Asians already suffered from this double disability. The black alien too, as we shall see, did not escape unscathed from this decision.

The logic of the exclusionists in Congress was seductively simple and seemingly impeccable: Why not bring immigration policy into consonance with the naturalization statutes? Why should aliens, ineligible to citizenship, be permitted to enter a country that they cannot hope to be part of? If they are allowed in, they insisted, such aliens become a nonassimilable plural community that ensconces itself in the normatively ill-defined institutional and geographic terrain located between the people's domain and the territorial limits of the country. There these aliens stand, the congressional exclusionists declared, in antagonistic competition to the people of the people's domain and pose at the least, an economic threat to the stability of the domain. If they are aliens from Japan, they continued, they are an even more serious political threat, inasmuch as their loyalty and ties to Japan make them a potent fifth column carrying out the imperialistic designs of their homeland.

As a result, once such ineligible aliens are allowed in, the congressional exclusionists contended, the only recourse for the people is to build a wall between the aliens and themselves and to use force if necessary to prevent the alien's gaining access to and possession of the resources of the people's domain. But this method of dealing with the problem, the exclusionists recognized, had certain constitutional constraints imposed upon it. They were fully aware, for example, that such an alien, once he was within the territorial limits of the United States, derived some benefit from the fundamental paradox that has historically characterized the legal-normative system of America: a paradox that generates contradictory cues as a result of the dialectical tension between the opposing racial and American creeds. As such, the racial creed may have deprived ineligible aliens of membership in the people's domain, but the American creed, as interpreted by the Supreme Court, had come to provide them with a modicum of protection of the normative code that prevails in the people's domain. For example, the Supreme Court has in some of its rulings spread the protective umbrella of the due process and equal treatment clauses of the Fourteenth Amendment over the alien. In addition, the racial creed may have prevented the alien from owning land as in the alien land laws of California, but the American creed has protected his constitutional right to work as decided by the Supreme Court in its *Truax* ruling.

Congressional exclusionists also recognized that limited though the protective mantle was for aliens, it became much more encompassing for their American-born children. No longer could the racial creed operate constitutionally to deny them membership in the people's domain, for the Fourteenth Amendment as interpreted by the Supreme Court, decreed that all such children born in America were to have the right of citizenship. And as citizens these children could not be deprived of the right to own property as their parents were under the racial creed. In short, the children of aliens ineligible to citizenship could themselves claim all the rights and immunities of membership in the people's domain and bask under the protective mantle of the American creed as spelled out in the Constitution and Declaration of Independence.*

This was viewed as an abomination by the congressional exclusionists particularly as it applied to the Japanese aliens and their offspring; for they saw the children as no better than the parents. Both generations were presumably dedicated and loyal subjects of the emperor. This notion was reinforced by Japanese laws on citizenship which made expatriation such an extremely complicated and difficult task that virtually all American-born Japanese, though citizens of the United States, were also considered to be citizens of Japan by virtue of having a Japanese father. (Japan dramatically dropped its claims on these children as it revised its citizenship laws in mid-1924, but this was too late to affect the deliberations on the Immigration Act of 1924; it had already been passed by Congress and signed by the president.)

Accordingly, the congressional exclusionists were convinced that the only way to avoid the normative paradox of America and the problem of American-born offspring was to construct an impermeable wall around the territorial limits of America which would prevent immigrants ineligible to citizenship from even stepping foot on American soil.

As the exclusion clause was formulated in the Act of 1924, it was obviously aimed, as we have already seen, against the Japanese. But what many scholars fail to realize is that the bill also sought to curtail if not eliminate immigration of the black alien as well, the only other nonwhite who showed any inclination to come to America. Protected as they were by the heritage from Reconstruction which gave them the right to become citizens, black aliens could not be kept out of the United States on the same basis as the Japanese. However, the author of the national origins section of the bill, Senator Reed of Pennsylvania, conceived of an ingenious scheme that would make relatively few black aliens eligible to enter this country. Consequently, if the numbers could be kept down, few would be in a position to take advantage of their inheritance from the past.

His scheme becomes evident once we deal with his fundamental category of "Inhabitants in the Continental United States" which was to serve as the population base from which immigration quotas were to be devised for the various nations. Included as "inhabitants" were the

---

*Actually this is an overstatement; for the *Plessy-Ferguson* decision had relegitimized the racial creed and helped create a plural structure segmented along racial lines within the social realm of the people's domain. In a benchmark case in 1927, the Supreme Court labeled the Chinese, hence all Asians, as nonwhite and therefore subject to the same Jim Crow restrictions in Mississippi as were the blacks.

foreign and native born, aliens as well as citizens. But he added one major exception to his original bill. He denied the identity of "inhabitant" to "descendants of such persons as were involuntary immigrants into the territory now included therein." With virtually all blacks being thereby excluded from the population base, Reed assured his colleagues that there would be few immigrants "from African sources." When the bill reached its final form, "aliens ineligible to citizenship and their descendants" and "descendants of aboriginal Americans," euphemisms for yellow men and red men, were also excluded from the category. That only left the *white race* as "Inhabitants in the Continental United States." (However in keeping with the tradition set in the writing of the Constitution, no explicit references to race were made in the bill, but no one could miss the meanings of the various euphemisms.)

Thus even in its first effort to deal comprehensively with immigration, America could not avoid the duality of its historic past. It created once again a plural structure along racial lines. On the one side of the racial divide were the whites. They comprised the "Inhabitants in the Continental United States" upon whom immigration quotas were to be based. On the other side of the divide were the nonwhites, and once again as in earlier encounters with dominant America, they were denied any identity. As such they might be called the noninhabitants in the Continental United States. Through endowing them with this invisibility Congress hoped they would not contribute anything to the immigrant flow into America.

Even with racial lines clearly drawn in the bill, most senators and representatives were not finished in this effort to purify and homogenize the flow of immigration into the United States. For example, they looked with askance at the flow of new immigrants from Southern and Eastern Europe. They continually referred to these immigrants as nonassimilable or difficult to assimilate and frequently called them undesirable. In sum, these immigrants were seen as a contaminating influence on a society that had been built and maintained by the Northern European who still constituted the majority of the American population.

Some congressmen accounted for the negative qualities of the new immigrants in purely cultural terms. Many others resorted to racial terms; they perceived the new immigrants as of an inferior racial stock to that of the Northern European. And some even saw them as no more desirable biologically than those of the yellow and black races. But virtually no one was prepared to rule them out of the white race, despite whatever inferiorities and undesirablenesses they were branded with. In addition, no one could find any constitutional basis for declaring them ineligible for citizenship, or any historic ground for considering them involuntary immigrants, or any grounds for calling them aboriginal Americans or any other equivalent masking device to label them. In short, no one could find any grounds for treating them as the nonwhite races were being treated.

As a result, the new immigrants had to be counted among the "Inhabitants in the Continental United States," and quotas assigned to the countries from which they came. In other words, the solution that was used to avoid giving quotas to nonwhite races was not available for dealing with the "inferior subraces of whites." The alternative solution that was finally tailored for them was to base the quotas first on the census of 1890 and then on the national origins of the "Inhabitants in the Continental United States" as recorded in 1920. In each instance, the quotas were much lower for immigrants from Southern and Eastern Europe than for immigrants from Northern and Western Europe. Thus, the solution was discriminatory treatment for the undesirable subraces of whites in contrast to the exclusionary treatment for the nonwhite races.

As the legislative process unfolded, the Japanese government maintained a close vigil over the deliberations and expressed its growing concern through its ambassador to the secretary of state and to other high government officials. They responded sympathetically, and between the two parties various stratagems were devised to salvage the Gentlemen's Agreement. The letter which included the phrase "grave consequences" was part of this endeavor, but unfortunately it backfired and produced a result opposite that intended by the Japanese ambassador. The final passage of the immigration bill with its exclusion clause elicited a solemn diplomatic protest from the Japanese government and angry public protests from the Japanese people, and for the next several decades it contaminated relations between the two countries.

Prelude to World War II

With the passage of the immigration act, blatant anti-Japanese agitation and violence subsided for the rest of the decade. On the international scene relative calm also enveloped the relations between the two countries. They even found themselves in agreement at several conferences on naval limitation. In short the double-edged yellow peril theme lapsed into a state of dormancy during this period.

By the mid-1930s however, the aggressive actions of Japan's ultranationalistic military leaders in Manchuria disrupted this veneer of calm and brought into focus once again the conflicting national interests of Japan and the United States. Even as the executive branch of the federal government was deploring these transgressions on international morality, an arm of the legislative branch was presumably uncovering at hearings on the West Coast the subversive threat of the Japanese immigrant. Testimony was heard alleging that under the guise of fishermen, Japanese immigrants were spying for Japan in naval vessels disguised as fishing boats. The rumors proved groundless, but this did not prevent the issue from being kept alive in the state politics of California for the rest of the decade.

By 1940 relations between the United States and Japan had deteriorated to such an extent that the United States abrogated the Commercial Treaty of 1911 and was on the verge of moving from a moral to an economic embargo of Japan. In turn, Japan was making military moves against the French and British possessions in the Far East and was about to announce a formal alignment with the other Axis powers. On the home front, particularly in California, the press abounded with stories of Japanese spies, and the double-edged yellow peril theme was reenergized to its full fury. Thus, on the eve of America's entry into World War II the deeply engrained theme of the yellow peril had become once again refurbished and revitalized, particularly on the West Coast, and its two branches were already in bloom when the Japanese struck Pearl Harbor.

World War II and the concentration camps

The surprise attack on Pearl Harbor did not precipitate an immediate angry and violent reaction against the Japanese in America. In addition, the federal government did not rush pell-mell into a campaign of across-the-board repression. Instead it followed, under the direction of the Department of Justice, a selective and relatively limited program of control and internment which was confined exclusively to the Japanese aliens; their American-born children were left untouched.

Three months later the climate changed completely. Anti-Japanese sentiment and demands for their evacuation mounted inexorably on the West Coast. In the middle of February, President Roosevelt reacted to these pressures by issuing an executive order authorizing the Army to exclude any or all persons from designated military areas. The War Department, however, had second thoughts about shouldering the full responsibility for the enforcement of the military restrictions and for the punishment of violations. Accordingly, it drafted and sent to Congress a bill, with the approval of the president, that would empower the federal courts to treat as a misdemeanor any violation of the restrictions.

A month later Congress passed the bill in the name of military necessity. In passing the bill, Congress draped the mantle of statutory legitimacy over the military to do what it would with the evacuation of the Japanese aliens and their American-born children, just as the president had cloaked it earlier with executive legitimacy. Still to come, however, was the mantle of constitutional legitimacy that was bestowed by the Supreme Court at a later date.

First, General De Witt, head of the Western Defense Command, tried a program of voluntary evacuation, but it was soon torpedoed by opposition from the interior communities in California. He then launched a program of compulsory evacuation of Japanese. They were to be sent initially to assembly centers for a short period of time and then to permanently constructed relocation centers. The first contingent of Japanese reached an assembly center before the first of April; and the last, by the end of 1942. During this period, over 110,000 Japanese— approximately two-thirds of whom were Nisei or American citizens— were ripped from the social fabric of their normal life, deprived of both legal and human rights, subjected to severe economic loss and shipped off to relocation centers, an euphemistic term for concentration camps, located in desolate and isolated places. For well over 90 percent of the evacuees this was to be their home for at least a year; and for over 50 percent, their home for two and one-half to 3 years. In these camps the evacuees were forced to come to terms with a strange and forbidding environment, to adapt to a barracks life-style at great personal discomfort and inconvenience, and to submit to a bureaucracy that set the terms of adaptation, forged patterns of dependency, and despite its self-image of benevolence could and would exercise its authority to coerce compliance.

By the middle of 1946 all relocation centers were closed and with the exception of the renunciants whose fates were still being decided, what "the American Civil Liberties Union called ... 'the worst single wholesale violation of civil rights of American citizens in our history'" drew to a close (Biddle 1962:213). But what made the wholesale violation take on a particularly Kafkaesque quality was its having been a consequence of governmental policies that were based on "collective representations" transmuted into propositions of truth and fact. The beliefs that had been used to construct the reality of the policy makers, particularly the military, were the myth of military necessity and the myth of the yellow peril.

The latter myth, which we have shown, had been deeply embedded in the "collective conscience" of the people of California and the cadre of military and civilian officials of the national government since the turn of the century. Each edge of the yellow peril found particular resonance in one of the two circles. Japan as a fearsome military power with whom America was likely to do battle at some point in time had been a preoccupation of the military for decades as President Roosevelt himself alluded to in describing the crisis of 1913. The people of California, especially their political leaders, had long made known their fifth column suspicions of the Japanese immigrant—a belief they used with telling effect in the drive for alien land laws in the second decade of the century.

Each edge—though of differing priority to each circle—was inextricably linked with the other in an historically coherent manner. Perhaps if Japan had not played such a consistently active role in protesting treatment of its nationals in America and if the "dual citizenship" issue had not been so readily available for extending the attack against the loyalty of Japanese immigrants to that of their children, then the linkage between Japan as a nation and the Japanese immigrants as aliens might have been less clearly perceived or perpetuated. But reality seemed to reinforce belief and together they forged a strong connection between the two aspects of the yellow peril.

As a result, whichever aspect was immediately highlighted by the events of the day, the other was sure to vibrate with attention before too long. And since Japan and the Japanese immigrant were continually relevant parts of America's foreign and domestic environments for the four decades prior to the attack on Pearl Harbor, small wonder that the two edges of the yellow peril were continuously being honed at the center of public and governmental attention during much of this period.

The attack on Pearl Harbor, despite its having caught America by surprise, was then like the long awaited but dreaded fulfillment of a Delphi-like prophesy that had been made decades before but which had left unsettled the exact time it was to happen. And with victory after victory for the Japanese forces in the Pacific during the early months after the attack, the image of "superpower" that had already been sketched by Fitzpatrick in the early 1900s was dusted off and brought up-to-date as the frightening picture of what the enemy was like. As a result, the traditional image and the present reality of defeats combined to make Japan seem more like an invincible foe than merely a formidable one.

As events in the Pacific seemed to confirm the awesomeness of Japan's military prowess, the second edge of the yellow peril—momentarily quiescent—began to revive and to find expression first among the committed exclusionists. It began to blossom into full fury with the publication of the report on the Japanese attack on Pearl Harbor by the Roberts commission which had been appointed by President Roosevelt. The theme became an obsessive preoccupation of many, even to the extent of affecting the flow of intelligence to the military policy makers on the coast and of contaminating their interpretation of this intelligence. The contaminating influence of this image reached the peak of absurdity when the absence of incidents of sabotage and espionage was taken by the military policy makers as "proof" of the organized fifth column designs of the Japanese on the coast. In this fashion, the yellow peril image reached Goliath-like proportions on the West Coast and became the prism through which the military command perceived the world of reality in which it had to act.

This prism, however, did more than distort the perceptions of the policy maker; it also fed into and fueled his sense of urgency that something had to be done about the yellow peril. As such it breathed vitality and drama into the second myth without which action against the yellow peril could not have been taken: the myth of military necessity.

In the early days following the attack on Pearl Harbor, it is understandable why military authorities, in California and Washington, were apprehensive about the intentions of the Japanese armed forces toward the Pacific Coast. Were they preparing some sort of assault, large or small? Accordingly, military necessity seemed to dictate the build-up of men and equipment; even the naming of the Western Defense Command as a Theater of Operations seemed a reasonable move or precaution. However, within a month the military command in Washington became convinced that no large-scale assault was imminent, only sporadic raids. They never changed this assessment. As a result, the command reduced the flow of men and equipment for the active defense of the Pacific Coast, though support for air defense retained some sort of priority. But despite this reassessment the command neglected to withdraw the label of Theater of Operations from the area.

Even as Washington was playing down the military threat to the Pacific Coast, General DeWitt and his staff remained convinced of its seriousness. They raised to the level of fact every report and rumor of enemy action and came to believe what they wanted to believe. In short, they remained convinced that enemy action posed a grave threat to American shipping and might even be a prelude to a large-scale attack in the future.

Certain that the external attack would materialize at some point in time, the general and his staff became increasingly uneasy about the internal threat of sabotage and subversion. Having swallowed the yellow peril thesis in its entirety, they were adamant in their insistence that the Japanese in America were merely biding their time before showng their dedication and loyalty to the homeland through subversive action. As a result, not even the absence of incidents could jar their faith in the internal threat of the yellow peril. To them the faith in the myth was itself sufficient proof of its own validity. They were certain that sabotage and subversion were bound to happen in the future given their conviction of the undying fealty of Japanese aliens and their children to the emperor of Japan.

To wait passively for what was predestined to happen would mean, according to them, risking military disaster for the country. Military necessity required decisive action against something certain to happen in the future. In this manner, the myth of military necessity was spawned phoenixlike from the myth of the yellow peril and both fed upon each other to germinate still a third myth: mass evacuation of aliens and citizens of Japanese ancestry was essential to the security and survival of the Western Theater of Operations.

Accordingly, General DeWitt and his staff embraced the policy of evacuation and as evidence of its effectiveness, they cited the absence of incidents of sabotage and subversion. The same data, in effect, were used both as an indication of the need for the policy, and later as a sign of how successfully the policy had met the need—an exercise in tautological reasoning if there ever was one.

Postwar metamorphosis: from concentration camp to the people's domain

With the lifting of the mass exclusion orders, evacuees began to drift back to their homes on the West Coast. A number were greeted with harassment and violence by the people of some of the communities to which they returned. Many also faced the threat of expropriation of their property through fraudulent practices by whites; virtually all sustained some personal or real property loss. Even the state government of California took advantage of the situation by filing escheat proceedings under the Alien Land Laws. The total property losses were estimated in the hundreds of millions.

However, within a month of the closing of the last relocation center, in the spring of 1946, the first significant sign of a change in the political climate became visible. At the fervent urgings of the Japanese American Citizens League, the Truman administration submitted a bill to Congress for establishing an Evacuation Claims Commission. This commission was to adjudicate claims of persons of Japanese ancestry against the United States for losses sustained from their evacuation and exclusion from the West Coast, Alaska, and Hawaii during World War II.

In the accompanying letter, the secretary of interior sounded a dual theme that was repeated continually during the next few years to justify the "political change of heart" toward the Japanese. First, he said, they deserved consideration because they had been loyal to the United States during their ordeal. As evidence, he cited the fact which just a few short years ago had been used by General DeWitt to "prove" the opposite and therefore to justify their incarceration: the absence of any incidents of sabotage or espionage during the war. Second, he pointed to the record of heroism and devotion to service of the 23,000 Japanese-Americans who served in the armed forces.

The judiciary committees of each house unanimously endorsed the bill before it, and speaker after speaker in each house virtually fell over each other in complimenting the work of the committee. The dual themes first mentioned by the secretary resounded throughout the walls of Congress. Finally in mid-1948 the bill was passed in amended form. It was subsequently revised several times; its final revision was completed in 1956; nine more years elapsed before the last claim was settled.

Finally the claims program came to an end. Its significance was more symbolic than remedial. For it provided only partial restitution at the rate of less than ten cents for every dollar lost. But perhaps more significantly the program signified that about five years after Americans had uprooted them from their homes and herded them into concentration camps, the Japanese immigrants (Issei) had been accorded once again "the right of situs" in the plural terrain of the American society; and their American-born children (Nisei), "the right of situs" in its people's domain. In relegitimizing their presence, the U.S. government expressed its regret for their suffering, but denied any regret for implementing a policy of evacuation that turned out to be both unnecessary and unjust. Congress, for example, persisted in reaffirming the myth of military necessity as justifying the policy. However, it did not say that subsequent events had validated the myth as General DeWitt had insisted in his final report written just two years before the claims program was first broached in Congress. Instead it defended the myth as having been a "reasonable expectation" that reasonable men would have had during the period that the policy was implemented. It conceded that the passage of time had "fortunately" proved the expectation to be in error. And so now Congress was willing to make some amends for the "necessary suffering." Only a few congressmen were prepared to call the suffering unnecessary and the policy a mistake.*

Once the legitimacy of their fellow ethnics' presence in their respective domains had been restored, the Japanese American Citizens League turned its attention to gaining access for their parents, the Issei, to the people's domain. By the end of the decade they had gained an important ally, President Truman. In his celebrated civil rights message of February 1948, he called on Congress to remove the racial barriers to

---

*These amends by Congress did not really lay the matter to rest for the Japanese-American. Many continued to express resentment at the stigma of collective disloyalty they had to bear during World War II. They finally succeeded in getting further congressional action—40 years later. In August 1988 Congress passed a law that offered a public apology for the forced internment and that also established a 1.25 billion dollar trust fund to pay reparations to the internees and their families. Leaders of the Japanese community expressed the hope that the bill would finally put an end to the shame and mental anguish Japanese-Americans have suffered for almost half a century from the World War II stigma.

naturalization. The House of Representatives responded to this call and enacted such a bill. Again the dual themes of loyalty of the Issei in the camps and valor of the Nisei on the battlefield played a major role in galvanizing support for the measure, even congressmen from California voiced their support. The bill foundered, though, in the Senate. The House made three more attempts in the next four years only to have its bill disappear in the Senate or as in 1950 to have it vetoed by the president because the Senate had added an objectionable provision.

Finally in January 1952, McCarran unveiled before the Senate a monumental omnibus bill on immigration, naturalization, and nationality. The bill reaffirmed the basic philosophy and national origins quota system of the 1924 Immigration Bill. It departed from the earlier bill however by abandoning exclusion for Japan and the other Asian countries; it gave them modest quotas. In still another radical departure from the 1924 Act, McCarran and his subcommittee finally articulated in their bill what the House had been espousing in vain for about four years. They dropped all racial barriers to naturalization after testimony had persuaded them that the time had come for delegitimizing the racial creed as an "un-American" way of blocking access to citizenship and to the people's domain.

The liberals in Congress condemned the bill for perpetuating the discriminatory and restrictive features of the 1924 Act. They offered instead the Humphrey-Lehman Bill as a more humane substitute. The battle over the two bills found the liberals and the Japanese on opposite sides once again much as they were in the struggle over the 1924 bill. Then, however, the liberals had rejected an alliance with the Japanese and joined the conservatives in Congress to pass the bill. Now the roles were reversed. It was the Japanese who rejected the overture of the liberals and who joined forces with the conservatives to urge passage of the McCarran Act. In the final showdown in Congress, the Humphrey-Lehman Bill lost by an overwhelming margin, the McCarran Act prevailed even over a presidential veto.

Once the battle for naturalization and for a quota had been won in 1952, the interests of the Japanese community began to converge with those of the liberals and white ethnic minorities on the issue of immigration. Ideologically their positions grew closer as all assailed the discriminatory allocation of quotas under the McCarran Act. Finally, they joined forces in 1965 to help bring about a radically new immigration law that abolished the national origins and quota features of the earlier acts.

In supporting the bill, the head of the Japanese American Citizens League no longer talked as though he were representing aliens and outsiders who wanted to gain access to the people's domain. That, he reminded the House Judiciary Committee in his testimony, was his and the JACL's lot in 1952 and accounted for their stand on the McCarran Act "in spite of its deficiencies." Now he talked as a representative of a racial and ethnic group that had become part of the people's domain, was living in accordance with the American creed, and had the credentials and achievements to prove it. And as representative of that group, he now wanted to eliminate the last vestiges of a racially discriminatory immigration policy that distinguished between Asians and white Europeans. Thus the enactment of the 1965 Immigration Bill signified to him the final step in the abolition of the racial creed as the established principle guiding America's historic policy of immigration. ("It would complete the objective of eliminating race as an accepted principle and practice in our immigration law" (US Congressional Record 1965:24,504).)

Overall, then, by enacting the immigration bill and the other civil rights acts of 1964 and 1965, America had finally delegitimized the racial creed as part of its legal-normative code for regulating the treatment of nonwhite minorities in any of their varied statuses: as potential or actual immigrant, as alien or as citizen. Only the American creed and its axiomatic premise of equal treatment was henceforth to be the regnant legal-normative code for all.

Puerto Rico: Colonial Dependency and Commonwealth Status

Territorial status and duality

With the acquisition of Puerto Rico, the United States came full circle to the point of its beginnings. Originally the product of the duality exported from the colonial power, England, it now became a colonial power in its own right with its own distinctive brand of duality to export to its political dependencies. This was legally an entirely new role for the United States. For, until Puerto Rico, it had treated new lands as colonist extensions of itself and granted them territorial status with the assurance of eventual incorporation into the Union as a state. Their people in the meantime were to be protected by most of the rights and immunities of the Constitution.

The model for relations with these "infant states" had been set 110 years earlier with the reaffirmation of the Northwest Ordinance by the First Congress, one year after the formation of the new nation. The only significant change during this interval was the addition to this model of an even more democratic third stage of territorial governance.

During this interval, however, the United States did confront dualities in its new territories, but these were by-products of its own "colonist-colonialist" past. For example, the U.S. government in retaining control of policy toward the Indian in these new acquisitions pursued and elaborated the particular kind of dualism that was set by the British government before the formation of the new nation. In addition, the United States had to deal with the dualities imported by the American settlers into these new territories. The most significant of which was the duality based on black slavery.

Although Congress barred slavery from the Northwest Territory in 1789, it did not interfere for the next 30 years with the extension of slavery into new territories, particularly those south of the Mason-Dixon line. However, in 1818 the balance between free and slave states became a preoccupation of a Congress divided between the two. It worried lest one side or the other become the predominant power in the setting of government policy on a national level. Congress subsequently passed the Missouri Compromise which drew the equivalent of a Mason-Dixon line west of the Mississippi River. North of this line slavery was to be barred from any territory entering as a state in the Union; south of this line slavery was to be permitted. For 30 years Congress monitored carefully the entry of new states according to the Missouri principle. But in 1854 Congress itself disrupted this accommodation through the Kansas-Nebraska bill, and three years later the Supreme Court drew the protective mantle of the Constitution around the extension into new territories of the duality based on slavery. In his opinion on *Dred Scott* in 1857, Chief Justice Taney declared that Congress had no constitutional right to ban slavery in any territory as it had done through the Missouri Compromise. The issue was to be left entirely up to the settlers in the territory. However, in approximately a decade the Taney opinion became moot as the enactment of the Thirteenth Amendment banned slavery in both the territories and states of the Union.

The Foraker Act and colonial status

With the passage of the Foraker Act in 1900, the United States was no longer merely acting out its own historical past. It officially joined the ranks of the colonialist powers and created its own version of duality that was to be exported to its political dependency, Puerto Rico. Unlike the old version that was instrumental in the founding of America and of other nations in the New World, the new version did not involve the colonization and settlement of large numbers of Americans in the new dependency and the creation by them of an entirely new political society in their image. In fact, of the relatively few Americans who migrated to the island, only a small handful ever settled there permanently. Most came to Puerto Rico as colonial administrators for the U.S. government and as managers for the absentee sugar corporations. They functioned as the kind of sojourner elite described in chapter 5. However unlike the sojourner elite who longed for their homeland but who remained permanently perched atop the colonial plural society, the American elite were frequently rotated. Most remained for a relatively short period of time on the island.

The new version then had little to do with the American settler; instead it had to do with the people of the island and with Puerto Rico as a political entity. In effect, the United States in enacting the Foraker Bill, had devised an entirely new legal relationship with a newly acquired land. As a colonial dependency or America's first legally defined "unincorporated territory," Puerto Rico could not look to eventual incorporation into the Union as a state. Its inhabitants were not to be included as part of the people of the United States as were those in incorporated territories and states of the Union. And finally both the island and the people were placed under the domination and control of the Congress.

The original and revised version of the Foraker Act

The act established a governance structure that was patterned after that of an incorporated territory, which was all that remained of any significance in the final bill from its original draft. The latter had been written as though territorial status was contemplated for Puerto Rico. Under this original draft, for example, all inhabitants of the island except those who retained their allegiance to Spain were to be deemed "citizens of the United States"; and collectively they were to "constitute a body politic with governmental powers ..." (Sec.3). In addition judicial and legal proceedings and processes conducted by this body politic were to run "in the name of 'The United States of America, island of Puerto Rico,' and all [of its] criminal or penal prosecutions shall be conducted in the name and by the authority of 'The United States of America, island of Puerto Rico'" (Sec.13). The bill also set the American Constitution as the basic legal-normative framework for the island; it and "all the laws of the United States locally applicable ... was to have the same force and effect in the island of Puerto Rico as elsewhere in the United States (Sec.10) (S2264 A Bill 1900:2,5).

The bill also established for the island a territorial governance structure of the second grade. In effect, the people were to elect representatives to one of the two legislative bodies, the House of Delegates; all other officials from the governor on down were to be appointed by the president. The bill also reaffirmed another feature of the second grade territorial governance structure. The island was to conduct a biennial election among qualified voters for "one Delegate to the House of

Representatives of the United States, who shall be entitled to a seat, but not to a vote, in that body, on the certificate of election of the governor of the island ..." (Sec.36) (S2264 A Bill 1900:18).

The revised bill that was reported back to the Senate after several weeks of hearings bore little resemblance to the original. The legal status of the island was completely altered. No longer was the island to be a territory incorporated into the United States, but it was to become a new kind of legal entity unique in American history. During the debate over the revised bill, Foraker was at a loss to identify what he had created. He rejected, though, the label brandished by his opponents. They insisted Puerto Rico had become a colonial dependency under the revised bill, which it indeed had. A year later the Supreme Court invented a more palatable label for the island; it became an "unincorporated territory" under the revised Foraker Bill.

Under the revised bill, Puerto Ricans were not identified as "citizens of the United States" as set forth in the original bill but as "citizens of Porto Rico, and as such entitled to the protection of the United States." Even their children were to be citizens of Porto Rico and not of the United States, despite the Fourteenth Amendment. And as "citizens of Porto Rico" the inhabitants were to "constitute a body politic under the name of The People of Porto Rico. ..." The revised bill also deleted all references to the American Constitution as the basic legal-normative framework for the island; it cast no protective mantle around the rights and immunities of the people of Porto Rico nor served as a standard by which the legitimacy of local laws could be assessed. The only standard that was to be applied was the "statutory laws of the United States, not locally inapplicable."

In addition, the bill as finally enacted deprived Puerto Rico of the right to elect "one Delegate to the House of Representatives of the United States, who shall be entitled to a seat, but not to a vote in that body"; instead the island was granted the right to elect "a resident commissioner to the United States, who shall be entitled to official recognition as such by all departments, upon presentation to the Department of State of a certificate of election of the governor of Porto Rico. ...."

Yet despite these various changes, the revised bill retained virtually intact most of the governance features of the original bill. In effect Puerto Rico was to be governed by a territorial governmental structure of the second grade, even though it had been stripped of the legal status of being a territory. To add to the anomalous situation, the revised bill retained the clause that the governor of Puerto Rico was to have "all the powers of governors of the Territories of the U.S." (HR8245 An Act 1900 56:1).

In retaining a territorial structure of governance, Congress built ambiguities and paradoxes into the newly created colonial edifice that gave it a hybrid dualism of its own. The transplantation of this governance structure, in effect, provided the Puerto Ricans with an institutional standard or "mirror" by which they could compare their own fate as a colonial people who were excluded from the people's domain with the fate of territorial people who were included in the domain.

The pressure for self-government and the parallel pathways

Once the ramifications of the revised Foraker Act became known, large segments of the island elite and citizens of Puerto Rico began to make these comparisons and to chafe under the act's "colonial" terms. And so began a five-decade campaign to pressure Congress into clarifying the ambiguities in the political-legal status of the island and into authorizing a greater measure of self-governance. Irrespective of the specific segment of the elite who was in saddle during this period, all wrapped the banner of the American creed and Constitution around their message of protest, but they differed markedly in the kind of ultimate status they advocated for the island. In most of the period, the ideological pendulum swung from advocacy of independent nationhood to statehood with the former receiving the more frequent play.

In turn, Congress, confounded by the ambiguous political and legal structure it had created sought to mark a passage through the uncharted political waters between the shoals of independence and statehood. In the process, it evolved an institutional pathway in the newly defined colonial domain of America that paralleled the established pathway for transforming a territory into a state of the Union. For example, slowly and hesitantly Congress granted the island the right to elect both of its houses of the legislature as would a territory in the third stage of governance. Almost 30 years later it endorsed the selection by the president of a governor from among the island's residents—an action that had previously been confined to the most advanced stage of territorial governance. Two years later Congress began to enact governance measures that traditionally marked the transmutation of a territory into a state in the Union. First it granted the island the right to elect its own governor in 1948. In 1950 it authorized Puerto Rico to write its own constitution. It stipulated as it would in the writing of a constitution for a new state, that Puerto Rico's document must provide for a republican form of government and contain a bill of rights. Within two years Puerto Rico completed a constitution that established the novel status of commonwealth for the island. Four months later Congress endorsed the status and approved the constitution after rejecting a portion of its expanded bill of rights.

Thus after a half century the United States finally completed a dual structure of governance for its territorial acquisitions. The novel structure mirrored many features of the older structure of governance, but it was built outside the people's domain. As a result, despite Puerto Rico's present "statelike" commonwealth status, it remains a colonial dependency of the United States.

The people of Puerto Rico and American citizenship

In the early days of building this structure, Congress also dissolved in 1917 its construct of people of Porto Rico and linked the island's inhabitants to the people of the United States by granting them American citizenship. In so doing Congress acted again in a paradoxical manner that compounded the ambiguous status of the Puerto Rican. The individual Puerto Rican could henceforth become a full member of the people's domain by migrating to a state of the Union and living there long enough to become a citizen of that state. But if he stayed in Puerto Rico, he would continue to be excluded from the people's domain despite his American citizenship. For a time there was no functional equivalent for territorial or state citizenship on the island. Almost a decade later Congress filled the void by restoring the construct, citizen of Puerto Rico. Thus, dual citizenship came to apply to the Puerto Ricans in Puerto Rico as it does to those Americans who are part of the people's domain on the mainland, but it was dual citizenship in a political community that itself remained outside the pale of the people's domain.

The uncertain future

In the final analysis, then, the Puerto Ricans have had to live with the various paradoxes and ambiguities imprinted in the dual structure of governance created by Congress in the shadow of the people's domain. How much longer they will wish to do so is open to question. Today discontent with this inherently unstable arrangement is increasingly coming to the surface. And unless Congress moves rapidly to dissolve this second structure and to incorporate the political community of Puerto Rico into the people's domain as a state in the Union, the pressure for independence may prove irresistible.

9   Blacks and the White Immigrants

Many social scientists find it difficult to accept the premise that the treatment of blacks and other racial minorities in America has been qualitatively different historically from that afforded non-Protestant white immigrants, particularly those from Southern and Eastern Europe. A number may agree that what happened to blacks in the Deep South may give some credence to this thesis, but to them the Deep South represented an aberrant and cancerous growth grafted onto what was truly the America of the Constitution and of the American creed.

However, once the blacks moved North during and after World War I, these scholars contend, their experience was similar to that of the white immigrants. They point to the fact that both experienced widespread discrimination and that both even engaged in joint efforts to combat this discrimination—at least until the early 1960s.

In this concluding chapter, we shall analyze the historical validity of the "immigrant analogy." Then, we shall examine the process whereby the progeny of the white immigrants (referred to today as white ethnics) and the blacks were transformed from allies in the struggle against discrimination into antagonists as the blacks persisted in their struggle against the continuing effects of America's historic duality.

The "Immigrant Analogy"

In the past several decades the "immigrant analogy" has gained a renewed measure of support from a number of social scientists. They insist that the northward migration of blacks during and after World War I bore a striking resemblance to the earlier flow of the non-Protestant white immigrants. Both groups of migrants are seen as unlettered and unskilled menials who crowded into urban ghettos and had to start at the bottom of the occupational ladder. In 1966, for example, Irving Kristol pursued this comparison in an article that he entitled "The Negro is Like the Immigrant Yesterday." A few years earlier Glazer and Moynihan had written, "These Americans [Negroes] of two centuries are as much immigrant as any European immigrant group, for the shift from the South to New York is as radical a change for the Negro as that faced by earlier immigrants" (Glazer and Moynihan 1963:26). This thesis has become increasingly popular among those scholars who have in the past several decades focused their attention on white ethnicity. It has been seriously challenged and discarded by other scholars who have concentrated during the same period on racial minorities.

According to the proponents of the immigrant analogy, both groups of migrants lived initially in poverty and followed a style of life that was alien to the larger society. They elicited anger and resentment from members of the established society who deemed their behavior disruptive to the public, social, and moral orders. Kristol describes in vivid detail the parallel response of hostility both to the immigrant of yesterday and to the urban black of today and the massive discrimination both faced on the job and housing markets (Kristol 1966).

By concentrating on the existential situation at the time of entry, these analysts seem intent on making the point that the white immigrant was no better off than the black, or its converse, the black was no worse off than the white. To support their case, these writers have no difficulty in showing the extreme hardship and contempt the white immigrants had to bear upon their arrival in a New World where people like themselves were first making their way. However, to make a similar point about the blacks, these analysts have virtually had to divest the blacks of any past history in the North and to treat their northward migration as though it took place on a blank tablet. Obviously Glazer, Kristol, and the others are aware of an earlier presence of blacks in the North, but they dismiss this presence as irrelevant to their thesis because they claim the numbers were too small to make a difference.

The Blacks and the Irish Immigrants

Yet whether few or many, their presence poses a serious challenge to the thesis that blacks and white immigrants faced similar conditions. Nowhere can this be better seen than in the unequal struggle that developed in the urban areas of New York and Boston in the mid-1800s between blacks and the first wave of non-Protestant white immigrants about whom Glazer and Moynihan have written: the Irish Catholic.

As freed men, blacks could no longer pursue the kind of artisan occupations that some were able to as slaves. Instead they were pushed into increasingly menial jobs such as on the docks, personal service, and the like. During the Napoleonic Wars they purportedly registered some gains only to have them taken away with the arrival of white immigrants. Thus, blacks were by and large already a relatively fixed underclass in the North by the time the first white immigrants disembarked. Their status was determined by the distinctive kind of duality imprinted in the North from colonial days on and legitimated by the Supreme Court prior to the Civil War and again later in the post-Reconstruction period.

In Ireland the political and economic status of the Irish Catholic was not too dissimilar from that of the black in the United States. Most scholars agree that their plight also resembled that of colonialized subjects. They experienced poverty, degradation, and the oppressive heel of the British. So deeply rooted was their hatred of the British that they carried it as part of their cultural and ideological baggage to the New World.

In the New World they suffered the indignities and discrimination which Glazer, Moynihan, and Kristol have vividly described. They had to struggle for economic survival and had to work at the most menial of jobs. But there was a difference on the political level. They did not have to accept the status of colonialized subject; instead, they soon made their presence felt in the political arena.

By the 1850s they comprised one-fourth to one-third of the voters in New York City and became a major force in the Democratic party. They were even partially successful in rolling back the pervasive control of the public school system by the Protestant establishment. They also became committed flag wavers of the American way of life—carefully drawing the distinction between that way of life and the English dominance and imprint on it.

Throughout this period their relations with the blacks became increasingly tense and hostile. In Ireland it's probable that few had known any blacks, and therefore had no fixed impression of blacks. But in the New World the Irish Catholics soon found themselves in a desperate competitive struggle with the blacks for the menial jobs that were available (Gibson 1951). No effort seemed to have been made to forge the kind of working-class coalition that Marx has written about; instead relations became increasingly conflictual and antagonistic.

The Irish, however, soon gained the upper hand in the struggle. They not only began to outnumber the blacks, but even more importantly they soon learned and adopted the basic rules of the institutional game in the America of the day: the rights of the white man were superior to those of the black man in all of the institutional arenas of society.

Armed with this claim to legal and moral superiority, the Irish soon pushed the blacks off of the docks and out of other occupations. They were even prepared to defend with violence the sphere of personal and political rights that the law and institutional system had allowed the Irish to carve out for themselves. Thus, when on occasion the blacks sought to counterattack by becoming scabs as in the case of a longshoreman's strike, the Irish struck back in full self-righteousness.

In a letter to Secretary of State Seward who was a friend of his, the Archbishop John Hughes of New York City sought to explain the violent reaction of his fellow Irishmen to the Draft Law of 1863 in precisely these terms. The discontented Irish were upset, he maintained, at what they perceived to be a concerted effort to make black labor the equal of white.

> We have had a week of trouble and apprehension in this city. I think the trouble is now over. The plea of the discontents is, on the surface, the draft. At its bottom, however, in my opinion, the discontent will be found in what the misguided people imagine to be a disposition on the part of a few here and elsewhere to make black labor equal to white labor, and put both on the same equality, with the difference that black labor shall have local patronage over the toil of the white man (Hughes 1863:938–939).

The Archbishop concluded with the statement "I have no opinion of my own to express on the subject" (Hughes 1863:939).

By the time the white immigrants from Southern and Eastern Europe began to arrive in the late nineteenth and early twentieth century, the struggle had more or less been decided. These immigrants were the beneficiaries of the struggle that the Irish Catholics had waged earlier to establish the claim that even non-Protestant white immigrants had superior rights to those of the blacks, despite the fact that the latter had arrived in this country generations earlier. As a result, blacks were locked out of the competitive arena. Their status of underclass was further sealed by the new versions of duality that legally and constitutionally evolved by the turn of the twentieth century.

The Northward Movement of Blacks

Thus the migration to the North of blacks during and after World War I did not take place in a legal-normative vacuum as Kristol and others seem to suggest. The stage was already set; the duality long imprinted in the North, in place. However, what was relatively new was the opening of a new job market for the blacks. No longer confined to the nonindustrial personal service sector of the economy, they were finally allowed into the manufacturing sector but only in its most menial and unskilled jobs. What is more, whites, including the immigrants—at virtually all levels—soon expressed concern at this influx and sought to breathe new life and vitality into the duality of the North. They solidified their virtually monopolistic control of the dual labor and housing markets with the general blessing, once again, of the courts.

As a result, blacks remained anchored to the lower reaches of the manufacturing and other sectors of the economy. For decades they functioned as an industrial reserve à la Marx that in recent years has become increasingly expendable as the economy itself has undergone dramatic technological and organizational changes. Under the circumstances, few blacks have been able to follow the path of upward mobility that Kristol and the other immigrant analogists predicted they would (Kristol 1966). These observers tend to interpret this as basically a failing of the blacks themselves. According to their way of thinking, if the blacks were to develop the necessary personal and communal resources—which some doubt they will—they should be able to overcome any obstacle and make their way up the occupational and societal ladder as did the white immigrant. These analysts continue to insist that whatever differences in historical barriers the two groups have had to face in their struggle upward, the differences were merely those of degree and not of kind. Both are, in their view, members of a society governed by the American creed which values individual achievement and effort over group prejudice.

To sustain this thesis, those observers have had to ignore or to deny, as has already become apparent, the full historical record of America's mistreatment of its racial minorities and of the sanctification of this mistreatment in the supreme law of the land. This pattern of mistreatment, as we have argued throughout this book, affected the life circumstances of blacks and of other nonwhite races in ways that made them qualitatively different from the conditions experienced by any white, including the non-Protestant immigrant.

As a result, to say "today's black is like yesterday's immigrant" is to utter an interesting metaphor that has little historical relevance. Perhaps closer to the historical mark is a metaphor that can be articulated from Rex's observations (1973). Namely, the northernbound black is like the colonial migrant of yesterday who had left the colony to live in the metropolitan society which in turn had its own colonial heritage.

The White Immigrants and Discrimination

Ironically, even as the white immigrants were benefitting from the duality that enabled them to establish their societal claims as superior to those of the blacks, they almost became its victims. They were caught in a massive web of discrimination that was an extension of the inequities built into the structure of duality. They even faced a concerted effort on the part of scientific, academic, and political circles in the dominant society to attach the label of race onto them. This label was used to stigmatize them as the biological inferiors of the white Anglo-Saxon race and to justify any attempt to clamp the duality as securely on them as it had already been clamped on blacks and on other nonwhites. To the extent that this attempt were to succeed, the white Anglo-Saxon Protestants could in good conscience treat these white immigrants much as they already were treating the blacks and other "inferior" nonwhite races.

These efforts were quite successful in various institutional arenas. The white immigrants were effectively barred from mainstream occupations; their access to institutions of academic and professional learning, seriously restricted. They also had little chance of moving into the better neighborhoods and of enhancing their social standing in the community. However, what the anti-immigrant forces could not do was to prevent their membership in the people's domain or to block their participation in the political arena. For despite the scope of their opposition, these forces had to admit that the immigrants were white albeit, according to them, an inferior subspecies of whites. And in being white the immigrants' rights of membership were protected by the law of 1790. Further, by the second decade of the twentieth century the number of immigrants had increased sufficiently to make them a political force to be reckoned with in New York and in other large cities.

Determined to remedy this "defect," the anti-immigrant forces shifted the battleground to immigration policy itself in the early decades of the twentieth century. If they could not keep the white immigrant from the people's domain, then they were going to try to bar him from entering the country or at least to reduce the numbers who could. Even on this front, though, these forces were not as successful as they were against racial minorities. In the Immigration Act of 1924, for example, they managed to bar all Japanese and other Asians from entering. They did so on the grounds that Asians, Japanese in particular, were ineligible for citizenship so why let them in. In support of this, they cited the 1790 law and the reaffirmation of this law by the U.S. Supreme Court in the *Ozawa* case of 1922. Such grounds, however, could not be used against the "new" immigrants from Southern and Eastern Europe so they had to settle for less. They made sure that the immigration quotas were much lower for immigrants from Southern and Eastern Europe than for those from Northern and Western Europe.

Both groups were, in effect, treated unfairly by the ruling WASP elite, but the unfairness each experienced was quite different. The "inferior" whites from Southern and Eastern Europe suffered discrimination; the "inferior" racial minorities, total exclusion.

Once again the fates of the "inferior" white immigrants and racial minorities were intertwined—but once again only up to a point. This is even more strikingly apparent in the course that debate on the bill took in Congress. Congressmen who favored more equitable treatment for the white immigrant from Southern and Eastern Europe abandoned the cause of the Japanese. They accepted exclusion for the Japanese in the hope of striking a better deal for their own side with the delegation from California—a tactic that failed.

The Joint Struggle against Discrimination

The intertwining of the fates of the white immigrants and racial minorities, blacks in particular, found further expression during the first half of the twentieth century in the efforts to push back the barriers of discrimination. Sometimes these efforts were performed jointly; other times, separately. The principal focus of attack was the legal and constitutional umbrella that protected and gave legitimacy to discriminatory and exclusionary policies of the federal, state, and local governments.

At the forefront of this struggle was the National Association for the Advancement of Colored People (NAACP). Organized in 1909, it resorted to legal contest and court action as its major vehicle of protest and challenge. Its ultimate goals were the reassertion of the claims of the blacks to full membership in the various realms of the people's domain lost after Reconstruction and the reaffirmation of the American creed as the regnant normative code for all Americans under the guarantees of the Constitution.

As Myrdal commented, "From the very beginning, the Association has laid stress on its legal redress work, and this has always been a most important and, certainly, the most spectacular part of its activity. The Association takes its stand on the legal equality of all the citizens of the country stipulated in the Constitution, and in most of the laws of the several states of the South and the North" (Myrdal 1944:828).

From its inception Jewish liberals have been actively involved with the NAACP. Over the decades they have contributed as donors, officers, and lawyers in addition to comprising a substantial portion of its white membership. Jewish organizations have also frequently joined the NAACP in its legal battles. For example, during the 1940s when the NAACP stepped up its litigation against segregated schools, the American Jewish Congress sent its own lawyers to volunteer their services for important cases. The NAACP and the Congress also jointly published a civil rights newsletter during this period. Will Maslow, who later became the director of the Congress, explained, "You cannot fight discrimination against one minority group without fighting it against others. It was logical for Jews and Negroes to cooperate" (Weisbrot 1984:22).

The cooperation between Jewish groups and the NAACP continued into the early 1960s. By then the scene had shifted from the courts to the streets of the South. According to Dr. Martin Luther King, Jr., by the time his civil rights campaign in Birmingham, Alabama became "a fuse [that] detonated revolution," he had gained the support of northern white liberals, Jews in particular (King 1964:114). They joined the ranks of the protesters and worked not only with Dr. King's Southern Christian Leadership Conference but also with the Congress of Racial Equality and the Student Nonviolent Coordinating Committee. They also contributed substantial funds to these various organizations. "In CORE, for example, most of the largest donors were Jewish, and the United Jewish Appeal even dispatched four skilled fundraisers to train CORE administrators ..." (Weisbrot 1984:22).

This interracial cooperation crested in late August 1963, when approximately a quarter of a million people from various parts of the country gathered in Washington, D.C. for a "march for jobs and freedom." The march brought together for one historical moment in time the divergent strands of the black civil rights movement, its various leaders and organizations. It also included an estimated 60,000 whites and received strong and vigorous support from the three major religious faiths. In fact Dr. Joachim Prinz of the American Jewish Congress was one of the day's chairmen. Whites and blacks joined together in a display of interracial harmony and amity over the issue of racial justice that had never been seen before and was to be seen but once more—in a lesser fashion—in Selma, Alabama. As Waskow comments, "The March on Washington was in many ways the high point of 'gladness' in the civil rights movement of the 1960s, and also the high point of coalition between the various elements in the country, white and black, that supported the demand for racial equality" (Waskow 1967:236).

The march ended with a mass meeting before the Lincoln Memorial where a number of demands were made, including a call to Congress and the president for comprehensive civil rights legislation, for training and jobs programs, for fair employment practices laws, and the like. The highlight of the meeting was the celebrated speech "I Have a Dream" by Dr. Martin Luther King, Jr.

Two years later, in March 1965, the epilogue to the drama of interracial unity and harmony that had climaxed in Washington was played out in the march from Selma to Montgomery, Alabama. This was the last major expression of interracial unity in the civil rights movement.

And so with the sustained pressure of the black revolution in the South and with the support of the northern white liberals, the stage was set for the passage of the Civil Rights Act of 1964 and the Voting Rights Act of 1965. With enactment of this and other civil rights legislation, such as the Immigration Act of 1965 and the Fair Housing Act of 1968, Congress dismantled the scaffolding that had served as the lingering legal and constitutional basis for discriminatory policies and practices. In so doing, Congress mandated that all the major institutional environments of the people's domain were to be governed under a common legal-normative framework based on equality of access and of opportunity.

The Jewish Immigrants and the Fulfillment of a Dream

Though the basic challenge that produced this legislation was racial, the statutes themselves stipulated that it was unlawful to discriminate not only on the grounds of race and color but also on the grounds of gender, religion, and national origins. For the progeny of the white immigrant this was a fitting climax to their decades-long struggle against discrimination. They now had the legal right to demand equal access to even the highest recesses of the various institutions and realms of the people's domain.

That was all they needed, they reasoned, in order for them to maximize their chances for success and to gain the full benefits of the American creed Myrdal wrote about. For, even without the legislation of the 1960s, they had made considerable progress. The most notable example is what happened to the Jewish immigrants and their children.

Even in the earliest days of their arrival when discrimination was at its peak, many of these immigrants were able to bypass at least some of these barriers. For example, a number of Eastern European Jews took advantage of America's expanding economy and became entrepreneurs in high-risk, low-capital business ventures, particularly in the garment industry. Their rapid rise from poverty to respectability has been trumpeted by the immigrant analogists as a model for all ethnic and racial groups. These observers have primarily attributed the success of the Jews to the strength of their inner communal and personal values and traits, and to the benign working of the American creed which provided the legal-normative support for the individual effort and achievement of the immigrant. These observers have failed, however, to give due weight to what Steinberg insists was crucial to their success: the set of urbanized occupational skills that they brought with them as part of their social and cultural baggage (Steinberg 1981). These skills, according to Steinberg, found a ready market in America's expanding economy. As a result, the East European Jew who decided to strike out on his own in the garment industry was able to tap a skilled labor supply which only he and his fellow ethnic entrepreneurs were in a position to exploit and to monopolize through the common language, the cultural and ethnic ties they shared. This gave him a competitive edge in the marketplace where he sold his product to customers who were primarily of the larger society and not of the impoverished ethnic group. In this manner, he gained access to the resources and wealth of the dominant society and began his rapid ascent on the ladder of success.

Only for a brief historical moment was the black in a comparable situation. Interestingly, this moment took place in the nineteenth and not in the twentieth century. For approximately four decades of that century, black entrepreneurs played an important role in the catering industry in Philadelphia and in New York City. They served a white elite that fashioned its tastes after the Southern plantation owner, and they exploited their fellow blacks as a skilled work force in the field of personal service. The brief moment came to an end by the last two decades of the century as the tastes of the white elite shifted toward the cuisine of the European aristocracy and as the white immigrant pushed the black service worker out of the fashionable into the second-rate hotels. As a result, by the turn of the century blacks were once again experiencing a double marginality: marginal jobs in marginal establishments in the field of personal service.

By the 1920s and 1930s the children of the Jewish immigrants breached still other discriminatory barriers, particularly in the area of higher education. Only a few may have been able to gain entrance into Harvard; Columbia also imposed restrictions. But many were able to attend City College and Hunter College in New York City. In addition, few may have been able to get into the best professional schools, but a number went to the second best. Further, instead of going into the corporate world, they went into family businesses.

By the end of World War II even more opportunities opened up in higher education. Not only did they become students; they also became teachers in public school systems and members of faculties in the social sciences, not necessarily in the top colleges or universities but in the fairly good ones. They also flocked to professional schools and became doctors and lawyers.

As a result, by the 1960s most of the occupational barriers had been breached. They still had trouble getting positions in the elite universities or gaining access to the higher circles of the professions and of business, and even less success in gaining membership in prestigious country clubs. Nevertheless, they were well ensconced in most of the institutional arenas of the people's domain, particularly in the economic, educational, and political sectors.

For them, then, the civil rights legislation was a way of opening the last doors to the higher reaches of the people's domain. Even more important was the symbolic significance of the legislation. It epitomized to them the final triumph of the American creed. They were convinced that America had at last become the kind of society the Founding Fathers hoped they were establishing through the Declaration of Independence and the Constitution.

The Jewish immigrants and their children were always confident even in the darkest days of discrimination that this was meant to be. They shared with Myrdal the optimistic belief that racism, prejudice, and discrimination were alien to the American creed and way of life. Jewish scholars, in particular, shared the premise that prejudice and discrimination were irrational and aberrant responses in a society whose core value system was the American creed. They were centrally involved in the classic studies of the authoritarian personality that were sponsored by the American Jewish Committee (Adorno 1950). They agreed with the conclusions that prejudice served important psychic and emotional needs for "sick" personalities; hence their need to scapegoat ethnic and racial minorities. In addition, they were appalled at the Deep South's treatment of its blacks and saw it as the major manifestation of this "sick" abnormality. They were confident that once this cancerous growth of Jim Crowism was excised from the body politic, America would be liberated from the major source that generated this abnormality and that contaminated the sentiments, beliefs, and behavior of the dominant whites in the South and in the rest of the country.

For many Jews, then, passage of the civil rights legislation—the Civil Rights Act of 1964, in particular—seemed to be the fulfillment of a dream. They cherished the gains that they had registered, were registering, and that they hoped to register in the future under the full beneficence of the American creed. They were, however, not prepared to recognize that for racial minorities, the blacks in particular, passage of the civil rights legislation did not mark the end of the struggle for equality but rather the beginning of another phase of the struggle.

The Black Challenge in the North

In the mid-1960s, blacks confronted the deeply rooted structure of racial discrimination and exclusion from America's past that continued to affect their life chances and to prevent them from equal and full access to the various institutional arenas of the people's domain despite the civil rights legislation and the American creed. The setting for this new challenge was no longer to be in the South but in the large cities of the North and the West.

It began in earnest in the streets of Watts in Los Angeles, even as the Voting Rights Act of 1965 was being enacted into law. For days rioting spread throughout the entire black area and took an increasingly devastating toll of life and property. The impact of Watts was so profound and traumatic that it sent shock waves throughout the nation and marked the beginning of the end of a mythological innocence about the historical character and meaning of the black encounter in the North. No longer would this encounter be seen in the simplistic and optimistic terms of the Jewish and other white liberals.

This new mood and resolve of the blacks in the North blossomed in 1966 through disorder, demonstration, and riot to the extent that the Kerner Commission observed, "The events of 1966 made it appear that domestic turmoil had become part of the American scene" (National Advisory Commission on Civil Disorders 1968:20). From these spontaneous and volcanic eruptions, a political rhetoric was articulated by the more militant of the black leaders. They called for black nationalism and black separatism. Their basic premise was that blacks had never had and never would have the benefits or protection of the American creed, Declaration of Independence, or Constitution. As a result, they insisted blacks were doomed to continued exploitation as a subordinated and segmented racial group in white America until and unless they were prepared to go to the streets, to demonstrate and to engage in militant action.

Finally in Mississippi in 1966, Stokely Carmichael fused the call for militance and nationalism into a simple slogan "black power" that captured the imagination of the black. From that time on the phrase "black power" came to dominate the language of protest, and Carmichael assumed the leading role as its interpreter.

Once having been proclaimed and enthusiastically embraced by young urban blacks, in particular, the slogan sent shudders through white America and elicited tirades of anger and laments of dismay each time it was repeated in the mass media. Among whites the slogan conjured up an image of massive and wanton destruction and violence by blacks that would spill over the boundaries of the ghettos into white neighborhoods and would take the form at its worst of guerilla warfare in city streets. These fears and anxieties were fed by the rapid spread of the urban riots through 1967 and 1968 with their climactic explosion in Newark and Detroit, and by the mounting crescendo of militant rhetoric. The assassination of Dr. King in 1968 added fuel to the fury. As a result, many Jewish liberals withdrew from the civil rights struggle and cut off their financial support. To placate whites, some of the more moderate black leaders sought to make the slogan more palatable. They claimed that it was nothing more than another version of the kind of ethnic solidarity that the white immigrants had also sought in their quest to become part of the American society.

Even after the street disturbances subsided, blacks continued to challenge their subordinated status and to press their challenge along territorial and institutional boundaries now being guarded by the newly commissioned sentries of "white ethnics"—the label increasingly employed to identify the progeny of the white immigrants from Southern and Eastern Europe. Thus, the stage was set for a series of confrontations between the two groups. What made the black challenge seem even more formidable and "unfair" to the white ethnics was the role that the government and its agencies played in supporting the challenge. The most hated opponents were the executive branch of the federal government and the federal courts.

The Response of the White Ethnic

Caught in what they saw as a vise that threatened their newly won gains and security, the white ethnics—including the Jews—moved increasingly toward a garrison mentality, and many Jews, in particular, jettisoned their empathy for the blacks and their own heritage of liberalism. Rieder examines this transformation in his study of lower middle-class Jewish and Italian residents of Canarsie in Brooklyn during the mid-1970s.

To the Italians and Jews of Canarsie the black challenge became increasingly defined as a glorified "hustle" or a "mugging" of the middle-class whites. They insisted that blacks wanted what they really did not deserve in the name of redressing some past injustice for which Canarsie whites were certainly not responsible. The Canarsie residents even saw the urban riots of the mid-1960s in these terms.

> The civil disorders of the 1960s represented such a mugging in a dramatic collective form. Canarsians tended to view rioting not as an outcry against grievous wrong but as a manifestation of the ghetto dwellers' tendency to scream for benefits, to wallow in self-pity about exploitation long past, and to use lofty ideals to mask thuggery. Instead of taking responsibility for themselves, rioters took the hard-earned surplus of others (Rieder 1985:108).

As a result, both Italians and Jews became increasingly annoyed, fearful, and defensive about the black presence along the borders of Canarsie. Any black who crossed into Canarsie was almost automatically defined as an intruder who had no right to be there, whether he was merely walking the streets of Canarsie or trying to buy a house there. Almost any means were seen as justified in order to protect the boundaries, whether the means involved vigilante justice or extra-legal pressuring of white property owners not to sell to blacks.

They blamed the circuitous path they had to follow in order to protect Canarsie from potential black property buyers on the laws banning housing discrimination. But they considered these laws more of a nuisance than a cause for major concern; they had learned how to circumvent them effectively through the various informal and extra-legal pressures. But they became outraged at a plan put forth by the New York City Board of Education in the early 1970s that would bus a small number of black children into a Canarsie public school from an adjacent area. Almost overnight they were transformed from a collection of individuals already under attack on other fronts into a community mobilized in defense of its most sacred symbol and value; the neighborhood school. They organized boycotts, demonstrations, sit-ins, talk-ins, and shouted against and reviled public officials.

The ardor subsided in time as negotiations with the Board of Education dragged on, and the plan was ultimately shelved for all practical purposes. But the awareness of shared values, norms, and interests persisted so that Canarsie became more of a moral community than it had before. In fact, the school crisis perhaps more than any other event proved to be the turning point for many Jewish residents. They now counted themselves among the full-fledged guardians of fortress Canarsie against the onslaught of liberalism, the government, and the blacks.

In creating a moral community, Canarsie residents parried the charge that they were in the final analysis acting as individuals motivated by selfish interest, greed, and racial hatred. Instead they saw themselves as defenders of a faith that was rooted in tradition and in the sanctity of home, hearth, and children. This faith imposed obligations on each of them and also bestowed upon them a sphere of personal rights that was legitimately their due. Their major obligation was to protect the faith from the demands of arbitrary authority and the unjustified claims of a vindictive and violent minority. This then was "the law" and "the order" that they felt they were obliged to protect even if it meant defying what to them was the wrongfully imposed law of the powerful and even if it meant countering the violence of the racial minority with their own. For after all, they insisted, their violence was "legitimate"; that of the minority, "illegitimate." They resolved not to become the passive victims of external forces that were determined to violate their rights.

For most residents of Canarsie the conflict was defined in local terms. They were defending themselves against busing, crime in the streets, blockbusting, and the like. But they pursued the ramifications of this local conflict onto the national political stage where they broke away from their residual loyalties to the New Deal coalition and to the Democratic party. For the Jews this was extremely difficult. Even in 1968 most remained loyal to the Democratic party and to Hubert Humphrey. By 1972 a significant shift occurred toward the Republican party with the election of Nixon. Momentarily stymied in 1976 with the election of Carter, the shift resumed in relatively full force with the election of Reagan in 1980.

The Controversy over Affirmative Action

Other than their defection to the Republican party in presidential elections, residents of Canarsie rarely framed the struggle in broader societal terms. That struggle was joined on a national scale in the early 1970s by Jewish intellectuals and academics who took a leading role in the unfolding drama. The issue was the policy of affirmative action that was being pursued by the executive branch of the federal government. What had set the stage for the outcry was the issuance of Revised Order No. 4 in 1971 by the Office of Federal Contract Compliance of the U.S. Department of Labor, but what had actually triggered it off was the concerted effort by the Office of Civil Rights of HEW (U.S. Department of Health, Education and Welfare) to apply the order to universities and colleges. Now they too would have to submit a written affirmative action program with goals and timetables for the recruitment of racial minorities to positions in which they were underutilized.

The academic reaction was intense and reverberated through the media, through periodicals such as *Commentary* and *Public Interest*, through books such as Glazer's *Affirmative Discrimination* (1975), and through groups specially organized to combat the program. The Committee on Academic Nondiscrimination and Integrity led by three nationally known academicians spearheaded the drive. The attacks against affirmative action generated the emotion and passion of a religious crusade.

The principal target of these critics was the "goals" and "timetables" of affirmative action programs. Only the critics called them "quotas" and insisted that there was no difference between the two terms. For example, Hook writing in *Freedom at Issue* scoffed at the effort of the assistant director for public affairs, Office of Civil Rights, HEW, to distinguish between the two concepts. He dismissed the notion that goals were more flexible than quotas and merely required "good faith" efforts, not compulsory fulfillment. He argued, "Quotas are numerical goals. A 'quota of 20 percent' is equivalent to 'a numerical goal of 20 percent.' The expressions are interchangeable" (Hook 1973:16438).

In their attack on "goals-quotas" the critics concentrated heavily on the theme that they violate basic tenets of the American creed and of the American Constitution. In the introduction to his book *Affirmative Discrimination*, Glazer argues that the passage of the civil rights legislation of the 1960s expressed a "national consensus" (Glazer 1975:3) that was "the culmination of the development of a distinctive American orientation to ethnic difference and diversity with a history of almost 200 years" (Glazer 1975:5). This orientation, he continues, was imprinted in the kind of inclusive color-blind society that the Founding Fathers intended to build with the writing of the Constitution but which took several centuries to complete.

In establishing racial quotas, he insists, the policy of affirmative action undermines this political society. In fact, it resurrects the "great Southern heresy" of racism "that had threatened the idea of American nationality as broadly inclusive" for much of America's history until the national consensus expunged it in the mid-1960s (Glazer 1975:15).

In fact, Glazer and other critics argue that racial goals and quotas violate the very law upon which they maintain affirmative action programs are based. To support their argument, they point to Section 703j of Title VII of the Civil Rights Act of 1964. That section forbids the granting of

> preferential treatment to any individual or to any group because of the race, color, religion, sex or national origin of such individual or group on account of an imbalance which may exist with respect to the total number or percentage of persons of any race, color, religion, sex, or national origin employed by any employer ... in comparison with the total number or percentage of persons of such race, color, religion, sex, or national origin in any community, State, section, or other area, or in the available workforce in any community, State, section or other area (US Statutes at Large 1964 78:257).

And what are affirmative action programs to these critics but attempts to give preferential treatment to racial minorities. They do so, according to these critics, on the highly questionable premise—also seemingly forbidden by the law—that racial imbalance in the work force is the result of discrimination and therefore requires remedial action. Glazer and the other critics, many of whom professed a liberal stance in the early days of the civil rights movement, scoff at this contention. They argue that only where such racial imbalance can be shown to be the product of willful intention can discrimination be claimed. And where such acts can be proved, they would favor remedial action on a case-by-case basis. As Glazer states unequivocally, "I oppose discrimination; I fully support the law. ... Where the EEOC [Equal Employment Opportunity Commission] takes up a case of discrimination and gets a job and compensation for the victim, I applaud it" (Glazer 1975:66–7).

But Glazer goes on to maintain that such cases of "discrimination" comprise only a fraction of the workload of government agencies. "The fact is that much of the work of the government agencies has nothing to do with discrimination. One may review these enormous governmental reports and legal cases at length and find scarcely a single reference to any act of discrimination against an individual" (Glazer 1975:67).

What he is really saying is that most instances of racial imbalance with which the government is dealing do not "fit" the definition of discrimination he favors. But, since he cannot deny the existence of these cases of racial imbalance, he explains them away in part as being the products of market or "natural" forces and factors of competition and selection. Glazer then goes on to mention another fact that seems to loom even larger in his causal explanation of racial imbalance: the internal characteristics of the minority, its "taste or, if you will, culture" (Glazer 1975:63). Elsewhere he refers to "life style." Hook (1973) extends the same mode of analysis to the disproportionately low number of women in professional occupations. He explains this primarily in terms of women's identification with and commitment to their domestic roles and of their corresponding reluctance to pursue careers in the occupational marketplace. There are also the critics who have resurrected the intelligence test and who interpret the racial differences in scores on these tests in terms of hereditary capabilities and capacities.

For Glazer and the other critics, then, racial imbalance is the product of discrimination only if it corresponds to the definition of discrimination they prefer. The key to their definition is *intent*. Where there is no apparent intent, they are eager to look elsewhere for an explanation of the persistence of racial imbalance. They are, in other words, extremely reluctant to accept even the possibility that racial imbalance can be a surviving and viable consequence of past discriminatory policies and practices.

As a result, they are inclined to look askance at the phrase "systemic discrimination" which the EEOC devised to cover this type of imbalance, and they have great difficulty with the phrase "institutional racism." This is evident in the way Glazer deals with the phrase in his book. He treats it disdainfully as a residual term. "It is obviously something devised in the absence of clear evidence of discrimination and prejudice." He expresses incredulity that, "It [institutional racism] suggests that, without intent, a group may be victimized"; for, he argues, "Racism, in common understanding, means an attitude of superiority, disdain, or prejudice toward another person because he is of another race, and a philosophy or ideology that justifies such attitudes on the basis of the inferiority— genetic, cultural, moral, or intellectual—of a race." He then attempts to turn the phrase against its users: "The rise of the popularity of the term 'institutional racism' points to one happy development, namely, that racism pure and simple is less often found or expressed." He concludes with a discussion of the way the phrase is used to label all cases of racial imbalance. He objects to this: "Each institutional form of exclusion must be judged in its own terms" (Glazer 1975:69). And yet even as he illustrates his point, Glazer reveals his deep-seated resistance toward defining as racist or discriminatory any act or policy that does not express intent and design as well. Consequently the term "institutional racism" remains for him a slogan and a fanciful piece of rhetoric.

In rejecting "institutional racism" and "systemic discrimination" as valid characterizations of the American society, Glazer and the other critics are not merely expressing their opposition to a particular version of the present, but are also questioning the general validity of the version of the historical past which such a conceptualization implies. They opt for the "immigrant analogy" and maintain that outside the South treatment of the blacks was not qualitatively different from that afforded to the white immigrants. They are convinced that with the passage of the civil rights legislation the reach of America's discriminatory past no longer extends automatically into the present. What remains of this past are sporadic and occasional intentional acts of discrimination that can be dealt with on a case-by-case basis under present law.

With such a version of the past and present racial situation, small wonder that Glazer and his fellow critics reserve their greatest sense of outrage for the decision by the EEOC and the federal courts to treat racial imbalance as prima facie evidence of an unlawful employment practice and for the policy of the OFCC to insist upon goals and timetables as remedies for the underutilization of affected classes. They consider such a decision and policy as flagrant examples of preferential treatment which according to their interpretation is unqualifiedly forbidden by Title VII of the Civil Rights Act of 1964. In addition, these critics are convinced that the decision and policy also violate the true intent of the Constitution even though the Supreme Court has ruled otherwise. For, as Glazer says, "public policy must be exercised without distinction of race, color, or national origin" (Glazer 1975:221). Or, as Hook maintains, they make inocent victims pay the price of past discrimination which they had nothing to do with (Hook 1973:16437).

Thus, it can be concluded that their version of the past and present encounters of racial minorities with the American society provides Glazer and his fellow critics a logical and reasonable argument for their opposition to quotas and affirmative action programs, but what it fails to do is to provide them or anyone else with a truly valid statement of the reality it purports to represent. For example, Ringer's monograph *"We the People" and Others* (1983) demonstrates that their version distorts and oversimplifies the historical character of these racial encounters. It maintains that the immigrant analogy alone does not suffice as an explanation of the black experience in the North and, on a more general level, neither does the classical assimilationist theory adequately account for the historical encounters of racial minorities in America.

Further, these critics' version of events also distorts and oversimplifies the historical development of affirmative action programs. Glazer, for example, mentions in passing some of the historical antecedents of the present program from President Roosevelt's executive orders on non-discrimination in government contracts to Kennedy's and Johnson's on affirmative action and equal employment opportunity. He does so, however, in the space of less than one paragraph. What he and his fellow critics have failed to do is to examine systematically and in detail the historical record as we have done. Had they done so, they might have concluded as we have that the present affirmative action program did not burst into its present form overnight but was instead the end product of a 30-year evolutionary process that gave bureaucratic substance and form to what was initially a mere abstract and vague policy of the executive branch of government. As we saw in Chapter 7, this process flowed through Republican and Democratic administrations alike with the former implementing what the latter had started. Throughout its early history the results were minimal, but the quest for increased effectiveness continued. Not until Kennedy reformulated the normative goals and Johnson supplied the basic structural components was a bureaucratic machinery finally in place that could do the job. Its initial efforts were still relatively inconsequential, and only as the Nixon administration refined the procedural mechanisms further and supplied such missing capstones as standards for assessing the underutilization of affected classes was it able to achieve a level of effectiveness that had long been its goal.

Viewed in this manner then, the decision of the OFCC to establish statistical goals and timetables takes on a significance and meaning different from that espoused by its critics. The decision can be seen as being organically related to the struggle by the OFCC and its predecessors to overcome a long history of ineffectualness through the development of procedures and standards that would transform it into an effective instrument of policy.

Such an interpretation directly contradicts that proferred by Glazer and others. They treat the imposition of statistical goals as having no coherent connection with the past and as being entirely a product of capricious and arbitrary decision-making by bureaucrats, intent upon flexing their muscles.

Just as Glazer and the others have misread the historical development of the policy of statistical goals, so in many respects have they given an overly simple and one-sided interpretation to the ban on preferential treatment as stated in Section 703(j) of Title VII. According to them, Congress intended this ban to take precedence over any other consideration, and they insist that the courts and the EEOC have circumvented this intention by ordering quotas as remedies for situations of racial imbalance.

What they fail to realize is that in early decisions on this provision, several lower courts followed almost to the letter their singularly simple line of reasoning. These courts went so far as to forbid any remedies for discriminatory action because they said such remedies ran afoul of the preferential treatment clause. Only as the issue reached higher courts was this simplistic interpretation of the law challenged. Higher courts took note of the fact that Congress had built into the law contradictory provisions. On the one hand, Section 703(j) forbade preferential treatment; on the other, Section 706(g) stipulated various kinds of relief for past discriminatory action which might give the aggrieved person or class preferential treatment in the future. Thus the courts increasingly defined their role as balancing these conflicting equities and as clarifying an ambiguous situation created by congressional action. In order to resolve this dilemma, they determined that remedial action for past discrimination did not constitute preferential treatment and did not accordingly fall under the proscription of Section 703(j).

Finally because Glazer and the other critics have so narrowly and rigidly construed the definition of discrimination, they have failed to grasp the significance and meaning of the reach of the past into the present. Specifically, they have discounted the continuing effects of past policies and practices of discrimination even after these public policies have been manifestly abandoned. They have even dismissed, often contemptuously, the efforts of the EEOC and the courts to grapple with the matter and have treated as mere rhetoric the labeling of such situations as systemic discrimination or institutional racism.

And yet as policies and practices of overtly intended discrimination have become increasingly things of the past in industry and elsewhere, the EEOC and the courts have had to confront on an ever larger scale the lingering effects of such policies and practices, let alone the effects of policies that have merely masked their discriminatory intent. They have observed how institutional arrangements and mechanisms perpetuate the consequences of these past discriminatory policies even though these arrangements may never have been manifestly devised for that purpose.

Interestingly, in early cases of this sort, the lower courts adhered to the same kind of narrow definition of discrimination as presently advocated by Glazer and the others. They ruled that in the absence of explicit intent by the employer, practices and policies could not be deemed legally discriminatory even if they had a disproportionately negative effect on racial minorities and/or created racial imbalances in his work force. However, as these and other cases wended their way through the higher courts, the courts discarded this simplistic approach and began to savor the full complexity of the problem to the extent of identifying and weighing the neutral institutional mechanisms that reinforced the discriminatory effects of the past. In the process, they moved increasingly toward a definition of discrimination that stressed consequences—as finally enunciated and legitimized by Justice Burger in the *Griggs* decision—and they cumulatively carved out the operational meanings of systemic discrimination and institutional racism in a variety of specific contexts. And in this way was the *Griggs* principle articulated, stating that employment practices, though neutral or fair in form, are unlawful if they perpetuate the effects of past discrimination. (A major exception to date is the limitation imposed by Section 703(h) of Title VII on applying the principle to seniority systems.)

Behind the specificity of the courts' focus, however, loomed a more general premise shared by the commission, that the debilitating effects of past discrimination were not merely confined to individual enterprises but were also spread throughout the societal system by a variety of neutral and not so neutral institutional mechanisms. In the *Griggs* decision, for example, Justice Burger traced the poor performance on tests of racial minorities to the inferior schooling they received because of past policies of segregation and discrimination in education. Added to this was an awareness by the EEOC and the courts that discriminatory effects were also being perpetuated throughout the occupational system by policies and practices that were professedly neutral but which masked a prejudicial intent.

With such a view of the present, it is understandable why the courts also accepted the premise of the EEOC that employment situations, which differentially affected racial minorities or expressed racial imbalance, were more probably than not linked to this persisting structure of discrimination, whether through overt or masked intention or through neutral mechanisms. Accordingly, the EEOC and the courts established as a matter of evidentiary procedure that where such situations of racial imbalance were found, the employer would have to bear the burden of proving that such a link did not exist.

Obviously Glazer and the other critics have been unable to accept this premise and procedure, for to do so would undermine their own interpretation of the present. But in his rejection of the premise and procedure, Glazer reveals once again that he cannot break out of his theoretical mold. The situation must be defined in terms of subjective intent. He attributes to those who support the premise the belief "that there is such a deeply ingrained prejudice in whites, leading to discrimination against blacks and other minorities, that it can be assumed prejudice is the operative cause in any case of differential treatment rather than concern about qualifications. To this assumption there can be no answer. One can only, as an individual, search one's own motives and actions, and those of the institutions and bodies with which one is involved" (Glazer 1975:68).

Since he denies the factual pervasiveness of such an attitude, citing results from public opinion polls as proof, Glazer is in effect saying that the premise and procedure of the EEOC and the courts are based on a distorted version of reality and are therefore "mythic" in character. And with the rapid rolling back of prejudice that he believes is happening, he is equally convinced that any remaining situations of racial imbalance are less likely than ever to be the result of overt discriminatory intent, or even covert intent, and more likely to be the product of "natural" forces of selection and competition. Under the circumstances he would completely reorient the evidentiary procedure of the EEOC. Instead of the employer, it would be the employee or EEOC who would have to bear the burden of proof. Thus Glazer would require that the latter prove discriminatory intent on the part of the employer in a case of racial imbalance; in the absence of such proof, racial imbalance would be deemed a product of "innocent forces."

By imputing to the EEOC and courts a definition of the situation that is actually his, not theirs, Glazer once again distorts and oversimplifies their position, this time on their rationale for the policy on racial imbalance. They make no claim, for example, as he says they do, that a deep and abiding race prejudice saturates the feelings of white Americans, although they probably believe that such prejudice is more prevalent among white Americans than Glazer would like to believe. But they have contended that persistence of systemic discrimination and institutionalized racism into the present make it probable that any given situation of racial imbalance is a product of this persistence and therefore this imbalance should be treated as prima facie evidence of discrimination.

It can accordingly be concluded that the academic opponents of affirmative action programs fail to comprehend the complexity and persistence of the historic and present-day structure of racial discrimination and inequality in America. They prefer to read and to interpret this history in terms similar to those they use for the history of white immigrants. As a result, they see no reason why the normative model that gave the latter access to full membership in the American society should not apply to the racial minorities as well. They firmly support policies of nondiscrimination as being an intrinsic part of the American creed and condemn affirmative action programs with their statistical goals as falling beyond the pale of the American creed, both morally and constitutionally.

But if these critics were to rid themselves of their moral and historical preconceptions and were instead to read and to understand more accurately the distinctive character of the racial encounters in America, then they would in all probability realize that the institutionally ingrained discriminatory effects of America's past as a plural society cannot be remedied by merely dismantling that society and its racial creed. More is needed, in effect, for fulfillment of the American creed with its normative goal of equal access and opportunity than merely opening up to all the institutional doors of the people's domain. That something more includes affirmative action programs—included, that is, at least until such time as the effects of America's dualistic past have been truly erased.

Overview

Even as the 1980s draw to a close, white reaction to the race riots of the 1960s and to the governmental policies of the 1970s has yet to run its course. Whites continue to close ranks against what they perceive to be the "unfair" and "unreasonable" challenge of the blacks with their "outmoded" charges of racism. The challenge, though, has gained little, if any, ground in recent years as the whites have reasserted their dominance in the various institutions of the people's domain. But the whites still do not believe the challenge is stalled. They continue to act as though they are the victims of a drive to take away what they consider as rightfully theirs. They also see themselves as beleaguered defenders of the "color blind" society that they insist was finally put into place by the civil rights acts of a quarter of a century ago and the true practitioners of the faith that all persons are created equal and what happens to them is a result of their own doing.

Accordingly, the dominant white society seems unwilling to afford some space or time on the national agenda for any public discourse on the continuing effects of America's historical racism and on what the federal government's responsibility should be in coping with them. The 1988 presidential campaign bore witness to the blanket of invisibility that has been cast over discussion of these racial inequities. One of the few glimpses of the "racial problem" that was allowed to break through was the negative imagery of the black man as a public threat—the subliminal, if not overt, message of Republican television commercials on the Massachusetts prison furlough program. Even the Democratic presidential candidate failed to address explicitly these racial inequities. Instead he subsumed them under a universal class appeal in which he inveighed against the rich and promised to deal with the needs of *all* of the poor, homeless, and economically disadvantaged.

How long the whites will continue to resist coming to terms with the persisting effects of America's historic duality and racism remains to be seen. In the meantime, the question is how do scholars study these continuing effects in a society whose dominant whites believe none exist.

References

Adorno, T. W., Frenkel-Brunswick, E., Levinson, D. J., and Sanford, R. N. 1950. *The Authoritarian Personality*. NY: Harper and Row.

Allen, R. L. 1970. *Black Awakening in Capitalist America*. Garden City, NY: Doubleday.

Allport, G. W. 1954. *The Nature of Prejudice*. Garden City, NY: Doubleday.

Berreman, G. D. 1967. "Stratification, pluralism and interaction: A comparative analysis of caste." In A. de Reuck and J. Knight (eds.), *CIBA Foundation Symposium: Caste and Race: Comparative Approaches*. Boston: Little, Brown.

Berry, B., and Tischler, H. L. 1978. *Race and Ethnic Relations*. 4th ed. Boston: Houghton Mifflin Co.

Biddle, F. 1962. *In Brief Authority*. Garden City, NY: Doubleday.

Blalock, Jr., H. M. 1967. *Toward a Theory of Minority-Group Relations*. NY: John Wiley & Sons.

Blauner, R. 1972. *Racial Oppression in America*. NY: Harper and Row.

Bogardus, E. S. 1930. "A Race Relations Cycle." *American Journal of Sociology* 35(4):612–617.

Braithwaite, L. 1952. "Social Stratification in Trinidad." *Social and Economic Studies*. 2(2):3–175.

Brown, W. O. 1934. "Culture Contact and Race Conflict." In E. B. Reuter (ed.), *Race and Culture Contacts*. NY: McGraw-Hill.

Cole, S. G., and Cole, M. W. 1954. *Minorities and the American Promise: The Conflict of Principle and Practice*. NY: Harper and Brothers.

Constitution of the United States of America with the Amendments, The. (1872). Washington, DC: Government Printing Office.

Cox, O. C. 1948. *Caste, Class and Race*. NY: Modern Reader Paperbacks.

Dahrendorf, R. 1959. *Class and Class Conflict in Industrial Society*. Stanford, CA: Stanford University Press.

Daniels, J. 1944. *The Wilson Era: Years of Peace. 1910–1917*. Chapel Hill, NC: The University of North Carolina Press.

Davis, A., Gardner, B. B., and Gardner, M. R. 1941. *Deep South: A Social Anthropological Study of Caste and Class.* Chicago, IL: The University of Chicago Press.

DeVos, G. 1967. "Discussion: Characterization of Caste and Class Systems." In A. deReuck and J. Knight (eds.), *Caste and Race: Comparative Approaches.* London, W.I.: J & A Churchill Ltd.

Dollard, J. 1949. *Caste and Class in a Southern Town.* NY: Harper and Brothers.

Durkheim, E. (1893) 1947. *The Division of Labor in Society.* Glencoe, Ill.: The Free Press.

Etzioni, A. 1964. *Modern Organizations.* Englewood Cliffs, NJ: Prentice-Hall.

Fanon, F. 1968. *The Wretched of the Earth.* NY: Grove Press.

Feagin, J. R. 1984. *Racial and Ethnic Relations.* Englewood Cliffs, NJ: Prentice-Hall.

Federal Convention of 1787, The. 1911. *The Records of Vols I, II, III.* New Haven, CN: Yale University Press.

Floyd, T. S. 1973. *The Columbus Dynasty in the Caribbean: 1492–1526.* Albuquerque, NM: University of New Mexico Press.

Foner, E. 1981. "Redemption II." *The New York Times*, November 7, p.23.

Francis, E. K. 1947. "The Nature of the Ethnic Group." *American Journal of Sociology* 52(5):393–400.

Frazier, E. F. 1957a. *Race and Culture Contacts in the Modern World.* Boston: Beacon Press.

———. 1957b. *Black Bourgeoisie.* NY: The Free Press.

Freyre, G. 1946. *The Masters and the Slaves.* NY: Alfred Knopf.

Furnivall, J. S. [1948] 1956. *Colonial Policy and Practice: A Comparative Study of Burma and Netherlands India.* NY: New York University Press.

Gans, H. J. 1962. *The Urban Villager.* NY: The Free Press.

Gibson, F. E. 1951. *The Attitudes of the New York Irish toward State and National Affairs 1848–1892.* NY: Columbia University Press.

Glazer, N. 1971. "Blacks and Ethnic Groups: The Difference and the Political Difference It Makes." *Social Problems* 18(Spring): 444–461.

———. 1975. *Affirmative Discrimination: Ethnic Inequality and Public Policy.* NY: Basic Books.

Glazer, N., and Moynihan, D. P. 1963. *Beyond the Melting Pot.* Cambridge, MA: The MIT Press.

———, (eds.) 1975. *Ethnicity: Theory and Experience.* Cambridge, MA: Harvard University Press.

Gordon, M. M. 1963. *Social Class in American Sociology.* NY: McGraw Hill.

———. 1964. *Assimilation in American Life.* NY: Oxford University Press.

Gumplowicz, L. [1899] 1963. *Outlines of Sociology.* NY: Paine-Whitman.

Hollingshead, A. B. 1952. "Social Stratification: A Case Study." *American Sociological Review*, 17(6): 679–686.

Hook, S. 1973. "HEW's Faculty 'Quotas' Inspire-Semantic Evasions." *US Congressional Record* 93:1: 16,437–16,438.

Hostetler, J. A. 1968. *Amish Society.* Baltimore, MD: The John Hopkins Press.

Hoult, T. F. 1969. *Dictionary of Modern Sociology*. Totowa, NJ: Littlefield, Adams & Co.

Hughes, Archbishop J. [1863] 1889. "Letter to Secretary of State Seward." In US War Dept. *The War of the Rebellion: A Compilation of the Official Records of the Union and Confederate Armies*, series I, vol. 27, part II. Washington, DC: Government Printing Office.

Hutton, J. H. 1963. *Caste in India: Its Nature, Function and Origins*. 4th ed. London: Oxford University Press.

Jordan, W. D. 1974. *The White Man's Burden: Historical Origins of Racism in the United States*. NY: Oxford University Press.

Kallen, H. M. 1924. *Culture and Democracy in the United States*. NY: Boni and Liveright.

Kamen, H. 1965. *The Spanish Inquisition*. NY: New American Library.

Keller, S. 1963. *Beyond the Ruling Class: Strategic Elites in Modern Society*. NY: Random House.

King, Jr., M. L. 1964. *Why We Can't Wait*. NY: New American Library.

Kluckholn, C., and Kluckholn, D. 1962. *The Navaho*. Rev. ed. Garden City, NY: Doubleday.

Kohn, H. 1961. *The Idea of Nationalism*. NY: Macmillan.

Kramer, J. R., and Leventman, S. 1961. *Children of the Gilded Ghetto: Conflict Resolutions of Three Generations of American Jews*. New Haven: Yale University Press.

Kristol, I. 1966. "The Negro Is Like the Immigrant Yesterday." *The New York Times Magazine*. September 11:50–1.

Lang, J. 1975. *Conquest and Commerce: Spain and England in the Americas*. NY: Academic Press.

Las Casas, Bartolome de. 1542. *Brevisima relacion de la destruccion de las Indias*.

Lelyveld, J. 1985. *Move Your Shadow: South Africa, Black and White*. NY: Times Books.

Lewin, K. 1948. *Resolving Social Conflicts*. NY: Harper and Brothers.

Lieberson, S. 1970. "Stratification and Ethnic Groups." In E. O. Laumann (ed.), *Social Stratification: Research and Theory for the 1970's*. NY: The Bobbs-Merrill Co.

———. 1975. "A Societal Theory of Race and Ethnic Relations." In N. R. Yetman and C. H. Steele (eds.), *Majority and Minority: The Dynamics of Racial and Ethnic Relations*. 2d ed. Boston: Allyn & Bacon.

Lipset, S. M. 1963. *The First New Nation*. NY: Basic Books.

Lowenthal, D. 1972. *West Indian Societies*. NY: Oxford University Press.

MacIver, R. M., and Page, C. H. 1949. *Society: An Introductory Analysis*. NY: Rinehart.

Marshall, T. H. 1964. *Class, Citizenship and Social Development*. Garden City, NY: Doubleday.

Marx, K., and Engels, F. [1848] 1935. *The Communist Manifesto*. In *A Handbook of Marxism*. NY: International Publishers.

McClatchy, V. S. 1920. *The Germany of Asia*. Sacramento Bee. (Pamphlet)

Memmi, A. 1965. *The Colonizer and the Colonized*. Boston: Beacon Press.

Mills, C. W. 1959. *The Power Elite*. NY: Oxford University Press.

Moreau de Saint-Mery, M-L-E. [1797] 1973. "Whites in a Slave Society." In L. Comitas and D. Lowenthal (eds.), *Slaves, Free Men, Citizens*. Garden City, NY: Doubleday.

Mörner, M. 1967. *Race Mixture in the History of Latin America*. Boston: Little, Brown.

Morris, H. S. 1968. "Ethnic Groups." *International Encyclopedia of the Social Sciences* 5:167–172

Myrdal, G. 1944. *An American Dilemma: The Negro Problem and Modern Democracy*. NY: Harper and Brothers.

National Advisory Commission on Civil Disorders, The. 1968. "Report." Washington, DC: Government Printing Office.

Newton, H. P. 1972. *To Die For the People*. NY: Random House.

Neumann, W. L. 1953. "Franklin D. Roosevelt and Japan, 1913–1933." *Pacific Historical Review* 22(2):143–153.

Oxaal, I. 1967. "The Intellectual Background to the Democratic Revolution in Trinidad." In W. Bell (ed.), *The Democratic Revolution in West Indies*. Cambridge, MA: Schenkman.

Park, R. E. 1950. *Race and Culture*. Glencoe, IL: Free Press.

Petersen, W. 1971. *Japanese Americans*. NY: Random House.

Parsons, T. 1970. "Equality and Inequality in Modern Society, or Social Stratification Revisited." In E. O. Laumann (ed.), *Social Stratification: Research and Theory for the 1970's*. NY: Bobbs-Merrill.

Race Relations Law Reporter. School of Law, Vanderbilt University.

Redfield, R. 1947. "The Folk Society." *American Journal of Sociology* 52(4):293–308.

Rex, J. 1970. *Race Relations in Sociological Theory*. NY: Schocken Books.

———. 1973. *Race, Colonialism and the City*. London: Routledge and Kegan Paul.

Rieder, J. 1985. *Canarsie: The Jews and Italians of Brooklyn against Liberalism*. Cambridge, MA: Harvard University Press.

Ringer, B. B. 1967. *The Edge of Friendliness: A Study of Jewish-Gentile Relations*. NY: Basic Books.

———. 1976. "Affirmative Action, Quotas and Meritocracy." *Society* 13(2):12, 22–25.

———. 1983. *"We the People" and Others: Duality and America's Treatment of its Racial Minorities*. London: Tavistock Publications.

Robinson, D. L. 1971. *Slavery in the Structure of American Politics 1765–1820*. NY: Harcourt Brace Jovanovich.

Rose, P. I. 1981. *They and We*. 3rd Ed. NY: Random House.

Roth, C. 1964. *The Spanish Inquisition*. NY: Norton.

Schermerhorn, R. A. 1970. *Comparative Ethnic Relations: A Framework for Theory and Research*. NY: Random House.

Shafer, B. C. 1955. *Nationalism: Myth and Reality*. NY: Harcourt Brace.

Shibutani, T., and Kwan, K. M. 1965. *Ethnic Stratification: A Comparative Approach*. NY: Macmillan.

Simmel, G. 1950. "The Secret and the Secret Society." In K. H. Wolff (ed.) *The Sociology of Georg Simmel* Glencoe, Ill.: The Free Press.

Simpson, G. E., and Yinger, J. M. 1965. *Racial and Cultural Minorities*. 3rd ed. NY: Harper and Row.

Sinha, S. 1967. "Caste in India: Its essential pattern of socio-cultural integration." In A. de Reuck and J. Knight (eds.), *CIBA Foundation Symposium: Caste and Race: Comparative Approaches.* Boston: Little, Brown.

Smith, M. G. 1965. *The Plural Society in the British West Indies.* Berkeley, CA: University of California Press.

Smith, R. T. 1956. *The Negro Family in British Guiana.* London: Routledge and Kegan Paul.

Sowell, T. 1981. *Ethnic America.* NY: Basic Books, Inc.

Stedman, J. G. [1806] 1973. "A Planter's Day." In L. Comitas and D. Lowenthal (eds.), *Slaves, Free Men, Citizens.* Garden City, NY: Doubleday.

Steinberg, S. 1981. *The Ethnic Myth.* NY: Atheneum.

Stonequist, E. V. 1937. *The Marginal Man.* NY: Charles Scribner's Sons.

Suttles, G. D. 1968. *The Social Order of the Slum.* Chicago, IL: The University of Chicago Press.

Tabb, W. K. 1970. *The Political Economy of the Black Ghetto.* NY: W. W. Norton.

Tawney, R. H. 1938. *Religion and the Rise of Capitalism.* Harmondsworth, England: Pelican Books.

Thompson, L., and Prior, A. 1982. *South African Politics.* New Haven: Yale University Press.

Tönnies, F. 1940. *Fundamental Concepts of Sociology (Gemeinschaft und Gesellschaft).* NY: American Book Co.

US Congress, *Debates and Proceedings,* 1790.

US Congressional Record (89:I, 1965).

US House of Representatives, An Act HR8245(1900) 56:I.

US Public Statutes at Large I.

US Reports. Cases Adjudged in The Supreme Court. Washington, DC. 30 US I (1831) *The Cherokee Nation v. The State of Georgia.*
  60 US 393 (1857)
    Dred Scott, Plaintiff in Error v. John F. A. Sandford.
  149 US 698 (1893)
    Fong Yue Ting v. U.S.
  163 US 228 (1896)
    Wong Wing v. U.S.
  163 US 538 (1896)
    Plessy v. Ferguson.
  169 US 649 (1898)
    U.S. v. Wong Kim Ark.
  347 US 483 (1954)
    Brown et al. v. Board of Education of Topeka et al.
  406 US 205 (1972)
    State of Wisconsin, Petitioner v. Jonas Yoder et al.

US Senate, A Bill S2264 (1900) 56:I

US Statutes at Large 78 (1964).

van den Berghe, P. L. 1967a. *Race and Racism: A Comparative Perspective.* NY: John Wiley & Sons.

————. 1967b. *South Africa: A Study in Conflict.* Berkeley, CA: University of California Press.

Veblen, T. 1899. *The Theory of the Leisure Class.* Macmillan

Wagley, C., and Harris, M. 1958. *Minorities in the New World.* NY: Columbia University Press.

Ware, C. F. 1937. "Ethnic Communities." *Encyclopaedia of the Social Sciences*, vols. 5–6:607–613.

Warner, W. L. 1949. *Democracy in Jonesville.* NY: Harper and Brothers.

————. [1949] 1960. *Social Class in America: The Evaluation of Status.* NY: Harper and Row.

Warner, W. L., and Lunt, P. S. 1941. *The Social Life of a Modern Community.* New Haven: Yale University Press.

Waskow, A. I. 1967. *From Race Riot to Sit-In.* Garden City, NY: Doubleday.

Weber, M. [1922] 1946. "Class, Status, and Party." In H. H. Gerth and C. W. Mills (eds.), *From Max Weber: Essays in Sociology.* NY: Oxford University Press.

————. [1922] 1947. *The Theory of Social and Economic Organization.* NY: Oxford University Press.

————. 1930. *The Protestant Ethic and the Spirit of Capitalism.* London: George Allen and Unwin, Ltd.

Weisbrot, R. 1984. "Black-Jewish Relations and the Civil Rights Movement: A Historical Perspective." *National Scene* July.

Wertenbaker, T. J. 1959. *The Planters of Colonial Virginia.* NY: Russell and Russell.

Williams, E. 1944. *Capitalism and Slavery.* Chapel Hill, NC: University of North Carolina Press.

Williams, Jr., R. M. 1964. *Strangers next Door.* Englewood Cliff, NJ: Prentice-Hall.

Wirth, L. 1945. "The Problem of Minority Groups." In R. Linton (ed.), *The Science of Man in the World Crisis.* NY: Columbia University Press.

————. 1966. *The Ghetto.* Chicago, IL: University of Chicago Press.

Znaniecki, F. 1952. *Modern Nationalities.* Urbana, IL: University of Illinois Press.

Index

234 Index

Germans, 4, 25, 141
Germany, 20, 138–139, 181
Gesellschaft, 3, 14, 64
The Ghetto, 10
Ghettos, 10, 13, 161, 210–202
Gibson, F.E., 203
Glazer, N., 15, 26–27, 202, 203; on
affirmative action, 215–220, 221–222
Gordon, Milton, 2, 3–5, 11, 12, 14, 17, 26,
144; on assimilation, 134–136, 149; on
social class, 40, 42–43, 47–48
Griggs decision, 221
Group Areas Act, 114–115
Gumplowicz, Ludwig, 16, 32–35, 77

(H)

Harris, M., 16, 17, 28, 29–30, 77, 84–85
Harvard University, 210
Hasidic community, 10
Hawaii, 123, 124
Hayes, Rutherford B., 172
Hearst newspapers, 180
Hearst William R., 181
Herrenvolk democracy, 118
Hindus, 2, 52, 139
Hispaniola, 96–97, 98, 99, 100, 101, 102
Hitler, Adolph, 6, 20, 85–86
Holland, 26, 114
Hollingshead, A.B., 42–43, 48
Hook, S., 215, 217, 218
Hostetler, J.A., 8, 12–13
Hoult, T.F., 76
Hughes, John, 204
Huguenots, 23
Humphrey, Hubert, 214
Humphrey-Lehman, Bill, 194
Hunter College, 210
Hutton, J.H., 53, 51–52

(I)

Immigrants, 26, 27, 124, 125, 132–134,
146, 149, 162; see also specific
immigrant groups; alliance with
blacks, 207; and American creed,
209; assimilation of, 134–136;
discrimination against, 30; first-
generation, 9–10, 13; as political
force, 206; and racial creed, 70
Immigration Act of 1924, 183–187, 194,
206

Immigration Act of 1965, 195, 209
Indentured servitude, 104–105, 123
India, 38, 50–55, 63, 139, 143
Indians, 21, 26, 98, 102, 103, 106, 113,
142, 143, 196; and Constitution, 151;
enslavement of, 96–97, 99–101, 124;
and racial creed, 171; and Spanish
conquistador, 96–97, 99–101; and the
Church, 99–100
Indonesia, 58, 122, 125
Intermarriage, 47, 100, 134, 135
*International Encyclopedia of the Social
Sciences*, 16
Ireland, 7, 203
Irish, 4, 6, 7, 30, 42, 46, 138; assimilation
of, 25; and English, 142
Irish immigrants, 10, 202–204
Isabella, Queen of Spain, 99, 102
Issei, 193
Italians, 1, 4, 10, 40, 43, 76, 141, 213–214

(J)

Jamaica, 59
Jamestown, 103, 113
Japan, 123, 185, 189; and Japanese
immigrants, 176–178, 180; and Pearl
Harbour, 188, 190, 191; and
relationship with U.S., 176–178,
187–188; and yellow peril, 180–182
Japanese, 40; incarceration in
concentration camps, 133–134,
188–193; and naturalization, 193–195
Japanese American Citizens League, 192,
193, 194–195
Japanese immigrants, 132, 133, 170, 171,
206, 207; and alien land laws,
178–180, 184; and American creed,
184–185; and California, 175–177,
178–180, 183, 188; and citizenship,
110, 182, 183; and Japan, 176–178,
180; and people's domain, 183,
184–185; and racial creed, 184–185;
and yellow peril, 180–182, 188
Jewish immigrants, 10, 209–211
Jews, 1, 2, 4, 7, 14, 40, 42, 43, 76, 209;
and American creed, 211; and
assimilation, 138; and blacks,
207–208; and civil rights, 210, 211,
213–214, 215; in czarist Russia, 142;
in medieval Europe, 23, 121, 137; as
middlemen, 121; in Nazi Germany, 6,